11-1/11-2 WORK TOGETHER, pp.

Journalizing transactions for starting a corporation
Journalizing transactions for stock subscriptions and preparing a balance sheet

CASH PAYMENTS JOURNAL
PAGE 1

DATE	ACCOUNT TITLE	CK. NO.	POST. REF.	GENERAL DEBIT	GENERAL CREDIT	ACCOUNTS PAYABLE DEBIT	PURCHASES DISCOUNT CREDIT	CASH CREDIT

CASH RECEIPTS JOURNAL
PAGE 1

DATE	ACCOUNT TITLE	DOC. NO.	POST. REF.	GENERAL DEBIT	GENERAL CREDIT	ACCOUNTS RECEIVABLE CREDIT	SALES CREDIT	SALES TAX PAYABLE DEBIT	SALES TAX PAYABLE CREDIT	SALES DISCOUNT DEBIT	CASH DEBIT

GENERAL JOURNAL
PAGE 1

DATE	ACCOUNT TITLE	DOC. NO.	POST. REF.	DEBIT	CREDIT

Chapter 11 Organizing a Corporation and Paying Dividends • 1

11-1/11-2 WORK TOGETHER (concluded)

[4]

Presidential Limousine, Inc.
Balance Sheet
April 30, 20--

ASSETS		
Current Assets:		
Cash		
Intangible Assets:		
Organization Costs		
Total Assets		
STOCKHOLDERS' EQUITY		
Paid-in Capital:		
Capital Stock—Common (		
shares, stated value)		
Total Stockholders' Equity		

11-1/11-2 ON YOUR OWN, pp. 305 and 309

Journalizing transactions for starting a corporation [8, 5]
Journalizing transactions for stock subscriptions and preparing a balance sheet

CASH PAYMENTS JOURNAL
PAGE 1

	DATE	ACCOUNT TITLE	CK. NO.	POST. REF.	GENERAL DEBIT	GENERAL CREDIT	ACCOUNTS PAYABLE DEBIT	PURCHASES DISCOUNT CREDIT	CASH CREDIT	
1										1
2										2
3										3
4										4
5										5
6										6
7										7
8										8
9										9

CASH RECEIPTS JOURNAL
PAGE 1

	DATE	ACCOUNT TITLE	DOC. NO.	POST. REF.	GENERAL DEBIT	GENERAL CREDIT	ACCOUNTS RECEIVABLE CREDIT	SALES CREDIT	SALES TAX PAYABLE DEBIT	SALES TAX PAYABLE CREDIT	SALES DISCOUNT DEBIT	CASH DEBIT	
1													1
2													2
3													3
4													4
5													5
6													6
7													7
8													8
9													9

GENERAL JOURNAL
PAGE 1

	DATE	ACCOUNT TITLE	DOC. NO.	POST. REF.	DEBIT	CREDIT	
1							1
2							2
3							3
4							4
5							5
6							6
7							7
8							8
9							9

11-1/11-2 ON YOUR OWN (concluded)

[6]

Sierra Corporation
Balance Sheet
June 30, 20--

ASSETS					
Current Assets:					
Cash					
Subscriptions Receivable					
Total Current Assets					
Intangible Asset:					
Organization Costs					
Total Assets					
STOCKHOLDERS' EQUITY					
Paid-in Capital:					
Capital Stock—Common (shares, $10.00 stated value)					
Stock Subscribed—Common (shares)					
Total Paid-in Capital					
Total Stockholders' Equity					

11-3 WORK TOGETHER, p. 313

Calculating and journalizing the dividends for a corporation [4]

Value of preferred stock:

[5]

Preferred stock dividend:

Common stock dividend:

[6]

GENERAL JOURNAL

PAGE 4

	DATE	ACCOUNT TITLE	DOC. NO.	POST. REF.	DEBIT	CREDIT	
1							1
2							2
3							3
4							4
5							5
6							6

11-3 WORK TOGETHER (concluded)

[7]

CASH PAYMENTS JOURNAL PAGE 11

DATE	ACCOUNT TITLE	CK. NO.	POST. REF.	GENERAL DEBIT	GENERAL CREDIT	ACCOUNTS PAYABLE DEBIT	PURCHASES DISCOUNT CREDIT	CASH CREDIT

11-3 ON YOUR OWN, p. 313

Calculating and journalizing the dividends for a corporation [8]

Value of preferred stock:

[9]

Preferred stock dividend:

Common stock dividend:

[10]

GENERAL JOURNAL
PAGE 7

	DATE	ACCOUNT TITLE	DOC. NO.	POST. REF.	DEBIT	CREDIT	
1							1
2							2
3							3
4							4
5							5
6							6

11-3 ON YOUR OWN (concluded)

[11]

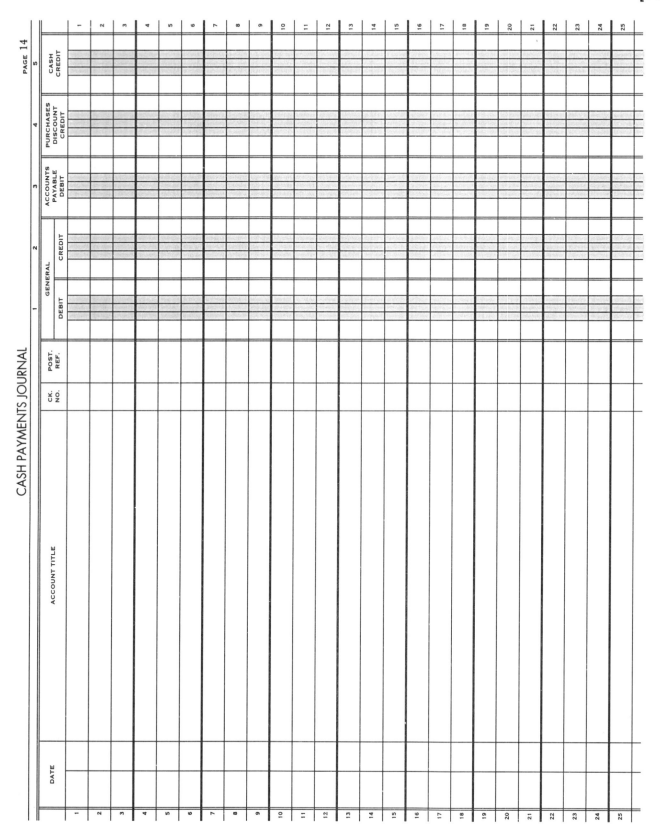

11-1/11-2 APPLICATION PROBLEMS, p. 315

Journalizing transactions for starting a corporation
Journalizing transactions for stock subscriptions and preparing a balance sheet

CASH PAYMENTS JOURNAL — PAGE 1

DATE	ACCOUNT TITLE	CK. NO.	POST. REF.	GENERAL DEBIT	GENERAL CREDIT	ACCOUNTS PAYABLE DEBIT	PURCHASES DISCOUNT CREDIT	CASH CREDIT

CASH RECEIPTS JOURNAL — PAGE 1

DATE	ACCOUNT TITLE	DOC. NO.	POST. REF.	GENERAL DEBIT	GENERAL CREDIT	ACCOUNTS RECEIVABLE CREDIT	SALES CREDIT	SALES TAX PAYABLE DEBIT	SALES TAX PAYABLE CREDIT	SALES DISCOUNT DEBIT	CASH DEBIT

GENERAL JOURNAL — PAGE 1

DATE	ACCOUNT TITLE	DOC. NO.	POST. REF.	DEBIT	CREDIT

11-1/11-2 APPLICATION PROBLEMS (concluded)

[2]

Pacific Technologies
Balance Sheet
March 2, 20--

ASSETS				
Current Assets:				
Cash				
Subscriptions Receivable				
Total Current Assets				
Intangible Asset:				
Organization Costs				
Total Assets				
STOCKHOLDERS' EQUITY				
Paid-in Capital:				
Capital Stock—Common (shares, $10.00 stated value)				
Stock Subscribed—Common (shares)				
Total Paid-in Capital				
Total Stockholders' Equity				

11-3 APPLICATION PROBLEM, p. 315

Calculating dividends for a corporation

[1]

	Edison	Carmac
Number of Preferred Shares		
Par Value		
Total Value of Preferred Stock		
Dividend Rate		
Total Annual Dividend—Preferred		

[2]

Edison Corporation

Year	Total Dividends	Preferred Dividends	Common Dividends
1			
2			
3			

Carmac Corporation

Year	Total Dividends	Preferred Dividends	Common Dividends
1			
2			
3			

Name _____ Date _____ Class _____

11-3 APPLICATION PROBLEM

Extra forms

Number of Preferred Shares		
Par Value		
Total Value of Preferred Stock		
Dividend Rate		
Total Annual Dividend—Preferred		

Year	Total Dividends	Preferred Dividends	Common Dividends
1			
2			
3			

Year	Total Dividends	Preferred Dividends	Common Dividends
1			
2			
3			

12 • Working Papers COPYRIGHT © SOUTH-WESTERN EDUCATIONAL PUBLISHING

11-4 APPLICATION PROBLEM, p. 316

Journalizing transactions for declaring and paying dividends

GENERAL JOURNAL — PAGE 8

DATE	ACCOUNT TITLE	DOC. NO.	POST. REF.	DEBIT	CREDIT

11-4 APPLICATION PROBLEM (concluded)

CASH PAYMENTS JOURNAL PAGE 21

DATE	ACCOUNT TITLE	CK. NO.	POST. REF.	GENERAL DEBIT	GENERAL CREDIT	ACCOUNTS PAYABLE DEBIT	PURCHASES DISCOUNT CREDIT	CASH CREDIT

11-5 MASTERY PROBLEM, p. 316

Journalizing transactions for starting a corporation, declaring and paying dividends, and preparing a balance sheet [1, 3]

CASH PAYMENTS JOURNAL — PAGE 1

DATE	ACCOUNT TITLE	CK. NO.	POST. REF.	GENERAL DEBIT	GENERAL CREDIT	ACCOUNTS PAYABLE DEBIT	PURCHASES DISCOUNT CREDIT	CASH CREDIT

CASH RECEIPTS JOURNAL — PAGE 1

DATE	ACCOUNT TITLE	DOC. NO.	POST. REF.	GENERAL DEBIT	GENERAL CREDIT	ACCOUNTS RECEIVABLE CREDIT	SALES CREDIT	SALES TAX PAYABLE DEBIT	SALES TAX PAYABLE CREDIT	SALES DISCOUNT DEBIT	CASH DEBIT

GENERAL JOURNAL — PAGE 1

DATE	ACCOUNT TITLE	DOC. NO.	POST. REF.	DEBIT	CREDIT

11-5 MASTERY PROBLEM (concluded)

[2]

SkyPark, Inc.
Balance Sheet
November 2, 20--

ASSETS			
Current Assets:			
Cash			
Subscriptions Receivable			
Total Current Assets			
Intangible Asset:			
Organization Costs			
Total Assets			
STOCKHOLDERS' EQUITY			
Paid-in Capital:			
Capital Stock—Common (　　　shares, stated value)			
Stock Subscribed—Common (　　　shares)			
Total Paid-in Capital			
Total Stockholders' Equity			

11-6 CHALLENGE PROBLEM, p. 317

Journalizing transactions for a corporation

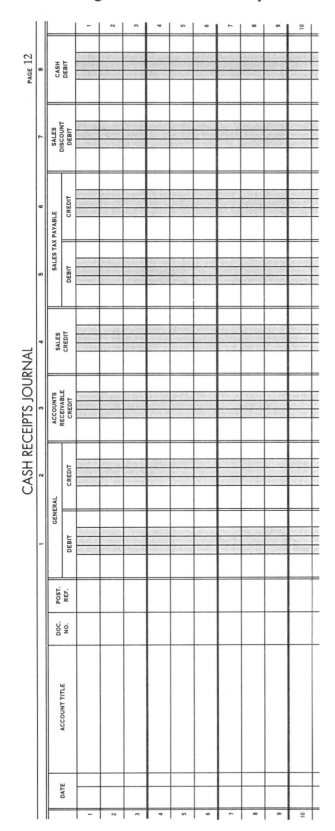

11-6 CHALLENGE PROBLEM (concluded)

GENERAL JOURNAL

PAGE 6

DATE	ACCOUNT TITLE	DOC. NO.	POST. REF.	DEBIT	CREDIT

12-1 WORK TOGETHER, p. 327

Journalizing capital stock transactions [6]

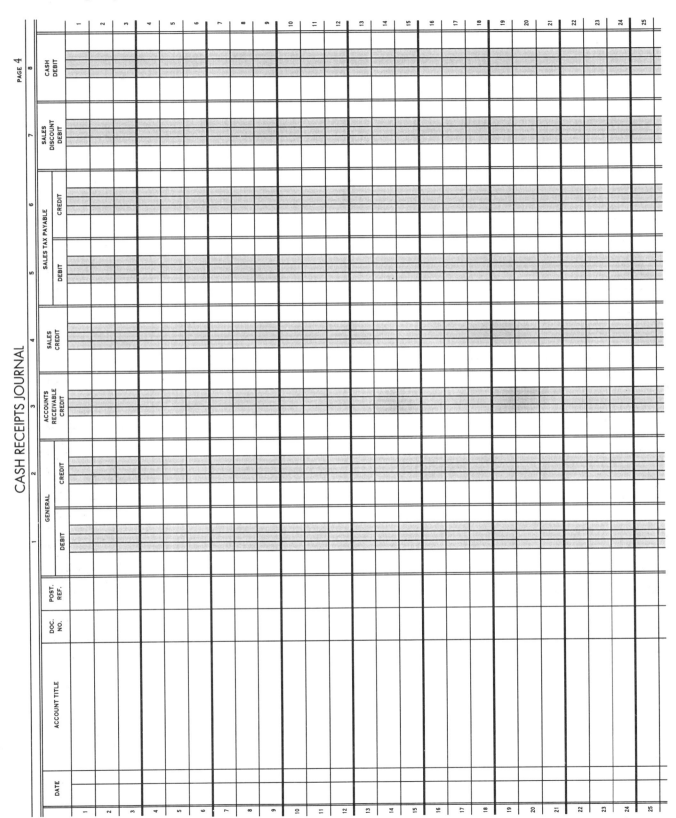

12-1 WORK TOGETHER (concluded)

[6]

GENERAL JOURNAL PAGE 2

DATE	ACCOUNT TITLE	DOC. NO.	POST. REF.	DEBIT	CREDIT

12-1 ON YOUR OWN, p. 328

Journalizing capital stock transactions [7]

CASH RECEIPTS JOURNAL — PAGE 5

DATE	ACCOUNT TITLE	DOC. NO.	POST. REF.	GENERAL DEBIT	GENERAL CREDIT	ACCOUNTS RECEIVABLE CREDIT	SALES CREDIT	SALES TAX PAYABLE DEBIT	SALES TAX PAYABLE CREDIT	SALES DISCOUNT DEBIT	CASH DEBIT

12-1 ON YOUR OWN (concluded)

[7]

GENERAL JOURNAL

PAGE 3

DATE	ACCOUNT TITLE	DOC. NO.	POST. REF.	DEBIT	CREDIT

12-2 WORK TOGETHER, p. 333

Journalizing treasury stock transactions [4]

CASH RECEIPTS JOURNAL PAGE 11

DATE	ACCOUNT TITLE	DOC. NO.	POST. REF.	GENERAL DEBIT	GENERAL CREDIT	ACCOUNTS RECEIVABLE CREDIT	SALES CREDIT	SALES TAX PAYABLE DEBIT	SALES TAX PAYABLE CREDIT	SALES DISCOUNT DEBIT	CASH DEBIT

Chapter 12 Acquiring Additional Capital for a Corporation • 23

12-2 WORK TOGETHER (concluded)

[4]

CASH PAYMENTS JOURNAL PAGE 8

DATE	ACCOUNT TITLE	CK. NO.	POST. REF.	GENERAL DEBIT	GENERAL CREDIT	ACCOUNTS PAYABLE DEBIT	PURCHASES DISCOUNT CREDIT	CASH CREDIT

12-2 ON YOUR OWN, p. 333

Journalizing treasury stock transactions [5]

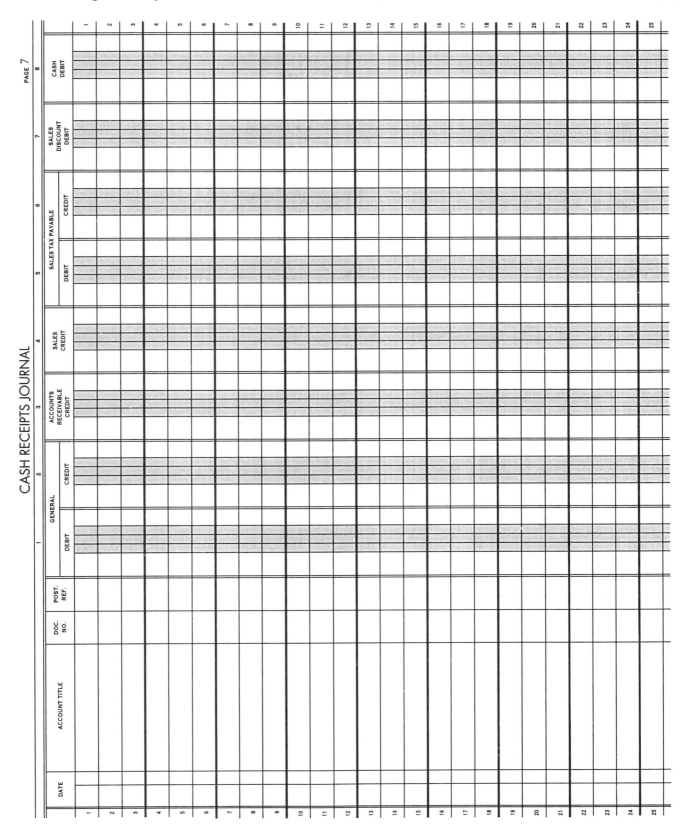

12-2 ON YOUR OWN (concluded)

[5]

CASH PAYMENTS JOURNAL — PAGE 6

DATE	ACCOUNT TITLE	CK. NO.	POST. REF.	GENERAL DEBIT	GENERAL CREDIT	ACCOUNTS PAYABLE DEBIT	PURCHASES DISCOUNT CREDIT	CASH CREDIT

12-3 WORK TOGETHER, p. 339

Journalizing bonds payable transactions [4]

CASH RECEIPTS JOURNAL — PAGE 4

CASH PAYMENTS JOURNAL — PAGE 5

12-3 WORK TOGETHER (concluded)

[4]

GENERAL JOURNAL PAGE 2

DATE	ACCOUNT TITLE	DOC. NO.	POST. REF.	DEBIT	CREDIT

12-3 ON YOUR OWN, p. 340

Journalizing bonds payable transactions [5]

CASH RECEIPTS JOURNAL — PAGE 11

CASH PAYMENTS JOURNAL — PAGE 10

12-3 ON YOUR OWN (concluded)

[5]

GENERAL JOURNAL — PAGE 9

	DATE	ACCOUNT TITLE	DOC. NO.	POST. REF.	DEBIT	CREDIT	
1							1
2							2
3							3
4							4
5							5
6							6
7							7
8							8
9							9
10							10
11							11
12							12
13							13
14							14
15							15
16							16
17							17
18							18
19							19
20							20
21							21
22							22
23							23
24							24
25							25
26							26
27							27
28							28
29							29
30							30
31							31

12-1 APPLICATION PROBLEM, p. 342

Journalizing capital stock transactions

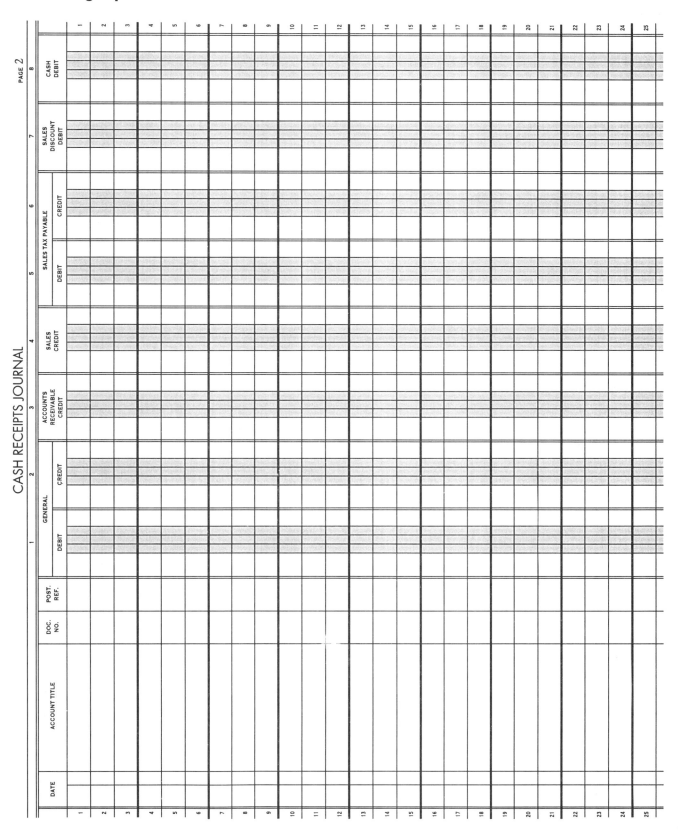

12-1 APPLICATION PROBLEM (concluded)

GENERAL JOURNAL PAGE 2

DATE	ACCOUNT TITLE	DOC. NO.	POST. REF.	DEBIT	CREDIT

12-2 APPLICATION PROBLEM, p. 342

Journalizing treasury stock transactions

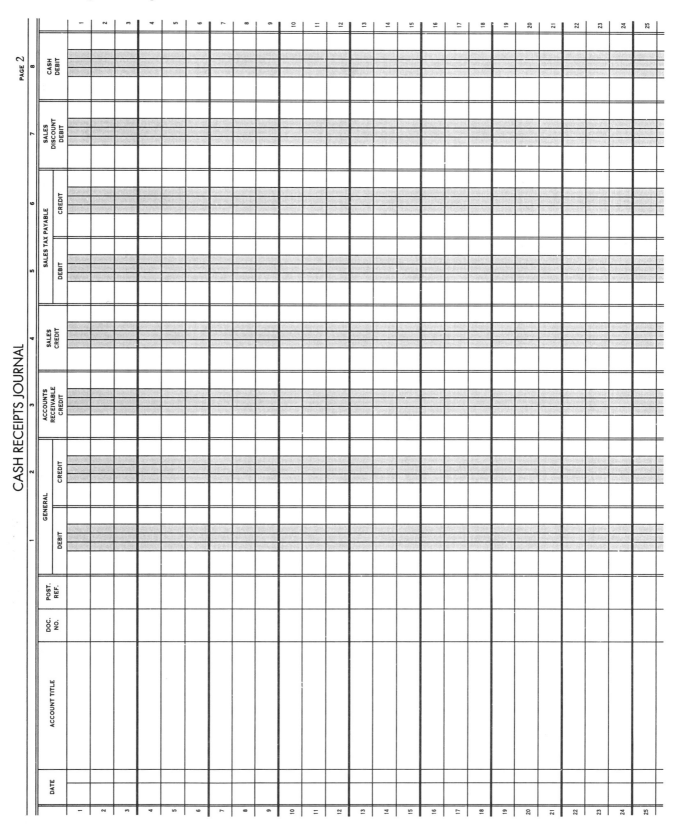

12-2 APPLICATION PROBLEM (concluded)

CASH PAYMENTS JOURNAL PAGE 3

DATE	ACCOUNT TITLE	CK. NO.	POST. REF.	GENERAL DEBIT	GENERAL CREDIT	ACCOUNTS PAYABLE DEBIT	PURCHASES DISCOUNT CREDIT	CASH CREDIT

12-3 APPLICATION PROBLEM, p. 343

Journalizing bonds payable transactions

CASH RECEIPTS JOURNAL — PAGE 1

CASH PAYMENTS JOURNAL — PAGE 8

12-3 APPLICATION PROBLEM (concluded)

GENERAL JOURNAL

PAGE 1

DATE	ACCOUNT TITLE	DOC. NO.	POST. REF.	DEBIT	CREDIT

12-4 MASTERY PROBLEM, p. 343

Journalizing stock and bonds transactions

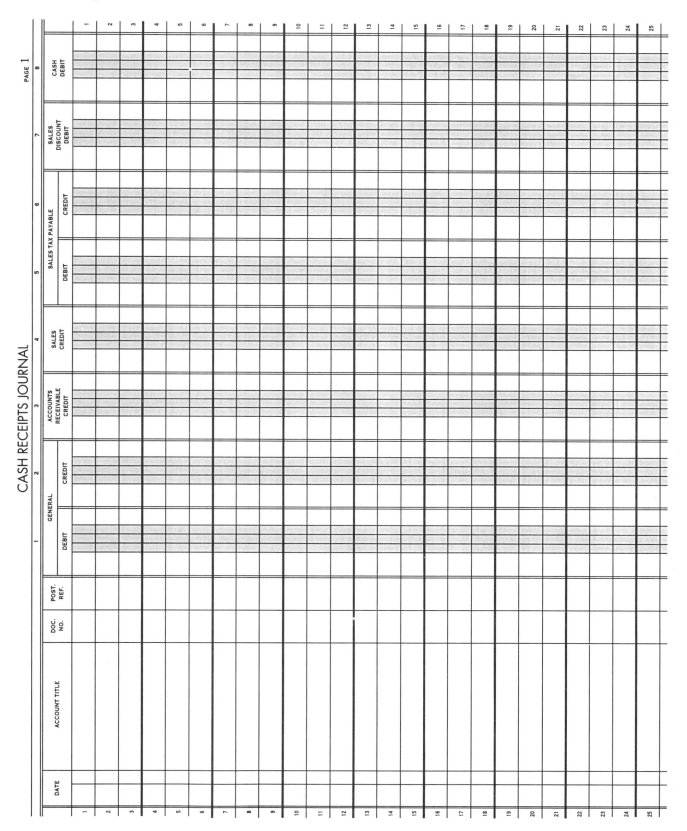

12-4 MASTERY PROBLEM (concluded)

CASH PAYMENTS JOURNAL — PAGE 8

DATE	ACCOUNT TITLE	CK. NO.	POST. REF.	GENERAL DEBIT	GENERAL CREDIT	ACCOUNTS PAYABLE DEBIT	PURCHASES DISCOUNT CREDIT	CASH CREDIT

GENERAL JOURNAL — PAGE 1

DATE	ACCOUNT TITLE	DOC. NO.	POST. REF.	DEBIT	CREDIT

12-5 CHALLENGE PROBLEM, p. 344

Journalizing stock and bond transactions

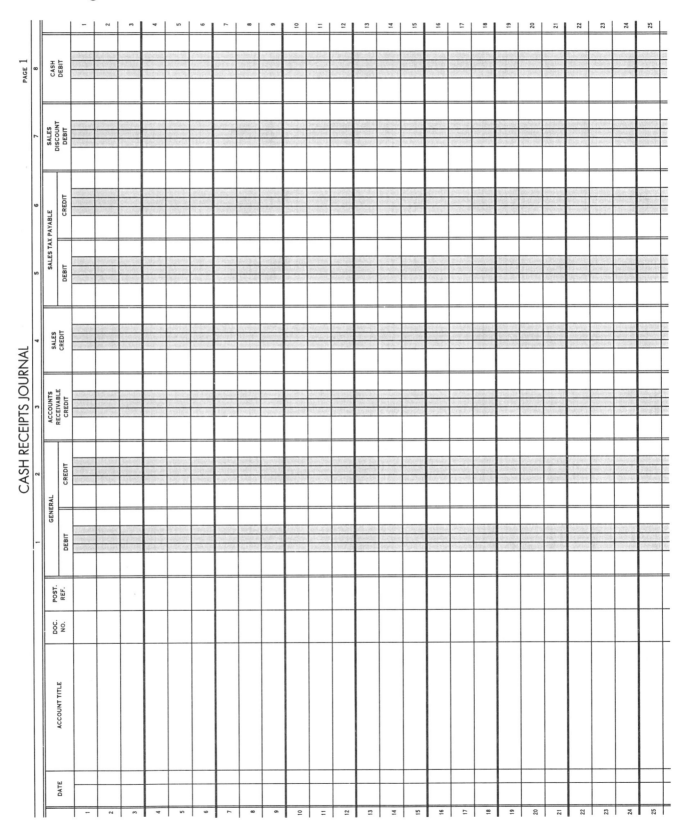

12-5 CHALLENGE PROBLEM (concluded)

CASH PAYMENTS JOURNAL PAGE 2

DATE	ACCOUNT TITLE	CK. NO.	POST. REF.	GENERAL DEBIT	GENERAL CREDIT	ACCOUNTS PAYABLE DEBIT	PURCHASES DISCOUNT CREDIT	CASH CREDIT

GENERAL JOURNAL PAGE 1

DATE	ACCOUNT TITLE	DOC. NO.	POST. REF.	DEBIT	CREDIT

13-1 WORK TOGETHER

The work sheet for this problem begins on page 42.

Extra form

13-1 WORK TOGETHER, p. 354

Calculating federal income tax expense, recording the adjustment, and completing a work sheet [3–7]

Provident Electronics
Work Sheet
For Year Ended December 31, 20--

#	ACCOUNT TITLE	TRIAL BALANCE DEBIT	TRIAL BALANCE CREDIT	ADJUSTMENTS DEBIT	ADJUSTMENTS CREDIT	INCOME STATEMENT DEBIT	INCOME STATEMENT CREDIT	BALANCE SHEET DEBIT	BALANCE SHEET CREDIT
1	Cash	2128012						2128012	
2	Petty Cash	25000						25000	
3	Notes Receivable	1073100						1073100	
4	Interest Receivable			(a) 13809				13809	
5	Accounts Receivable	3802943						3802943	
6	Allowance for Uncollectible Accts.		110025		(b) 1067 22				117747
7	Merchandise Inventory	4407220			(c) 13715			4393505	
8	Supplies—Sales	804428			(d) 363376			441052	
9	Supplies—Administrative	514130			(e) 343121			171009	
10	Prepaid Insurance	343037			(f) 120544			222493	
11	Store Equipment	4297458						4297458	
12	Accum. Depr.—Store Equipment		516400		(g) 482100				998500
13	Office Equipment	5214294						5214294	
14	Accum. Depr.—Office Equipment		1110448		(h) 159224				2696 72
15	Building	2400000						2400000	
16	Accum. Depr.—Building		2614 00		(i) 130700				392100
17	Land	4100000						4100000	
18	Notes Payable		152000						152000
19	Interest Payable				(j) 15200				15200
20	Accounts Payable		523427						523427
21	Employee Income Tax Payable		20800						20800
22	Federal Income Tax Payable								
23	Social Security Tax Payable		100065		(k) 5745				158 10
24	Medicare Tax Payable		2687		(k) 1342				4029
25	Salaries Payable				(l) 6743 4				67434
26	Sales Tax Payable		31450						31450
27	Unemploy. Tax Payable—Federal		1834		(k) 201				2035
28	Unemploy. Tax Payable—State		28582		(k) 4890				33472
29	Health Ins. Premiums Payable		7306						7306
30	Dividends Payable		746288						746288
31	Capital Stock		12837600						12837600
32	Paid-in Capital in Exc. St. Val.		1590100						1590100
33	Retained Earnings		4014397						4014397

13-1 WORK TOGETHER (concluded)

[3-7]

	ACCOUNT TITLE	TRIAL BALANCE DEBIT	TRIAL BALANCE CREDIT	ADJUSTMENTS DEBIT	ADJUSTMENTS CREDIT	INCOME STATEMENT DEBIT	INCOME STATEMENT CREDIT	BALANCE SHEET DEBIT	BALANCE SHEET CREDIT
34	Dividends	7 4 5 6 00						7 4 5 6 00	
35	Income Summary			(c) 1 3 7 15		1 3 7 15			
36	Sales		29 8 3 7 2 50				29 8 3 7 2 50		
37	Sales Discount	2 9 4 00				2 9 4 00			
38	Sales Returns & Allowances	4 5 7 69				4 5 7 69			
39	Purchases	14 7 3 3 2 99				14 7 3 3 2 99			
40	Purchases Discount		1 3 2 3 15				1 3 2 3 15		
41	Purchases Returns & Allowances		4 7 2 64				4 7 2 64		
42	Advertising Expense	2 5 9 0 45				2 5 9 0 45			
43	Credit Card Fee Expense	2 2 4 1 03				2 2 4 1 03			
44	Depr. Expense—Store Equip.			(g) 4 8 2 1 00		4 8 2 1 00			
45	Miscellaneous Exp.—Sales	3 4 2 6 00				3 4 2 6 00			
46	Salary Expense—Sales	17 0 7 2 30		(j) 6 7 4 34		17 7 4 6 64			
47	Supplies Expense—Sales			(d) 3 6 3 3 76		3 6 3 3 76			
48	Depr. Expense—Office Equip.	3 1 5 6 90		(h) 1 5 9 2 24		4 7 4 9 14			
49	Depr. Expense—Building	1 2 0 0 00		(i) 1 3 0 7 00		2 5 0 7 00			
50	Insurance Expense			(f) 1 2 0 5 44		1 2 0 5 44			
51	Miscellaneous Exp.—Administrative	3 2 4 4 12				3 2 4 4 12			
52	Payroll Taxes Expense	2 2 0 5 22		(k) 1 2 1 78		2 3 2 7 00			
53	Property Tax Expense	1 1 0 0 00				1 1 0 0 00			
54	Salary Expense—Administrative	4 5 0 9 00				4 5 0 9 00			
55	Supplies Expense—Administrative			(e) 3 4 3 1 21		3 4 3 1 21			
56	Uncollectible Accounts Expense			(b) 1 0 6 7 22		1 0 6 7 22			
57	Utilities Expense	9 2 3 9 46				9 2 3 9 46			
58	Interest Income				(a) 1 3 8 09		1 3 8 09		
59	Interest Expense	2 2 0 5 00		(i) 1 5 2 00		2 3 5 7 00			
60	Federal Income Tax Expense	10 0 0 0 00							
61		508 8 2 6 38	508 8 2 6 38						

13-1 WORK TOGETHER

Extra form

13-1 ON YOUR OWN

The work sheet for this problem begins on page 46.

Extra form

13-1 ON YOUR OWN, p. 354

Calculating federal income tax expense, recording the adjustment, and completing a work sheet [8-12]

BRE Corporation
Work Sheet
For Year Ended December 31, 20--

	ACCOUNT TITLE	TRIAL BALANCE DEBIT	TRIAL BALANCE CREDIT	ADJUSTMENTS DEBIT	ADJUSTMENTS CREDIT	INCOME STATEMENT DEBIT	INCOME STATEMENT CREDIT	BALANCE SHEET DEBIT	BALANCE SHEET CREDIT
1	Cash	4256024						4256024	
2	Petty Cash	50000						50000	
3	Notes Receivable	2146200						2146200	
4	Interest Receivable			(a) 13809				13809	
5	Accounts Receivable	7605886						7605886	
6	Allowance for Uncollectible Accts.		22050		(b) 106722				128772
7	Merchandise Inventory	8814440			(c) 13715			8800725	
8	Supplies—Sales	1608856			(d) 363376			1245480	
9	Supplies—Administrative	1028260			(e) 343121			685139	
10	Prepaid Insurance	686074			(f) 120544			565530	
11	Store Equipment	8594916						8594916	
12	Accum. Depr.—Store Equipment		1032800		(g) 482100				1514900
13	Office Equipment	10428588						10428588	
14	Accum. Depr.—Office Equipment		2220896		(h) 1592224				3801200
15	Building	4800000						4800000	
16	Accum. Depr.—Building		522800		(i) 130700				653500
17	Land	8200000						8200000	
18	Notes Payable		304000						304000
19	Interest Payable				(j) 15200				15200
20	Accounts Payable		1046854						1046854
21	Employee Income Tax Payable		41600						41600
22	Federal Income Tax Payable								
23	Social Security Tax Payable		20130		(k) 5745				25875
24	Medicare Tax Payable		5374		(k) 1342				6716
25	Salaries Payable				(l) 67434				67434
26	Sales Tax Payable		62900						62900
27	Unemploy. Tax Payable—Federal		3668		(k) 201				3869
28	Unemploy. Tax Payable—State		57164		(k) 4890				62054
29	Health Ins. Premiums Payable		14612						14612
30	Dividends Payable		1492576						1492576
31	Capital Stock		25675000						25675000
32	Paid-in Capital in Exc. St. Val.		3180400						3180400
33	Retained Earnings		10028794						10028794

13-1 ON YOUR OWN (concluded)

[8–12]

	ACCOUNT TITLE	TRIAL BALANCE DEBIT	TRIAL BALANCE CREDIT	ADJUSTMENTS DEBIT	ADJUSTMENTS CREDIT	INCOME STATEMENT DEBIT	INCOME STATEMENT CREDIT	BALANCE SHEET DEBIT	BALANCE SHEET CREDIT
34	Dividends	14 912 00						14 912 00	
35	Income Summary			(c) 1 377 15		1 377 15			
36	Sales		596 745 00				596 745 00		
37	Sales Discount	5 880 0				5 880 0			
38	Sales Returns & Allowances	9 153 8				9 153 8			
39	Purchases	294 665 98				294 665 98			
40	Purchases Discount		2 646 30				2 646 30		
41	Purchases Returns & Allowances		945 28				945 28		
42	Advertising Expense	5 180 90				5 180 90			
43	Credit Card Fee Expense	4 482 06				4 482 06			
44	Depr. Expense—Store Equip.			(g) 4 821 00		4 821 00			
45	Miscellaneous Exp.—Sales	6 852 00				6 852 00			
46	Salary Expense—Sales	34 114 60		(f) 674 34		34 788 94			
47	Supplies Expense—Sales			(d) 3 633 76		3 633 76			
48	Depr. Expense—Office Equip.	6 313 80		(h) 1 592 24		7 906 04			
49	Depr. Expense—Building	2 400 00		(i) 1 307 00		3 707 00			
50	Insurance Expense			(f) 1 205 44		1 205 44			
51	Miscellaneous Exp.—Administrative	6 488 24				6 488 24			
52	Payroll Taxes Expense	4 410 44		(k) 121 78		4 532 22			
53	Property Tax Expense	2 200 00				2 200 00			
54	Salary Expense—Administrative	9 018 00				9 018 00			
55	Supplies Expense—Administrative			(e) 3 431 21		3 431 21			
56	Uncollectible Accounts Expense			(b) 1 067 22		1 067 22			
57	Utilities Expense	18 478 92				18 478 92			
58	Interest Income				(a) 138 09		138 09		
59	Interest Expense	4 410 00		(j) 152 00		4 562 00			
60	Federal Income Tax Expense	4 000 00							
61		1 037 652 76	1 037 652 76						

Name _____ Date _____ Class _____

13-1 ON YOUR OWN

Extra form

(Blank work sheet with columns: Account Title, Trial Balance (Debit/Credit), Adjustments (Debit/Credit), Income Statement (Debit/Credit), Balance Sheet (Debit/Credit); 33 rows)

48 • Working Papers COPYRIGHT © SOUTH-WESTERN EDUCATIONAL PUBLISHING

13-2 WORK TOGETHER, p. 362

Analyzing financial statements [4]

The work sheet prepared in Work Together 13-1 is needed to complete this problem.

Provident Electronics
Income Statement
For Year Ended December 31, 20--

					% OF NET SALES
Operating Revenue:					
Sales				298 3 7 2 50	
Less: Sales Discount		2 9 4 00			
Sales Ret. & Allow.		4 5 7 69		7 5 1 69	
Net Sales					297 6 2 0 81
Cost of Merchandise Sold:					
Mdse. Inventory, January 1, 20--				44 0 7 2 20	
Purchases			147 3 3 2 99		
Less: Purchases Discount	1 3 2 3 15				
Purch. Ret. & Allow.	4 7 2 64		1 7 9 5 79		
Net Purchases				145 5 3 7 20	
Total Cost of Mdse. Avail for Sale				189 6 0 9 40	
Less Mdse. Inventory, Dec. 31, 20--				43 9 3 5 05	
Cost of Merchandise Sold					145 6 7 4 35
Gross Profit on Operations					151 9 4 6 46
Operating Expenses:					
Selling Expenses:					
Advertising Expense			2 5 9 0 45		
Credit Card Fee Expense			2 2 4 1 03		
Depr. Expense—Store Equip.			4 8 2 1 00		
Miscellaneous Expense—Sales			3 4 2 6 00		
Salary Expense—Sales			17 7 4 6 64		
Supplies Expense—Sales			3 6 3 3 76		
Total Selling Expenses				34 4 5 8 88	
Administrative Expenses:					
Depr. Expense—Office Equip.			4 7 4 9 14		
Depr. Expense—Building			2 5 0 7 00		
Insurance Expense			1 2 0 5 44		
Miscellaneous Expense—Admin.			3 2 4 4 12		
Payroll Taxes Expense			2 3 2 7 00		

13-2 WORK TOGETHER (continued)

[4]

Provident Electronics
Income Statement (continued)
For Year Ended December 31, 20--

					% OF NET SALES
Property Tax Expense	1 1 0 0 00				
Salary Expense—Admin.	4 5 0 9 00				
Supplies Expense—Admin.	3 4 3 1 21				
Uncoll. Accounts Expense	1 0 6 7 22				
Utilities Expense	9 2 3 9 46				
Total Admin. Expense		33 3 7 9 59			
Total Operating Expenses			67 8 3 8 47		
Income from Operations			84 1 0 7 99		
Other Revenue:					
Interest Income		1 3 8 09			
Other Expenses:					
Interest Expense		2 3 5 7 00			
Net Deduction			2 2 1 8 91		
Net Income before Fed. Income Tax			81 8 8 9 08		
Less Federal Income Tax Expense			16 0 9 2 29		
Net Income after Fed. Income Tax			65 7 9 6 79		

[5]

Earnings per share:

13-2 WORK TOGETHER (continued)

Provident Electronics
Statement of Stockholders' Equity
For Year Ended December 31, 20--

Paid-in Capital:			
Capital Stock, $12.00 Stated Value:			
January 1, 20--, 10,000 Shares Issued	120 000 00		
Issued during Current Year, 698 Shares	8 376 00		
Balance, Dec. 31, 20--, 10,698 Shares Issued		128 376 00	
Total Value of Capital Stock Issued			128 376 00
Additional Paid-in Capital:			
Pd.-in-Cap. in Exc. of St. Value			15 901 00
Total Paid-in Capital			144 277 00
Retained Earnings:			
Balance, January 1, 20--		40 143 97	
Net Income after Federal Income Tax for 20--	65 796 79		
Less Dividends Declared during 20--	7 456 00		
Net Increase during 20--		58 340 79	
Balance, December 31, 20--			98 484 76
Total Stockholders' Equity, Dec. 31, 20--			242 761 76

[6a]

Equity per share:

[6b]

Price-earnings ratio:

Market Price

$31.75

13-2 WORK TOGETHER (continued)

Provident Electronics
Balance Sheet
December 31, 20--

ASSETS			
Current Assets:			
Cash		21 2 8 0 12	
Petty Cash		2 5 0 00	
Notes Receivable		10 7 3 1 00	
Interest Receivable		1 3 8 09	
Accounts Receivable	38 0 2 9 43		
Less Allow. for Uncollectible Accounts	1 1 7 7 47	36 8 5 1 96	
Merchandise Inventory		43 9 3 5 05	
Supplies—Sales		4 4 1 0 52	
Supplies—Administrative		1 7 1 0 09	
Prepaid Insurance		2 2 2 4 93	
Total Current Assets			121 5 3 1 76
Plant Assets:			
Store Equipment	42 9 7 4 58		
Less Accum. Depr.—Store Equip.	9 9 8 5 00	32 9 8 9 58	
Office Equipment	52 1 4 2 94		
Less Accum. Depr.—Office Equipment	2 6 9 6 72	49 4 4 6 22	
Building	24 0 0 0 00		
Less Accum. Depr.—Building	3 9 2 1 00	20 0 7 9 00	
Land		41 0 0 0 00	
Total Plant Assets			143 5 1 4 80
Total Assets			265 0 4 6 56

13-2 WORK TOGETHER (continued)

Provident Electronics
Balance Sheet (continued)
December 31, 20--

LIABILITIES		
Current Liabilities:		
Notes Payable	1 5 2 0 00	
Interest Payable	1 5 2 00	
Accounts Payable	5 2 3 4 27	
Employee Income Tax Payable	2 0 8 00	
Federal Income Tax Payable	6 0 9 2 29	
Social Security Tax Payable	1 5 8 10	
Medicare Tax Payable	4 0 29	
Salaries Payable	6 7 4 34	
Sales Tax Payable	3 1 4 50	
Unemploy. Tax Payable—Federal	2 0 35	
Unemploy. Tax Payable—State	3 3 4 72	
Health Insurance Premiums Payable	7 3 06	
Dividends Payable	7 4 6 2 88	
Total Liabilities		22 2 8 4 80
STOCKHOLDERS' EQUITY		
Total Stockholders' Equity		242 7 6 1 76
Total Liabilities & Stockholders' Equity		265 0 4 6 56

13-2 WORK TOGETHER (concluded)

[7a]

Accounts receivable turnover ratio:

January 1 Book Value

$42,684.28

Net Sales on Account

$238,698.00

[7b]

Rate earned on average stockholders' equity:

January 1 Equity

$171,613.97

[7c]

Rate earned on average total assets:

January 1 Assets

$249,980.25

13-2 ON YOUR OWN, p. 362

Analyzing financial statements [8]

The work sheet prepared in On Your Own 13-1 is needed to complete this problem.

BRE Corporation
Income Statement
For Year Ended December 31, 20--

					% OF NET SALES
Operating Revenue:					
Sales				596 745 00	
Less: Sales Discount			588 00		
Sales Ret. & Allow.			915 38	1 503 38	
Net Sales					595 241 62
Cost of Merchandise Sold:					
Mdse. Inventory, January 1, 20--				88 144 40	
Purchases			294 665 98		
Less: Purchases Discount	2 646 30				
Purch. Ret. & Allow.	945 28	3 591 58			
Net Purchases				291 074 40	
Total Cost of Mdse. Avail for Sale				379 218 80	
Less Mdse. Inventory, Dec. 31, 20--				88 007 25	
Cost of Merchandise Sold					291 211 55
Gross Profit on Operations					304 030 07
Operating Expenses:					
Selling Expenses:					
Advertising Expense			5 180 90		
Credit Card Fee Expense			4 482 06		
Depr. Expense—Store Equip.			4 821 00		
Miscellaneous Expense—Sales			6 852 00		
Salary Expense—Sales			34 818 94		
Supplies Expense—Sales			3 633 76		
Total Selling Expenses				59 788 66	
Administrative Expenses:					
Depr. Expense—Office Equip.			7 906 04		
Depr. Expense—Building			3 707 00		
Insurance Expense			1 205 44		
Miscellaneous Expense—Admin.			6 488 24		
Payroll Taxes Expense			4 532 22		

13-2 ON YOUR OWN (continued)

[8]

BRE Corporation
Income Statement (continued)
For Year Ended December 31, 20--

				% OF NET SALES
Property Tax Expense	2 200 00			
Salary Expense—Admin.	9 018 00			
Supplies Expense—Admin.	3 431 21			
Uncoll. Accounts Expense	1 067 22			
Utilities Expense	18 478 92			
Total Admin. Expense		58 034 29		
Total Operating Expenses			117 822 95	
Income from Operations			186 207 12	
Other Revenue:				
Interest Income		138 09		
Other Expenses:				
Interest Expense		4 562 00		
Net Deduction			4 423 91	
Net Income before Fed. Income Tax			181 783 21	
Less Federal Income Tax Expense			54 145 45	
Net Income after Fed. Income Tax			127 637 76	

[9]

Earnings per share:

13-2 ON YOUR OWN (continued)

BRE Corporation
Statement of Stockholders' Equity
For Year Ended December 31, 20--

Paid-in Capital:			
Capital Stock, $10.00 Stated Value:			
January 1, 20--, 20,000 Shares Issued	200 000 00		
Issued during Current Year, 5,675 Shares	56 750 00		
Balance, Dec. 31, 20--, 25,675 Shares Issued		256 750 00	
Total Value of Capital Stock Issued			256 750 00
Additional Paid-in Capital:			
Pd.-in-Cap. in Exc. of St. Value			31 804 00
Total Paid-in Capital			288 554 00
Retained Earnings:			
Balance, January 1, 20--		100 287 94	
Net Income after Federal Income Tax for 20--	127 637 76		
Less Dividends Declared during 20--	14 912 00		
Net Increase during 20--		112 725 76	
Balance, December 31, 20--			213 013 70
Total Stockholders' Equity, Dec. 31, 20--			501 567 70

[10a]

Equity per share:

[10b]

Price-earnings ratio:

Market Price
  $48.25

13-2 ON YOUR OWN (continued)

BRE Corporation
Balance Sheet
December 31, 20--

ASSETS				
Current Assets:				
Cash			42 560 24	
Petty Cash			500 00	
Notes Receivable			21 462 00	
Interest Receivable			138 09	
Accounts Receivable	76 058 86			
Less Allow. for Uncoll. Accounts	1 287 72		74 771 14	
Merchandise Inventory			88 007 25	
Supplies—Sales			12 454 80	
Supplies—Administrative			6 851 39	
Prepaid Insurance			5 655 30	
Total Current Assets				252 400 21
Plant Assets:				
Store Equipment	85 949 16			
Less Accum. Depr.—Store Equip.	15 149 00		70 800 16	
Office Equipment	104 285 88			
Less Accum. Depr.—Office Equipment	3 801 20		100 484 68	
Building	48 000 00			
Less Accum. Depr.—Building	6 535 00		41 465 00	
Land			82 000 00	
Total Plant Assets				294 749 84
Total Assets				547 150 05

13-2 ON YOUR OWN (continued)

<u>BRE Corporation</u>
<u>Balance Sheet (continued)</u>
<u>December 31, 20--</u>

LIABILITIES		
Current Liabilities:		
Notes Payable	3 0 4 0 00	
Interest Payable	1 5 2 00	
Accounts Payable	10 4 6 8 54	
Employee Income Tax Payable	4 1 6 00	
Federal Income Tax Payable	14 1 4 5 45	
Social Security Tax Payable	2 5 8 75	
Medicare Tax Payable	6 7 16	
Salaries Payable	6 7 4 34	
Sales Tax Payable	6 2 9 00	
Unemploy. Tax Payable—Federal	3 8 69	
Unemploy. Tax Payable—State	6 2 0 54	
Health Insurance Premiums Payable	1 4 6 12	
Dividends Payable	14 9 2 5 76	
Total Liabilities		45 5 8 2 35
STOCKHOLDERS' EQUITY		
Total Stockholders' Equity		501 5 6 7 70
Total Liabilities & Stockholders' Equity		547 1 5 0 05

13-2 ON YOUR OWN (concluded)

[11a]

Accounts receivable turnover ratio:

January 1 Book Value
$69,250.50

Net Sales on Account
$505,955.30

[11b]

Rate earned on average stockholders' equity:

January 1 Equity
$300,287.94

[11c]

Rate earned on average total assets:

January 1 Assets
$538,140.20

13-3 WORK TOGETHER, p. 369

End-of-fiscal period work for a corporation [4]

The work sheet from Work Together 13-1 is needed to complete this problem.

GENERAL JOURNAL — PAGE 14

DATE	ACCOUNT TITLE	DOC. NO.	POST. REF.	DEBIT	CREDIT

13-3 WORK TOGETHER (continued)

[5]

GENERAL JOURNAL — PAGE 15

DATE	ACCOUNT TITLE	DOC. NO.	POST. REF.	DEBIT	CREDIT

13-3 WORK TOGETHER (continued)

[6]

Provident Electronics
Post-Closing Trial Balance
December 31, 20--

ACCOUNT TITLE	DEBIT	CREDIT

13-3 WORK TOGETHER (concluded)

[7]

GENERAL JOURNAL PAGE 16

DATE	ACCOUNT TITLE	DOC. NO.	POST. REF.	DEBIT	CREDIT

13-3 ON YOUR OWN, p. 369

End-of-fiscal period work for a corporation [8]

The work sheet from On Your Own 13-1 is needed to complete this problem.

GENERAL JOURNAL — PAGE 14

	DATE	ACCOUNT TITLE	DOC. NO.	POST. REF.	DEBIT	CREDIT	
1							1
2							2
3							3
4							4
5							5
6							6
7							7
8							8
9							9
10							10
11							11
12							12
13							13
14							14
15							15
16							16
17							17
18							18
19							19
20							20
21							21
22							22
23							23
24							24
25							25
26							26
27							27
28							28
29							29
30							30

13-3 ON YOUR OWN (continued)

[9]

GENERAL JOURNAL
PAGE 15

	DATE	ACCOUNT TITLE	DOC. NO.	POST. REF.	DEBIT	CREDIT	
1							1
2							2
3							3
4							4
5							5
6							6
7							7
8							8
9							9
10							10
11							11
12							12
13							13
14							14
15							15
16							16
17							17
18							18
19							19
20							20
21							21
22							22
23							23
24							24
25							25
26							26
27							27
28							28
29							29
30							30
31							31

13-3 ON YOUR OWN (continued)

[10]

BRE Corporation
Post-Closing Trial Balance
December 31, 20--

ACCOUNT TITLE	DEBIT	CREDIT

13-3 ON YOUR OWN (concluded)

[11]

GENERAL JOURNAL   PAGE 16

DATE	ACCOUNT TITLE	DOC. NO.	POST. REF.	DEBIT	CREDIT

13-1 APPLICATION PROBLEM, p. 371

The work sheet for this problem begins on page 70.

Preparing a work sheet for a corporation

	ACCOUNT TITLE	TRIAL BALANCE DEBIT	TRIAL BALANCE CREDIT	ADJUSTMENTS DEBIT	ADJUSTMENTS CREDIT	INCOME STATEMENT DEBIT	INCOME STATEMENT CREDIT	BALANCE SHEET DEBIT	BALANCE SHEET CREDIT
59	Depr. Expense—Office Equip.								
60	Insurance Expense								
61	Miscellaneous Expense—Admin.	3 268 03							
62	Payroll Taxes Expense	2 381 86							
63	Property Tax Expense	2 300 00							
64	Salary Expense—Admin.	5 395 33							
65	Supplies Expense—Admin.								
66	Uncollectible Accounts Expense								
67	Utilities Expense	5 518 66							
68	Interest Income		1 233 3						
69	Interest Expense	2 620 59							
70	Organization Expense								
71	Federal Income Tax Expense	5 500 00							
72		44 662 426	44 662 426						

13-1 APPLICATION PROBLEM (continued)

The work sheet prepared in Application Problem 13-1 is needed to complete Application Problems 13-3 and 13-4.

Trexler, Inc.
Work Sheet
For Year Ended December 31, 20--

	ACCOUNT TITLE	TRIAL BALANCE DEBIT	TRIAL BALANCE CREDIT	ADJUSTMENTS DEBIT	ADJUSTMENTS CREDIT	INCOME STATEMENT DEBIT	INCOME STATEMENT CREDIT	BALANCE SHEET DEBIT	BALANCE SHEET CREDIT
1	Cash	42789 60							
2	Petty Cash	500 00							
3	Notes Receivable	18924 91							
4	Interest Receivable								
5	Accounts Receivable	30830 48							
6	Allowance for Uncollectible Accts.		92 49						
7	Merchandise Inventory	516100 22							
8	Supplies—Sales	2898 07							
9	Supplies—Administrative	5025 37							
10	Prepaid Insurance	4069 62							
11	Prepaid Interest								
12	Bond Sinking Fund	4000 00							
13	Store Equipment	13627 07							
14	Accum. Depr.—Store Equip.		1308 20						
15	Building	58000 00							
16	Accum. Depr.—Building		3219 00						
17	Office Equipment	3049 134							
18	Accum. Depr.—Office Equip.		3079 63						
19	Land	31488 84							
20	Organization Costs	200 00							
21	Notes Payable		3083 0						
22	Interest Payable								
23	Accounts Payable		19427 6						
24	Employee Income Tax Payable		2466 4						
25	Federal Income Tax Payable								
26	Social Security Tax Payable		1209 0						
27	Medicare Tax Payable		279 0						
28	Salaries Payable								

13-1 APPLICATION PROBLEM (continued)

	ACCOUNT TITLE	TRIAL BALANCE		ADJUSTMENTS		INCOME STATEMENT		BALANCE SHEET	
		DEBIT	CREDIT	DEBIT	CREDIT	DEBIT	CREDIT	DEBIT	CREDIT
29	Sales Tax Payable		431 63						
30	Unemploy. Tax Payable—Federal		49 21						
31	Unemploy. Tax Payable—State		332 78						
32	Health Insur. Prem. Payable		92 49						
33	Dividends Payable		9073 50						
34	Bonds Payable		40000 00						
35	Capital Stock—Common		109000 00						
36	Pd.-in Cap. in Exc. St. Val.—Common		2400 00						
37	Capital Stock—Preferred		42000 00						
38	Pd.-in.Cap. in Exc. Par—Preferred		1100 00						
39	Disc. on Sale of Preferred Stock	2000 00							
40	Treasury Stock	700 00							
41	Pd.-in Cap. from Sale of Tr. Stock		140 00						
42	Retained Earnings		13411 26						
43	Dividends—Common	4873 50							
44	Dividends—Preferred	4200 00							
45	Income Summary								
46	Sales		194401 19						
47	Sales Discount	388 80							
48	Sales Returns & Allowances	583 20							
49	Purchases	92306 46							
50	Purchases Discount		1569 21						
51	Purchases Returns & Allowances		553 84						
52	Advertising Expense	2343 12							
53	Credit Card Fee Expense	2651 42							
54	Depr. Expense—Store Equip.								
55	Miscellaneous Expense—Sales	1140 73							
56	Salary Expense—Sales	13997 04							
57	Supplies Expense—Sales								
58	Depr. Expense—Building								

13-1 APPLICATION PROBLEM (concluded)

Extra form

13-2 APPLICATION PROBLEM, p. 371

Calculating federal income taxes

Corporation A	Net Income Before Taxes	Tax Rate	Federal Income Tax Amount
15% of the first $50,000			
25% of the next $25,000			
34% of the next $25,000			
39% of the next $235,000			
34% of the net income about $335,000			
Totals			

Corporation B	Net Income Before Taxes	Tax Rate	Federal Income Tax Amount
15% of the first $50,000			
25% of the next $25,000			
34% of the next $25,000			
39% of the next $235,000			
34% of the net income about $335,000			
Totals			

Corporation C	Net Income Before Taxes	Tax Rate	Federal Income Tax Amount
15% of the first $50,000			
25% of the next $25,000			
34% of the next $25,000			
39% of the next $235,000			
34% of the net income about $335,000			
Totals			

Name _____ Date _____ Class _____

13-2 APPLICATION PROBLEM

Extra forms

	Net Income Before Taxes	Tax Rate	Federal Income Tax Amount
15% of the first $50,000			
25% of the next $25,000			
34% of the next $25,000			
39% of the next $235,000			
34% of the net income about $335,000			
Totals			

	Net Income Before Taxes	Tax Rate	Federal Income Tax Amount
15% of the first $50,000			
25% of the next $25,000			
34% of the next $25,000			
39% of the next $235,000			
34% of the net income about $335,000			
Totals			

	Net Income Before Taxes	Tax Rate	Federal Income Tax Amount
15% of the first $50,000			
25% of the next $25,000			
34% of the next $25,000			
39% of the next $235,000			
34% of the net income about $335,000			
Totals			

13-3 APPLICATION PROBLEM, p. 371

Preparing financial statements for a corporation [1]

The work sheet prepared in Application Problem 13-1 is needed to complete this problem.

Trexler, Inc.
Income Statement
For Year Ended December 31, 20--

					% OF NET SALES
Operating Revenue:					
Sales					
Less: Sales Discount					
Sales Ret. & Allow.					
Net Sales					
Cost of Merchandise Sold:					
Mdse. Inventory, January 1, 20--					
Purchases					
Less: Purchases Discount					
Purch. Ret. & Allow.					
Net Purchases					
Total Cost of Mdse. Avail. for Sale					
Less Mdse. Inventory, Dec. 31, 20--					
Cost of Merchandise Sold					
Gross Profit on Operations					
Operating Expenses:					
Selling Expenses:					
Advertising Expense					
Credit Card Fee Expense					
Depr. Expense—Store Equip.					
Miscellaneous Expense—Sales					
Salary Expense—Sales					
Supplies Expense—Sales					
Total Selling Expenses					
Administrative Expenses:					
Depr. Expense—Building					
Depr. Expense—Office Equip.					
Insurance Expense					
Miscellaneous Expense—Admin.					
Payroll Taxes Expense					

13-3 APPLICATION PROBLEM (continued)

[1]

Trexler, Inc.

Income Statement (continued)

For Year Ended December 31, 20--

				% OF NET SALES
Property Tax Expense				
Salary Expense—Admin.				
Supplies Expense—Admin.				
Uncoll. Accounts Expense				
Utilities Expense				
Total Admin. Expense				
Total Operating Expenses				
Income from Operations				
Other Revenue:				
Interest Income				
Other Expenses:				
Interest Expense				
Organization Expense				
Total Other Expenses				
Net Deduction				
Net Income before Fed. Income Tax				
Less Federal Income Tax Expense				
Net Income after Fed. Income Tax				

[4]

Earnings per share:

Name _____ Date _____ Class _____

13-3 APPLICATION PROBLEM (continued)

Income statement analysis [2, 3]

		Acceptable %	Actual %	Positive Result		Recommended Action If Needed
				Yes	No	
a.	Cost of merchandise sold	Not more than 40.0%				
b.	Gross profit on operations	Not less than 60.0%				
c.	Total selling expenses	Not more than 13.5%				
d.	Total administrative expenses	Not more than 18.5%				
e.	Total operating expenses	Not more than 32.0%				
f.	Income from operations	Not less than 28.0%				
g.	Net deduction from other revenue and expenses	Not more than 4.0%				
h.	Net income before federal income tax	Not less than 24.0%				

Chapter 13 Financial Analysis and Reporting for a Corporation • 77

13-3 APPLICATION PROBLEM (continued)

[5]

Trexler, Inc.
Statement of Stockholders' Equity
For Year Ended December 31, 20--

Paid-in Capital:					
Common Stock, Stated Value:					
January 1, 20--, Shares Issued					
Issued during Current Year, Shares					
Balance, Dec. 31, 20--, Shares Issued					
Preferred Stock, , Par Value:					
January 1, 20--, Shares Issued					
Issued during Current Year, Shares					
Balance, Dec. 31, 20--, Shares Issued					
Total Value of Capital Stock Issued					
Additional Paid-in Capital:					
Pd.-in-Cap. in Exc. of St. Value—Common					
Pd.-in-Cap. in Exc. of Par—Preferred					
Pd.-in-Cap. from Sale of Treasury Stock					
Less Disc. on Sale of Preferred Stock					
Total Additional Paid-in Capital					
Total Paid-in Capital					
Retained Earnings:					
Balance, January 1, 20--					
Net Income after Federal Income Tax for 20--					
Less Dividends Declared during 20--					
Net Increase during 20--					
Balance, December 31, 20--					
Total Pd.-in Capital & Retained Earnings					
Less Treasury Stock, Shares of					
Common Stock, December 31, 20--					
Total Stockholders' Equity, Dec. 31, 20--					

13-3 APPLICATION PROBLEM (continued)

[6a]

Equity per share:

[6b]

Price-earnings ratio:

[7]

Trexler, Inc.

Balance Sheet

December 31, 20--

ASSETS					
Current Assets:					
Cash					
Petty Cash					
Notes Receivable					
Interest Receivable					
Accounts Receivable					
Less Allow. for Uncoll. Accounts					
Merchandise Inventory					
Supplies—Sales					
Supplies—Administrative					
Prepaid Insurance					
Prepaid Interest					
Total Current Assets					
Long-Term Investment:					
Bond Sinking Fund					
Plant Assets:					
Store Equipment					
Less Accum. Depr.—Store Equip.					

13-3 APPLICATION PROBLEM (continued)

[7]

Trexler, Inc.
Balance Sheet (continued)
December 31, 20--

Building				
Less Accum. Depr.—Building Equipment				
Office				
Less Accum. Depr.—Office				
Land				
Total Plant Assets				
Intangible Asset:				
Organization Costs				
Total Assets				
LIABILITIES				
Current Liabilities:				
Notes Payable				
Interest Payable				
Accounts Payable				
Employee Income Tax Payable				
Federal Income Tax Payable				
Social Security Tax Payable				
Medicare Tax Payable				
Salaries Payable				
Sales Tax Payable				
Unemploy. Tax Payable—Federal				
Unemploy. Tax Payable—State				
Health Insurance Premiums Payable				
Dividends Payable				
Total Current Liabilities				
Long-Term Liability:				
Bonds Payable				
Total Liabilities				
STOCKHOLDERS' EQUITY				
Total Stockholders' Equity				
Total Liabilities & Stockholders' Equity				

13-3 APPLICATION PROBLEM (continued)

[8a]

Accounts receivable turnover ratio:

[8b]

Rate earned on average stockholders' equity:

[8c]

Rate earned on average total assets:

13-3 APPLICATION PROBLEM

Extra form

13-4 APPLICATION PROBLEM, p. 372

[1]

The work sheet prepared in Application Problem 13-1 is needed to complete this problem.

DATE	ACCOUNT TITLE	DOC. NO.	POST. REF.	DEBIT	CREDIT

GENERAL JOURNAL — PAGE 13

13-4 APPLICATION PROBLEM (continued)

[2]

GENERAL JOURNAL — PAGE 14

DATE	ACCOUNT TITLE	DOC. NO.	POST. REF.	DEBIT	CREDIT

13-4 APPLICATION PROBLEM (concluded)

[3]

GENERAL JOURNAL — PAGE 1

	DATE	ACCOUNT TITLE	DOC. NO.	POST. REF.	DEBIT	CREDIT	
1							1
2							2
3							3
4							4
5							5
6							6
7							7
8							8
9							9
10							10
11							11
12							12
13							13
14							14
15							15
16							16
17							17
18							18
19							19
20							20
21							21
22							22
23							23
24							24
25							25
26							26
27							27
28							28
29							29
30							30
31							31
32							32
33							33
34							34
35							35

13-4 APPLICATION PROBLEM

Extra form

GENERAL JOURNAL

PAGE

DATE	ACCOUNT TITLE	DOC. NO.	POST. REF.	DEBIT	CREDIT

13-5 MASTERY PROBLEM

Extra form

GENERAL JOURNAL PAGE

DATE	ACCOUNT TITLE	DOC. NO.	POST. REF.	DEBIT	CREDIT

13-5 MASTERY PROBLEM, p. 373

Completing end-of-fiscal period work for a corporation [1]

Lander, Inc.
Work Sheet
For Year Ended December 31, 20--

	ACCOUNT TITLE	TRIAL BALANCE DEBIT	TRIAL BALANCE CREDIT	ADJUSTMENTS DEBIT	ADJUSTMENTS CREDIT	INCOME STATEMENT DEBIT	INCOME STATEMENT CREDIT	BALANCE SHEET DEBIT	BALANCE SHEET CREDIT
1	Cash	42 560 24							
2	Petty Cash	500 00							
3	Notes Receivable	2 156 17							
4	Interest Receivable								
5	Accounts Receivable	56 058 86							
6	Allowance for Uncollectible Accounts		156 18						
7	Merchandise Inventory	87 146 53							
8	Supplies—Sales	17 088 54							
9	Supplies—Administrative	10 485 59							
10	Prepaid Insurance	6 871 77							
11	Prepaid Interest								
12	Bond Sinking Fund	7 000 00							
13	Store Equipment	67 974 77							
14	Accum. Depr.—Store Equip.		8 035 91						
15	Building	48 000 00							
16	Accum. Depr.—Building		5 328 00						
17	Office Equipment	53 010 02							
18	Accum. Depr.—Office Equip.		2 208 96						
19	Land	104 285 03							
20	Organization Costs	300 00							
21	Notes Payable		5 205 9						
22	Interest Payable								
23	Accounts Payable		10 468 53						
24	Employee Income Tax Payable		416 47						
25	Federal Income Tax Payable								
26	Social Security Tax Payable		204 15						
27	Medicare Tax Payable		47 11						
28	Salaries Payable								

13-5 MASTERY PROBLEM (continued)

[1]

	ACCOUNT TITLE	TRIAL BALANCE DEBIT	TRIAL BALANCE CREDIT	ADJUSTMENTS DEBIT	ADJUSTMENTS CREDIT	INCOME STATEMENT DEBIT	INCOME STATEMENT CREDIT	BALANCE SHEET DEBIT	BALANCE SHEET CREDIT	
29	Sales Tax Payable		7 2 8 82							29
30	Unemploy. Tax Payable—Federal		8 3 09							30
31	Unemploy. Tax Payable—State		5 6 1 92							31
32	Health Ins. Prem. Payable		1 5 6 18							32
33	Dividends Payable		14 9 2 2 80							33
34	Bonds Payable		70 0 0 0 00							34
35	Capital Stock—Common		184 0 0 0 00							35
36	Pd.-in Cap. in Exc. St. Val.—Common		30 0 0 0 00							36
37	Capital Stock—Preferred		72 0 0 0 00							37
38	Pd.-in.Cap. in Exc. Par—Preferred		1 8 0 0 00							38
39	Disc. on Sale of Preferred Stock	3 0 0 0 00								39
40	Treasury Stock	1 2 0 0 00								40
41	Pd.-in Cap. from Sale of Tr. Stock		2 4 0 00							41
42	Retained Earnings		22 6 4 5 60							42
43	Dividends—Common	7 7 2 2 80								43
44	Dividends—Preferred	7 2 0 0 00								44
45	Income Summary									45
46	Sales		376 7 3 5 50							46
47	Sales Discount	5 9 3 47								47
48	Sales Returns & Allowances	8 9 0 21								48
49	Purchases	155 6 5 5 99								49
50	Purchases Discount		2 6 4 6 15							50
51	Purchases Returns & Allow.		9 3 3 94							51
52	Advertising Expense	3 9 5 6 47								52
53	Credit Card Fee Expense	4 4 7 7 06								53
54	Depr. Expense—Store Equip.									54
55	Miscellaneous Expense—Sales	6 9 7 5 89								55
56	Salary Expense—Sales	34 1 5 0 61								56
57	Supplies Expense—Sales									57
58	Depr. Expense—Building									58

13-5 MASTERY PROBLEM (continued)

[1]

	ACCOUNT TITLE	TRIAL BALANCE DEBIT	TRIAL BALANCE CREDIT	ADJUSTMENTS DEBIT	ADJUSTMENTS CREDIT	INCOME STATEMENT DEBIT	INCOME STATEMENT CREDIT	BALANCE SHEET DEBIT	BALANCE SHEET CREDIT	
59	Depr. Expense—Office Equip.									59
60	Insurance Expense									60
61	Miscellaneous Expense—Admin.	6518 24								61
62	Payroll Taxes Expense	4710 44								62
63	Property Tax Expense	2300 00								63
64	Salary Expense—Admin.	9110 30								64
65	Supplies Expense—Admin.									65
66	Uncollectible Accounts Expense									66
67	Utilities Expense	9318 54								67
68	Interest Income		208 24							68
69	Interest Expense	4425 00								69
70	Organization Expense									70
71	Federal Income Tax Expense	20000 00								71
72		80504 8 14	80504 8 14							72
73										73
74										74
75										75
76										76
77										77
78										78
79										79
80										80
81										81
82										82
83										83
84										84
85										85
86										86
87										87
88										88

13-5 MASTERY PROBLEM (continued)

[2-4]

Lander, Inc.
Income Statement
For Year Ended December 31, 20--

					% OF NET SALES
Operating Revenue:					
Sales					
Less: Sales Discount					
Sales Ret. & Allow.					
Net Sales					
Cost of Merchandise Sold:					
Mdse. Inventory, January 1, 20--					
Purchases					
Less: Purchases Discount					
Purch. Ret. & Allow.					
Net Purchases					
Total Cost of Mdse. Avail. for Sale					
Less Mdse. Inventory, Dec. 31, 20--					
Cost of Merchandise Sold					
Gross Profit on Operations					
Operating Expenses:					
Selling Expenses:					
Advertising Expense					
Credit Card Fee Expense					
Depr. Expense—Store Equip.					
Miscellaneous Expense—Sales					
Salary Expense—Sales					
Supplies Expense—Sales					
Total Selling Expenses					
Administrative Expenses:					
Depr. Expense—Building					
Depr. Expense—Office Equip.					
Insurance Expense					
Miscellaneous Expense—Admin.					
Payroll Taxes Expense					
Property Tax Expense					
Salary Expense—Admin.					

13-5 MASTERY PROBLEM (continued)

[2]

Lander, Inc.
Income Statement (continued)
For Year Ended December 31, 20--

					% OF NET SALES
Supplies Expense—Admin.					
Uncollectible Accounts Expense					
Utilities Expense					
Total Admin. Expense					
Total Operating Expenses					
Income from Operations					
Other Revenue:					
Interest Income					
Other Expenses:					
Interest Expense					
Organization Expense					
Total Other Expenses					
Net Deduction					
Net Income before Fed. Income Tax					
Less Federal Income Tax Expense					
Net Income after Fed. Income Tax					

[4]

Earnings per share:

13-5 MASTERY PROBLEM (continued)

Income statement analysis [3]

		Acceptable %	Actual %	Positive Result		Recommended Action If Needed
				Yes	No	
a.	Cost of merchandise sold	Not more than 42.0%				
b.	Gross profit on operations	Not less than 58.0%				
c.	Total selling expenses	Not more than 13.0%				
d.	Total administrative expenses	Not more than 15.5%				
e.	Total operating expenses	Not more than 28.5%				
f.	Income from operations	Not less than 29.5%				
g.	Net deduction from other revenue and expenses	Not more than 3.5%				
h.	Net income before federal income tax	Not less than 26.0%				

13-5 MASTERY PROBLEM (continued)

[5]

Lander, Inc.
Statement of Stockholders' Equity
For Year Ended December 31, 20--

Paid-in Capital:					
Common Stock, Stated Value:					
January 1, 20--, Shares Issued					
Issued during Current Year, Shares					
Balance, Dec. 31, 20--, Shares Issued					
Preferred Stock, , Par Value:					
January 1, 20--, Shares Issued					
Issued during Current Year, Shares					
Balance, Dec. 31, 20--, Shares Issued					
Total Value of Capital Stock Issued					
Additional Paid-in Capital:					
Pd.-in-Cap. in Exc. of St. Value—Common					
Pd.-in-Cap. in Exc. of Par—Preferred					
Pd.-in-Cap. from Sale of Treasury Stock					
Less Disc. on Sale of Preferred Stock					
Total Additional Paid-in Capital					
Total Paid-in Capital					
Retained Earnings:					
Balance, January 1, 20--					
Net Income after Federal Income Tax for 20--					
Less Dividends Declared during 20--					
Net Increase during 20--					
Balance, December 31, 20--					
Total Pd.-in Capital & Retained Earnings					
Less Treasury Stock, Shares of					
Common Stock, December 31, 20--					
Total Stockholders' Equity, Dec. 31, 20--					

13-5 MASTERY PROBLEM (continued)

[6a]

Equity per share:

[6b]

Price-earnings ratio:

[7]

Lander, Inc.

Balance Sheet

December 31, 20--

ASSETS												
Current Assets:												
Cash												
Petty Cash												
Notes Receivable												
Interest Receivable												
Accounts Receivable												
Less Allow. for Uncoll. Accounts												
Merchandise Inventory												
Supplies—Sales												
Supplies—Administrative												
Prepaid Insurance												
Prepaid Interest												
Total Current Assets												
Long-Term Investment:												
Bond Sinking Fund												
Plant Assets:												
Store Equipment												
Less Accum. Depr.—Store Equip.												

13-5 MASTERY PROBLEM (continued)

[7]

Lander, Inc.

Balance Sheet (continued)

December 31, 20--

Building					
Less Accum. Depr.—Building Equipment					
Office Equipment					
Less Accum. Depr.—Office Equipment					
Land					
Total Plant Assets					
Intangible Asset:					
Organization Costs					
Total Assets					
<div align="center">LIABILITIES</div>					
Current Liabilities:					
Notes Payable					
Interest Payable					
Accounts Payable					
Employee Income Tax Payable					
Federal Income Tax Payable					
Social Security Tax Payable					
Medicare Tax Payable					
Salaries Payable					
Sales Tax Payable					
Unemploy. Tax Payable—Federal					
Unemploy. Tax Payable—State					
Health Insurance Premiums Payable					
Dividends Payable					
Total Current Liabilities					
Long-Term Liability:					
Bonds Payable					
Total Liabilities					
<div align="center">STOCKHOLDERS' EQUITY</div>					
Total Stockholders' Equity					
Total Liabilities & Stockholders' Equity					

Name _____ Date _____ Class _____

13-5 MASTERY PROBLEM (continued)

[8a]

Accounts receivable turnover ratio:

[8b]

Rate earned on average stockholders' equity:

[8c]

Rate earned on average total assets:

13-5 MASTERY PROBLEM (continued)

[9]

GENERAL JOURNAL PAGE 13

DATE	ACCOUNT TITLE	DOC. NO.	POST. REF.	DEBIT	CREDIT

13-5 MASTERY PROBLEM (continued)

[10]

GENERAL JOURNAL PAGE 14

	DATE	ACCOUNT TITLE	DOC. NO.	POST. REF.	DEBIT	CREDIT	
1							1
2							2
3							3
4							4
5							5
6							6
7							7
8							8
9							9
10							10
11							11
12							12
13							13
14							14
15							15
16							16
17							17
18							18
19							19
20							20
21							21
22							22
23							23
24							24
25							25
26							26
27							27
28							28
29							29
30							30
31							31
32							32
33							33
34							34
35							35

13-5 MASTERY PROBLEM (concluded)

[11]

GENERAL JOURNAL

PAGE 1

DATE	ACCOUNT TITLE	DOC. NO.	POST. REF.	DEBIT	CREDIT

13-6 CHALLENGE PROBLEM, p. 374

Preparing a Form 1120, U.S. Corporation Income Tax Return

Goldstein, Inc.

Income Statement

For Year Ended December 31, 20--

					% OF NET SALES
Operating Revenue:					
Sales			873 902 40		
Less: Sales Discount		1 887 45			
Sales Ret. & Allow.		3 000 45	4 887 90		
Net Sales				869 014 50	100.0
Cost of Merchandise Sold:					
Mdse. Inventory, January 1, 20--			267 453 09		
Purchases		426 596 48			
Less: Purchases Discount	3 625 65				
Purch. Ret. & Allow.	5 754 70	9 380 35			
Net Purchases			417 216 13		
Total Cost of Mdse. Avail. for Sale			684 669 22		
Less Mdse. Inventory, Dec. 31, 20--			258 755 19		
Cost of Merchandise Sold				425 914 03	49.0
Gross Profit on Operations				443 100 47	51.0
Operating Expenses:					
Selling Expenses:					
Advertising Expense		8 021 20			
Credit Card Fee Expense		12 632 30			
Depr. Expense—Store Equip.		14 256 30			
Miscellaneous Expense—Sales		17 352 30			
Salary Expense—Sales		48 643 40			
Supplies Expense—Sales		18 464 31			
Total Selling Expenses			119 369 81		13.7
Administrative Expenses:					
Depr. Expense—Building		10 500 00			
Depr. Expense—Office Equip.		5 854 50			
Insurance Expense		6 234 20			
Miscellaneous Expense—Admin.		17 432 20			
Payroll Taxes Expense		7 523 30			
Property Tax Expense		16 918 84			
Salary Expense—Admin.		21 754 30			

13-6 CHALLENGE PROBLEM (continued)

Goldstein, Inc.
Income Statement (continued)
For Year Ended December 31, 20--

				% OF NET SALES
Supplies Expense—Admin.		16 4 3 2 60		
Uncoll. Accounts Expense		3 7 4 5 20		
Utilities Expense		20 5 3 2 60		
Total Admin. Expense			126 9 2 7 74	14.6
Total Operating Expenses			246 2 9 7 55	28.3
Income from Operations			196 8 0 2 92	22.6
Other Revenue:				
Interest Income			5 1 1 33	
Other Expenses:				
Interest Expense		35 7 5 5 45		
Organization Expense		7 2 0 00		
Total Other Expenses			36 4 7 5 45	
Net Deduction from Other Rev. & Exp.			35 9 6 4 12	4.1
Net Income before Fed. Income Tax			160 8 3 8 80	18.5
Less Federal Income Tax Expense			45 9 7 7 13	5.3
Net Income after Fed. Income Tax			114 8 6 1 67	13.2

13-6 CHALLENGE PROBLEM (concluded)

[1–6]

Form 1120 — U.S. Corporation Income Tax Return
Department of the Treasury, Internal Revenue Service
OMB No. 1545-0123
20--

For calendar year 20-- or tax year beginning ...., 20--, ending ...., 20 ...
▶ Instructions are separate. See page 1 for Paperwork Reduction Act Notice.

A Check if a:
(1) Consolidated return (attach Form 851) ☐
(2) Personal holding co. (attach Sch. PH) ☐
(3) Personal service corp. (as defined in Temporary Regs. sec. 1.441-4T—see instructions) ☐

Use IRS label. Otherwise, please print or type.
Name
Number, street, and room or suite no. (If a P.O. box, see page 6 of instructions.)
City or town, state, and ZIP code

B Employer identification number
C Date incorporated
D Total assets (see Specific Instructions) $

E Check applicable boxes: (1) ☐ Initial return (2) ☐ Final return (3) ☐ Change in address

Income

1a	Gross receipts or sales _____ b Less returns and allowances _____ c Bal ▶	1c
2	Cost of goods sold (Schedule A, line 8)	2
3	Gross profit. Subtract line 2 from line 1c	3
4	Dividends (Schedule C, line 19)	4
5	Interest	5
6	Gross rents	6
7	Gross royalties	7
8	Capital gain net income (attach Schedule D (Form 1120))	8
9	Net gain or (loss) from Form 4797, Part II, line 20 (attach Form 4797)	9
10	Other income (see instructions—attach schedule)	10
11	**Total income.** Add lines 3 through 10 ▶	11

Deductions (See instructions for limitations on deductions.)

12	Compensation of officers (Schedule E, line 4)	12
13a	Salaries and wages _____ b Less jobs credit _____ c Balance ▶	13c
14	Repairs	14
15	Bad debts	15
16	Rents	16
17	Taxes	17
18	Interest	18
19	Charitable contributions (see instructions for 10% limitation)	19
20	Depreciation (attach Form 4562) 20	
21	Less depreciation claimed on Schedule A and elsewhere on return ... 21a	21b
22	Depletion	22
23	Advertising	23
24	Pension, profit-sharing, etc., plans	24
25	Employee benefit programs	25
26	Other deductions (attach schedule)	26
27	**Total deductions.** Add lines 12 through 26 ▶	27
28	Taxable income before net operating loss deduction and special deductions. Subtract line 27 from line 11	28
29	Less: a Net operating loss deduction (see instructions) 29a	
	b Special deductions (Schedule C, line 20) 29b	29c
30	**Taxable income.** Subtract line 29c from line 28	30
31	**Total tax** (Schedule J, line 10)	31

Tax and Payments

32	Payments: a 20-- overpayment credited to 20-- ... 32a	
b	20-- estimated tax payments .. 32b	
c	Less 20-- refund applied for on Form 4466 32c ( ) d Bal ▶ 32d	
e	Tax deposited with Form 7004	32e
f	Credit from regulated investment companies (attach Form 2439)	32f
g	Credit for Federal tax on fuels (attach Form 4136). See instructions	32g
		32h
33	Estimated tax penalty (see instructions). Check if Form 2220 is attached ▶ ☐	33
34	**Tax due.** If line 32h is smaller than the total of lines 31 and 33, enter amount owed	34
35	**Overpayment.** If line 32h is larger than the total of lines 31 and 33, enter amount overpaid	35
36	Enter amount of line 35 you want: Credited to 20-- estimated tax ▶ Refunded ▶	36

Please Sign Here
Under penalties of perjury, I declare that I have examined this return, including accompanying schedules and statements, and to the best of my knowledge and belief, it is true, correct, and complete. Declaration of preparer (other than taxpayer) is based on all information of which preparer has any knowledge.
▶ Signature of officer   Date   ▶ Title

Paid Preparer's Use Only
Preparer's signature ▶   Date   Check if self-employed ☐   Preparer's social security number
Firm's name (or yours if self-employed) and address ▶   E.I. No. ▶   ZIP code ▶

Name _____ Date _____ Class _____

13-6 CHALLENGE PROBLEM

Extra form

Form **1120**	**U.S. Corporation Income Tax Return**	OMB No. 1545-0123
Department of the Treasury Internal Revenue Service	For calendar year 20-- or tax year beginning ...., 20--, ending ...., 20 ... ▶ Instructions are separate. See page 1 for Paperwork Reduction Act Notice.	**20--**

A Check if a:
(1) Consolidated return (attach Form 851) ☐
(2) Personal holding co. (attach Sch. PH) ☐
(3) Personal service corp. (as defined in Temporary Regs. sec. 1.441-4T— see instructions) ☐

Use IRS label. Otherwise, please print or type.
- Name
- Number, street, and room or suite no. (If a P.O. box, see page 6 of instructions.)
- City or town, state, and ZIP code

B Employer identification number
C Date incorporated
D Total assets (see Specific Instructions) $

E Check applicable boxes: (1) ☐ Initial return (2) ☐ Final return (3) ☐ Change in address

Income

1a	Gross receipts or sales _____ b Less returns and allowances _____ c Bal ▶	1c	
2	Cost of goods sold (Schedule A, line 8)	2	
3	Gross profit. Subtract line 2 from line 1c	3	
4	Dividends (Schedule C, line 19)	4	
5	Interest	5	
6	Gross rents	6	
7	Gross royalties	7	
8	Capital gain net income (attach Schedule D (Form 1120))	8	
9	Net gain or (loss) from Form 4797, Part II, line 20 (attach Form 4797)	9	
10	Other income (see instructions—attach schedule)	10	
11	**Total income.** Add lines 3 through 10 ▶	11	

Deductions (See instructions for limitations on deductions.)

12	Compensation of officers (Schedule E, line 4)	12	
13a	Salaries and wages _____ b Less jobs credit _____ c Balance ▶	13c	
14	Repairs	14	
15	Bad debts	15	
16	Rents	16	
17	Taxes	17	
18	Interest	18	
19	Charitable contributions (**see instructions for 10% limitation**)	19	
20	Depreciation (attach Form 4562) 20		
21	Less depreciation claimed on Schedule A and elsewhere on return . . 21a	21b	
22	Depletion	22	
23	Advertising	23	
24	Pension, profit-sharing, etc., plans	24	
25	Employee benefit programs	25	
26	Other deductions (attach schedule)	26	
27	**Total deductions.** Add lines 12 through 26 ▶	27	
28	Taxable income before net operating loss deduction and special deductions. Subtract line 27 from line 11	28	
29	**Less: a** Net operating loss deduction (see instructions) . . . 29a		
	b Special deductions (Schedule C, line 20) . . . 29b	29c	
30	**Taxable income.** Subtract line 29c from line 28	30	
31	Total tax (Schedule J, line 10)	31	

Tax and Payments

32	**Payments: a** 20-- overpayment credited to 20-- 32a		
b	20-- estimated tax payments . . 32b		
c	Less 20-- refund applied for on Form 4466 32c ( ) d Bal ▶ 32d		
e	Tax deposited with Form 7004 32e		
f	Credit from regulated investment companies (attach Form 2439) 32f		
g	Credit for Federal tax on fuels (attach Form 4136). See instructions 32g	32h	
33	Estimated tax penalty (see instructions). Check if Form 2220 is attached ▶ ☐	33	
34	**Tax due.** If line 32h is smaller than the total of lines 31 and 33, enter amount owed	34	
35	**Overpayment.** If line 32h is larger than the total of lines 31 and 33, enter amount overpaid	35	
36	Enter amount of line 35 you want: **Credited to 20-- estimated tax** ▶ **Refunded** ▶	36	

Please Sign Here
Under penalties of perjury, I declare that I have examined this return, including accompanying schedules and statements, and to the best of my knowledge and belief, it is true, correct, and complete. Declaration of preparer (other than taxpayer) is based on all information of which preparer has any knowledge.
▶ Signature of officer   Date   ▶ Title

Paid Preparer's Use Only
Preparer's signature ▶	Date	Check if self-employed ☐	Preparer's social security number
Firm's name (or yours if self-employed) and address ▶		E.I. No. ▶	
		ZIP code ▶	

104 • Working Papers   COPYRIGHT © SOUTH-WESTERN EDUCATIONAL PUBLISHING

2 REINFORCEMENT ACTIVITY, p. 378

[1, 2]

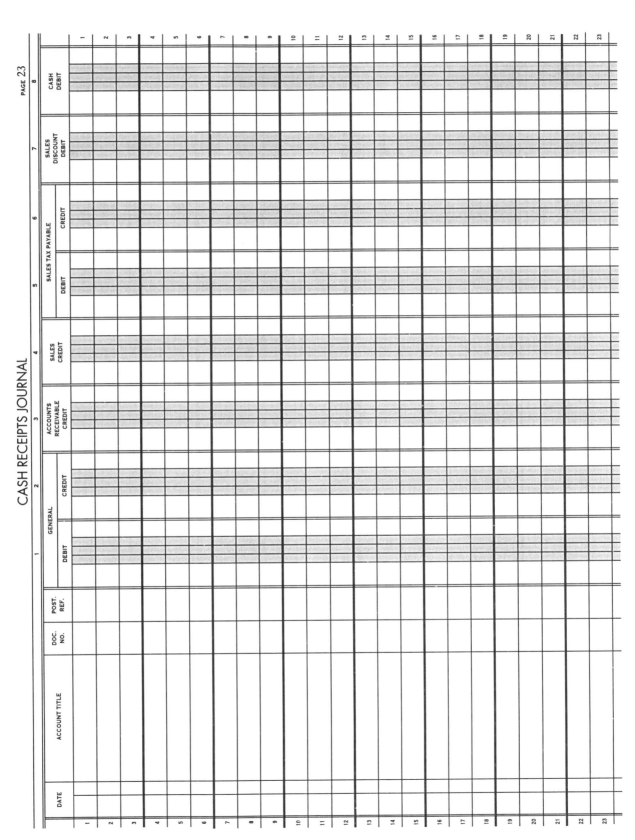

2 **REINFORCEMENT ACTIVITY (continued)**

[1, 2]

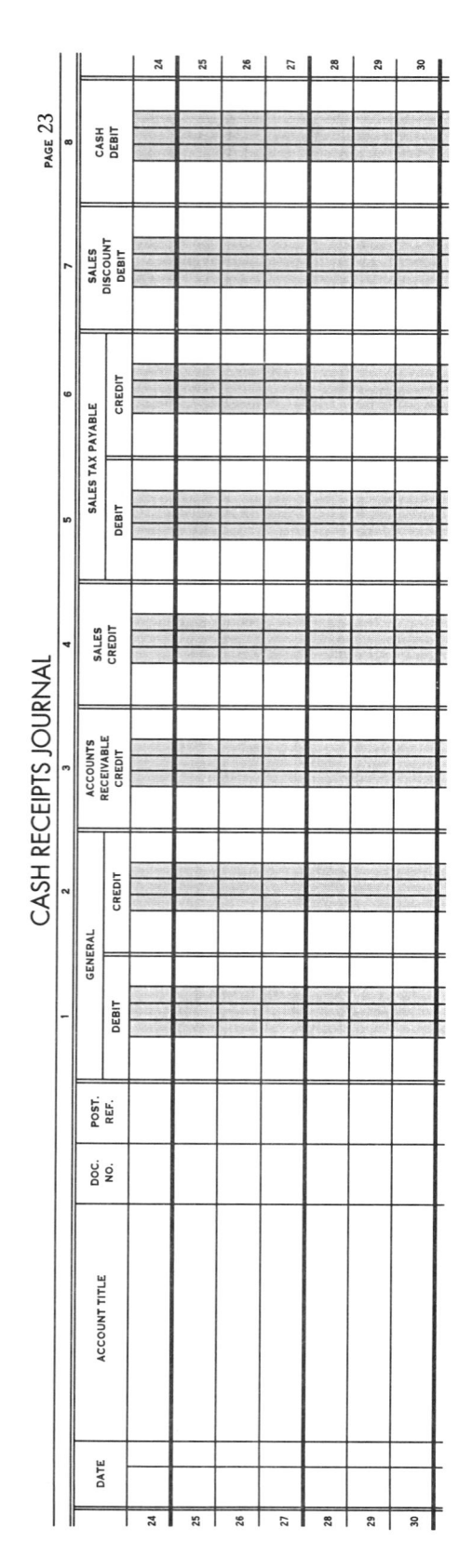

CASH RECEIPTS JOURNAL

CASH PAYMENTS JOURNAL

2 REINFORCEMENT ACTIVITY (continued)

[1]

GENERAL JOURNAL — PAGE 12

DATE	ACCOUNT TITLE	DOC. NO.	POST. REF.	DEBIT	CREDIT

REINFORCEMENT ACTIVITY (continued)

[3]

Whitehurst, Inc.
Work Sheet
For Year Ended December 31, 20--

#	ACCOUNT TITLE	TRIAL BALANCE DEBIT	TRIAL BALANCE CREDIT	ADJUSTMENTS DEBIT	ADJUSTMENTS CREDIT	INCOME STATEMENT DEBIT	INCOME STATEMENT CREDIT	BALANCE SHEET DEBIT	BALANCE SHEET CREDIT
1	Cash	24 86 15 9							
2	Petty Cash	300 00							
3	Notes Receivable	500 00							
4	Interest Receivable								
5	Accounts Receivable	40 95 7 65							
6	Allowance for Uncollectible Accounts		419 28						
7	Subscriptions Receivable								
8	Merchandise Inventory	218 84 6 33							
9	Supplies—Sales	3 40 6 78							
10	Supplies—Administrative	1 94 7 28							
11	Prepaid Insurance	1 76 4 00							
12	Prepaid Interest								
13	Bond Sinking Fund	6 000 00							
14	Store Equipment	9 340 00							
15	Accum. Depr.—Store Equip.		2 802 00						
16	Building	80 000 00							
17	Accum. Depr.—Building		4 500 00						
18	Office Equipment	3 156 80							
19	Accum. Depr.—Office Equip.		947 040						
20	Land	20 000 00							
21	Organization Costs	600 00							
22	Notes Payable		15 000 00						
23	Interest Payable								
24	Accounts Payable		12 420 00						
25	Employee Inc. Tax Payable		1 634 40						
26	Federal Income Tax Payable								
27	Social Security Tax Payable		152 52						
28	Medicare Tax Payable		35 20						

REINFORCEMENT ACTIVITY (continued)

[3]

	ACCOUNT TITLE	TRIAL BALANCE		ADJUSTMENTS		INCOME STATEMENT		BALANCE SHEET	
		DEBIT	CREDIT	DEBIT	CREDIT	DEBIT	CREDIT	DEBIT	CREDIT
29	Salaries Payable								
30	Sales Tax Payable		9 5 1 4 2						
31	Unearned Rent								
32	Unemploy. Tax Pay.—Federal		1 0 7 2						
33	Unemploy. Tax Pay.—State		7 2 3 6						
34	Health Ins. Prem. Payable		2 1 5 40						
35	Dividends Payable								
36	Bonds Payable		200 0 0 0 00						
37	Capital Stock—Common		126 8 0 0 00						
38	Stock Subscribed—Common								
39	Pd.-in Cap. in Exc. Stated Va.—Common		3 0 0 0 00						
40	Capital Stock—Preferred		44 4 0 0 00						
41	Stock Subscribed—Preferred								
42	Pd.-in Cap. in Exc. Stated Val.—Preferred		1 5 0 0 00						
43	Treasury Stock	4 5 0 0 00							
44	Pd.-in Cap. from Sale of Tr. Stock		4 0 00						
45	Retained Earnings		26 7 5 9 39						
46	Dividends—Common	11 7 8 0 00							
47	Dividends—Preferred	4 0 4 0 00							
48	Income Summary								
49	Sales		625 6 1 5 96						
50	Sales Discount	4 2 7 57							
51	Sales Ret. & Allowances	4 4 1 5 16							
52	Purchases	346 1 2 6 27							
53	Purchases Discount		1 7 4 2 32						
54	Purchases Ret. & Allow.		2 1 1 2 17						
55	Advertising Expense	3 1 9 44							
56	Credit Card Fee Expense	6 7 2 1 83							
57	Depr. Exp.—Store Equip.	5 9 4 00							
58	Misc. Expense—Sales	4 7 6 30							

2 REINFORCEMENT ACTIVITY (continued)

[3]

ACCOUNT TITLE	TRIAL BALANCE DEBIT	TRIAL BALANCE CREDIT	ADJUSTMENTS DEBIT	ADJUSTMENTS CREDIT	INCOME STATEMENT DEBIT	INCOME STATEMENT CREDIT	BALANCE SHEET DEBIT	BALANCE SHEET CREDIT
59 Salary Expense–Sales	84 033 00							
60 Supplies Expense–Sales								
61 Depr. Expense–Building								
62 Depr. Exp.–Office Equip.	2 000 00							
63 Insurance Expense								
64 Misc. Expense–Admin.	3 900 00							
65 Payroll Taxes Expense	9 660 15							
66 Property Tax Expense	4 000 00							
67 Salary Expense–Admin.	13 555 138							
68 Supplies Expense–Admin.								
69 Uncollectible Accounts Expense								
70 Utilities Expense	3 411 87							
71 Gain on Plant Assets		240 00						
72 Interest Income		1 611 29						
73 Rent Income		10 800 00						
74 Interest Expense	2 413 423							
75 Loss on Plant Assets	640 00							
76 Organization Expense								
77 Federal Income Tax Expense	22 200 00							
78	1117 522 83	1117 522 83						

Name _____ Date _____ Class _____

2 REINFORCEMENT ACTIVITY (continued)

Income statement analysis [5]

	Acceptable %	Actual %	Positive Result Yes	Positive Result No	Recommended Action If Needed
Cost of merchandise sold	Not more than 55.0%				
Gross profit on operations	Not less than 45.0%				
Total selling expenses	Not more than 20.0%				
Total administrative expenses	Not more than 8.0%				
Total operating expenses	Not more than 28.0%				
Income from operations	Not less than 17.0%				
Net deduction from other revenue and expenses	Not more than 3.0%				
Net income before federal income tax	Not less than 14.0%				

[6]

Earnings per share:

Reinforcement Activity 2 • 111

2 REINFORCEMENT ACTIVITY (continued)

[4]

Whitehurst, Inc.
Income Statement
For Year Ended December 31, 20--

					% OF NET SALES
Operating Revenue:					
Sales					
Less: Sales Discount					
Sales Ret. & Allow.					
Net Sales					
Cost of Merchandise Sold:					
Mdse. Inventory, January 1, 20--					
Purchases					
Less: Purchases Discount					
Purch. Ret. & Allow.					
Net Purchases					
Total Cost of Mdse. Avail. for Sale					
Less Mdse. Inventory, Dec. 31, 20--					
Cost of Merchandise Sold					
Gross Profit on Operations					
Operating Expenses:					
Selling Expenses:					
Advertising Expense					
Credit Card Fee Expense					
Depr. Expense—Store Equip.					
Miscellaneous Expense—Sales					
Salary Expense—Sales					
Supplies Expense—Sales					
Total Selling Expenses					
Administrative Expenses:					
Depr. Expense—Building					
Depr. Expense—Office Equip.					
Insurance Expense					
Miscellaneous Expense—Admin.					
Payroll Taxes Expense					
Property Tax Expense					
Salary Expense—Admin.					

REINFORCEMENT ACTIVITY (continued)

[4]

Whitehurst, Inc.
Income Statement (continued)
For Year Ended December 31, 20--

					% OF NET SALES
Supplies Expense—Admin.					
Uncollectible Accounts Expense					
Utilities Expense					
Total Admin. Expense					
Total Operating Expenses					
Income from Operations					
Other Revenue:					
Gain on Plant Assets					
Interest Income					
Rent Income					
Total Other Revenue					
Other Expenses:					
Interest Expense					
Loss on Plant Assets					
Organization Expense					
Total Other Expenses					
Net Deduction from Other Rev. & Exp.					
Net Income before Fed. Income Tax					
Less Federal Income Tax Expense					
Net Income after Fed. Income Tax					

2 REINFORCEMENT ACTIVITY (continued)

[7]

Whitehurst, Inc.
Statement of Stockholders' Equity
For Year Ended December 31, 20--

Paid-in Capital:				
Common Stock, $10.00 Stated Value:				
January 1, 20--, 11,780 Shares Issued				
Issued during Current Year, 900 Shares				
Balance, Dec. 31, 20--, 12,680 Shares Issued				
Preferred Stock, 10.0%, $100.00 Par Value:				
January 1, 20--, 404 Shares Issued				
Issued during Current Year, 40 Shares				
Balance, Dec. 31, 20--, 444 Shares Issued				
Total Value of Capital Stock Issued				
Additional Paid-in Capital:				
Pd.-in-Cap. in Exc. of St. Value—Common				
Pd.-in-Cap. in Exc. of Par Value—Preferred				
Pd.-in-Cap. from Sale of Treasury Stock				
Total Additional Paid-in Capital				
Total Paid-in Capital				
Retained Earnings:				
Balance, January 1, 20--				
Net Income after Federal Income Tax for 20--				
Less Dividends Declared during 20--				
Net Increase during 20--				
Balance, December 31, 20--				
Total Pd.-in Capital & Retained Earnings				
Less Treasury Stock, 50 Shares of				
Common Stock, December 31, 20--				
Total Stockholders' Equity, Dec. 31, 20--				

2 REINFORCEMENT ACTIVITY (continued)

[8]

a. Equity per share:

b. Price-earnings ratio:

[9]

Whitehurst, Inc.
Balance Sheet
December 31, 20--

ASSETS				
Current Assets:				
Cash				
Petty Cash				
Notes Receivable				
Interest Receivable				
Accounts Receivable				
Less Allow. for Uncoll. Accounts				
Merchandise Inventory				
Supplies—Sales				
Supplies—Administrative				
Prepaid Insurance				
Prepaid Interest				
Total Current Assets				
Long-Term Investment:				
Bond Sinking Fund				
Plant Assets:				
Store Equipment				
Less Accum. Depr.—Store Equip.				
Building				
Less Accum. Depr.—Building				
Office Equipment				
Less Accum. Depr.—Office Equip.				

REINFORCEMENT ACTIVITY 2 (continued)

[9]

Whitehurst, Inc.
Balance Sheet (continued)
December 31, 20--

Land			
Total Plant Assets			
Intangible Asset:			
Organization Costs			
Total Assets			
LIABILITIES			
Current Liabilities:			
Notes Payable			
Interest Payable			
Accounts Payable			
Employee Income Tax Payable			
Federal Income Tax Payable			
Social Security Tax Payable			
Medicare Tax Payable			
Salaries Payable			
Sales Tax Payable			
Unearned Rent			
Unemploy. Tax Payable—Federal			
Unemploy. Tax Payable—State			
Health Insurance Premiums Payable			
Total Current Liabilities			
Long-Term Liability:			
Bonds Payable			
Total Liabilities			
STOCKHOLDERS' EQUITY			
Total Stockholders' Equity			
Total Liabilities & Stockholders' Equity			

2 REINFORCEMENT ACTIVITY (continued)

[10a]

Accounts receivable turnover ratio:

[10b]

Rate earned on average stockholders' equity:

[10c]

Rate earned on average total assets:

2 REINFORCEMENT ACTIVITY (continued)

[11]

GENERAL JOURNAL
PAGE 13

DATE	ACCOUNT TITLE	DOC. NO.	POST. REF.	DEBIT	CREDIT

2 REINFORCEMENT ACTIVITY (continued)

[11, 12]

GENERAL JOURNAL — PAGE 14

	DATE	ACCOUNT TITLE	DOC. NO.	POST. REF.	DEBIT	CREDIT	
1							1
2							2
3							3
4							4
5							5
6							6
7							7
8							8
9							9
10							10
11							11
12							12
13							13
14							14
15							15
16							16
17							17
18							18
19							19
20							20
21							21
22							22
23							23
24							24
25							25
26							26
27							27
28							28
29							29
30							30
31							31
32							32

2 REINFORCEMENT ACTIVITY (concluded)

[12]

GENERAL JOURNAL — PAGE 15

DATE	ACCOUNT TITLE	DOC. NO.	POST. REF.	DEBIT	CREDIT

[13]

GENERAL JOURNAL — PAGE 1

DATE	ACCOUNT TITLE	DOC. NO.	POST. REF.	DEBIT	CREDIT

14-1 WORK TOGETHER, p. 392

Analyzing a comparative income statement [4]

Cost/Expense Item	Percentage of Increase (Decrease)	Favorable/Unfavorable
Cost of Merchandise Sold	11.0%	
Advertising Expense	15.1%	
Salary Expense	12.5%	
Utilities Expense	(1.2%)	

14-1 ON YOUR OWN, p. 392

Analyzing a comparative income statement [5]

Cost/Expense Item	Percentage of Increase (Decrease)	Favorable/Unfavorable
Cost of Merchandise Sold	11.0%	
Advertising Expense	7.3%	
Insurance Expense	(4.5%)	
Rent Expense	2.0%	

14-1 WORK TOGETHER / ON YOUR OWN

Extra form

	Budget 1st Qtr.	Actual 1st Qtr.	Increase (Decrease) Amount	Increase (Decrease) Percentage
Unit Sales				
Operating Revenue:				
Net Sales				
Cost of Merchandise Sold				
Gross Profit on Operations				
Operating Expenses:				
Selling Expenses:				
Advertising Expense				
Delivery Expense				
Depr. Expense—Delivery Equipment				
Depr. Expense—Warehouse Equipment				
Miscellaneous Expense—Sales				
Salary Expense—Commissions				
Salary Expense—Regular				
Supplies Expense—Sales				
Total Selling Expenses				
Administrative Expenses:				
Depr. Expense—Office Equipment				
Insurance Expense				
Miscellaneous Expense—Adminstrative				
Payroll Taxes Expense				
Rent Expense				
Salary Expense—Administrative				
Supplies Expense—Administrative				
Uncollectible Accounts Expense				
Utilities Expense				
Total Administrative Expenses				
Total Operating Expenses				
Income from Operations				
Other Expenses:				
Interest Expense				
Net Income before Federal Income Tax				
Federal Income Tax Expense				
Net Income after Federal Income Tax				

14-2 WORK TOGETHER, p. 401

Planning for a budgeted income statement [3–6]

3. Units projected to be sold during first quarter of 20X2: _____

   Projected sales for first quarter of 20X2: _____

4. Number of units needed for first quarter: _____

5. Units purchased during first quarter: _____

6. Projected cost of purchases: _____

14-2 WORK TOGETHER

Extra space for calculations

14-2 ON YOUR OWN, p. 401

Planning for a budgeted income statement [7–10]

7. Units projected to be sold during first quarter of 20X2: _____

   Projected sales for first quarter of 20X2: _____

8. Number of units needed for first quarter: _____

9. Units purchased during first quarter: _____

10. Projected cost of purchases: _____

14-2 ON YOUR OWN

Extra space for calculations

14-3 WORK TOGETHER, p. 408

Planning for a cash budget [4–6]

4. Total amount of cash received during second quarter: _____

5. Total cash payments for second quarter: _____

6. Ending cash balance for second quarter: _____

14-3 WORK TOGETHER

Extra space for calculations

Name _____ Date _____ Class _____

14-3 ON YOUR OWN, p. 408

Planning for a cash budget [7–9]

7. Total amount of cash received during second quarter: _____

8. Total cash payments for second quarter: _____

9. Ending cash balance for second quarter: _____

14-3 ON YOUR OWN

Extra space for calculations

14-1 APPLICATION PROBLEM, p. 410

Preparing a sales budget schedule and a purchase budget schedule [1]

PhotoMax, Inc.
Sales Budget Schedule
For Year Ended December 31, 20X3
Schedule 1

	Annual Budget	Quarter 1st	Quarter 2d	Quarter 3d	Quarter 4th
Actual Unit Sales, 20X2					
Sales Percentage by Quarter					
Projected Unit Sales, 20X3					
Times Unit Sales Price					
Net Sales					

[2]

PhotoMax, Inc.
Purchases Budget Schedule
For Year Ended December 31, 20X3
Schedule 2

	Quarter 1st	Quarter 2d	Quarter 3d	Quarter 4th
Ending Inventory				
Unit Sales for Quarter				
Total Units Needed				
Less Beginning Inventory				
Purchases				
Times Unit Cost				
Cost of Purchases				

Extra space for calculations

14-1 APPLICATION PROBLEM

Extra forms

	Annual Budget	Quarter			
		1st	2d	3d	4th
Actual Unit Sales, 20X2					
Sales Percentage by Quarter					
Projected Unit Sales, 20X3					
Times Unit Sales Price					
Net Sales					

Schedule 1

	Quarter			
	1st	2d	3d	4th
Ending Inventory				
Unit Sales for Quarter				
Total Units Needed				
Less Beginning Inventory				
Purchases				
Times Unit Cost				
Cost of Purchases				

Schedule 2

Extra space for calculations

14-2 APPLICATION PROBLEM, p. 410

Preparing a budgeted income statement

[1]

<table>
<tr><td colspan="6">Coffee Oasis
Selling Expenses Budget Schedule
For Year Ended December 31, 20X3   Schedule 3</td></tr>
<tr><td></td><td rowspan="2">Annual Budget</td><td colspan="4">Quarter</td></tr>
<tr><td></td><td>1st</td><td>2d</td><td>3d</td><td>4th</td></tr>
<tr><td>Advertising Expense............</td><td></td><td></td><td></td><td></td><td></td></tr>
<tr><td>Delivery Expense ....</td><td></td><td></td><td></td><td></td><td></td></tr>
<tr><td>Depr. Expense—Del. Equip.</td><td></td><td></td><td></td><td></td><td></td></tr>
<tr><td>Depr. Expense—Store Equipment.</td><td></td><td></td><td></td><td></td><td></td></tr>
<tr><td>Miscellaneous Expense—Sales....</td><td></td><td></td><td></td><td></td><td></td></tr>
<tr><td>Salary Expense—Sales...........</td><td></td><td></td><td></td><td></td><td></td></tr>
<tr><td>Supplies Expense—Sales ....</td><td></td><td></td><td></td><td></td><td></td></tr>
<tr><td>Total Selling Expenses ....</td><td></td><td></td><td></td><td></td><td></td></tr>
</table>

[2]

<table>
<tr><td colspan="6">Coffee Oasis
Administrative Expenses Budget Schedule
For Year Ended December 31, 20X3   Schedule 4</td></tr>
<tr><td></td><td rowspan="2">Annual Budget</td><td colspan="4">Quarter</td></tr>
<tr><td></td><td>1st</td><td>2d</td><td>3d</td><td>4th</td></tr>
<tr><td>Depr. Expense—Office Equipment..</td><td></td><td></td><td></td><td></td><td></td></tr>
<tr><td>Insurance Expense..............</td><td></td><td></td><td></td><td></td><td></td></tr>
<tr><td>Miscellaneous Expense—Admin....</td><td></td><td></td><td></td><td></td><td></td></tr>
<tr><td>Payroll Taxes Expense............</td><td></td><td></td><td></td><td></td><td></td></tr>
<tr><td>Rent Expense ....</td><td></td><td></td><td></td><td></td><td></td></tr>
<tr><td>Salary Expense—Administrative....</td><td></td><td></td><td></td><td></td><td></td></tr>
<tr><td>Supplies Expense—Administrative..</td><td></td><td></td><td></td><td></td><td></td></tr>
<tr><td>Uncollectible Accounts Expense....</td><td></td><td></td><td></td><td></td><td></td></tr>
<tr><td>Utilities Expense ....</td><td></td><td></td><td></td><td></td><td></td></tr>
<tr><td>Total Administrative Expenses.....</td><td></td><td></td><td></td><td></td><td></td></tr>
</table>

14-2 APPLICATION PROBLEM (concluded)

[3]

<table>
<tr><td colspan="6" align="center">Coffee Oasis
Budgeted Income Statement
For Year Ended December 31, 20X3</td></tr>
<tr><td></td><td rowspan="2">Annual Budget</td><td colspan="4" align="center">Quarter</td></tr>
<tr><td></td><td>1st</td><td>2d</td><td>3d</td><td>4th</td></tr>
<tr><td>Operating Revenue:
  Net Sales (Schedule 1)..........</td><td></td><td></td><td></td><td></td><td></td></tr>
<tr><td>Cost of Merchandise Sold:
  Beginning Inventory............</td><td></td><td></td><td></td><td></td><td></td></tr>
<tr><td> Purchases (Schedule 2)..........</td><td></td><td></td><td></td><td></td><td></td></tr>
<tr><td> Total Merchandise Available.....</td><td></td><td></td><td></td><td></td><td></td></tr>
<tr><td> Less Ending Inventory..........</td><td></td><td></td><td></td><td></td><td></td></tr>
<tr><td> Cost of Merchandise Sold.......</td><td></td><td></td><td></td><td></td><td></td></tr>
<tr><td>Gross Profit on Operations........</td><td></td><td></td><td></td><td></td><td></td></tr>
<tr><td>Operating Expenses:
  Selling Expenses (Schedule 3)....</td><td></td><td></td><td></td><td></td><td></td></tr>
<tr><td> Administrative Expenses
  (Schedule 4)..................</td><td></td><td></td><td></td><td></td><td></td></tr>
<tr><td> Total Operating Expenses.......</td><td></td><td></td><td></td><td></td><td></td></tr>
<tr><td>Net Income before Federal Income Tax..............................</td><td></td><td></td><td></td><td></td><td></td></tr>
<tr><td> Federal Income Tax Expense.....</td><td></td><td></td><td></td><td></td><td></td></tr>
<tr><td>Net Income after Federal Income Tax..............................</td><td></td><td></td><td></td><td></td><td></td></tr>
</table>

Space for calculations:

14-3 APPLICATION PROBLEM, p. 411

Preparing a cash budget with supporting schedules [1]

SeaWest Fabrication
Cash Receipts Budget Schedule
For Year Ended December 31, 20X3   Schedule A

	Quarter			
	1st	2d	3d	4th
From Sales:				
Prior Year's 4th Quarter ($639,200)				
1st Quarter Sales ($646,300)				
2d Quarter Sales ($674,900)				
3d Quarter Sales ($661,800)				
4th Quarter Sales ($681,600)				
Total Receipts from Sales				
From Other Sources:				
Note Payable to Bank				
Total Cash Receipts				

[2]

SeaWest Fabrication
Cash Payments Budget Schedule
For Year Ended December 31, 20X3   Schedule B

	Quarter			
	1st	2d	3d	4th
For Merchandise:				
Prior Year's 4th Quarter Purchases ($548,240) . . .				
1st Quarter Purchases ($558,300)				
2d Quarter Purchases ($571,600)				
3d Quarter Purchases ($561,200)				
4th Quarter Purchases ($582,300)				
Total Cash Payments for Purchases				
From Operating Expenses:				
Cash Selling Expenses				
Cash Administrative Expenses				
Total Cash Operating Expenses				
For Other Cash Payments:				
Federal Income Tax Expense				
Equipment Purchases				
Cash Dividend				
Note Payable and Interest				
Total Other Cash Payments				
Total Cash Payments				

14-3 APPLICATION PROBLEM (concluded)

[3]

	Quarter			
SeaWest Fabrication Cash Budget For Year Ended December 31, 20X3	1st	2d	3d	4th
Cash Balance—Beginning....................				
Cash Receipts (Schedule A)....................				
Cash Available...............................				
Less Cash Payments (Schedule B).............				
Cash Balance—Ending.......................				

Space for calculations:

14-4 MASTERY PROBLEM, p. 412

Preparing a budgeted income statement and a cash budget with supporting budget schedules

[a]

<table>
<tr><td colspan="6">Zylar, Inc.
Sales Budget Schedule
For Year Ended December 31, 20X3   Schedule 1</td></tr>
<tr><td></td><td rowspan="2">Annual Budget</td><td colspan="4">Quarter</td></tr>
<tr><td></td><td>1st</td><td>2d</td><td>3d</td><td>4th</td></tr>
<tr><td>Actual Unit Sales, 20X2 . . . .</td><td></td><td></td><td></td><td></td><td></td></tr>
<tr><td>Sales Percentage by Quarter . . . . .</td><td></td><td></td><td></td><td></td><td></td></tr>
<tr><td>Projected Unit Sales, 20X3 . . . .</td><td></td><td></td><td></td><td></td><td></td></tr>
<tr><td>Times Unit Sales Price . . . .</td><td></td><td></td><td></td><td></td><td></td></tr>
<tr><td>Net Sales . . . .</td><td></td><td></td><td></td><td></td><td></td></tr>
</table>

[b]

<table>
<tr><td colspan="5">Zylar, Inc.
Purchases Budget Schedule
For Year Ended December 31, 20X3   Schedule 2</td></tr>
<tr><td></td><td colspan="4">Quarter</td></tr>
<tr><td></td><td>1st</td><td>2d</td><td>3d</td><td>4th</td></tr>
<tr><td>Ending Inventory . . . .</td><td></td><td></td><td></td><td></td></tr>
<tr><td>Unit Sales for Quarter . . . .</td><td></td><td></td><td></td><td></td></tr>
<tr><td>Total Units Needed . . . .</td><td></td><td></td><td></td><td></td></tr>
<tr><td>Less Beginning Inventory . . . .</td><td></td><td></td><td></td><td></td></tr>
<tr><td>Purchases . . . .</td><td></td><td></td><td></td><td></td></tr>
<tr><td>Times Unit Cost . . . .</td><td></td><td></td><td></td><td></td></tr>
<tr><td>Cost of Purchases . . . .</td><td></td><td></td><td></td><td></td></tr>
</table>

Space for calculations:

14-4 MASTERY PROBLEM (continued)

[c]

Zylar, Inc.
Selling Expenses Budget Schedule
For Year Ended December 31, 20X3
Schedule 3

	Annual Budget	Quarter			
		1st	2d	3d	4th
Advertising Expense............					
Delivery Expense					
Depr. Expense—Del. Equipment..					
Depr. Expense—Store Equipment.					
Miscellaneous Expense—Sales....					
Salary Expense—Sales...........					
Supplies Expense—Sales					
Total Selling Expenses					

[d]

Zylar, Inc.
Administrative Expenses Budget Schedule
For Year Ended December 31, 20X3
Schedule 4

	Annual Budget	Quarter			
		1st	2d	3d	4th
Depr. Expense—Office Equipment..					
Insurance Expense..............					
Miscellaneous Expense—Admin....					
Payroll Taxes Expense					
Rent Expense					
Salary Expense—Administrative....					
Supplies Expense—Administrative..					
Uncollectible Accounts Expense....					
Utilities Expense					
Total Administrative Expenses.....					

[e]

Zylar, Inc.
Other Revenue and Expenses Budget Schedule
For Year Ended December 31, 20X3
Schedule 5

	Annual Budget	Quarter			
		1st	2d	3d	4th
Other Expenses					
Interest Expense					

14-4 MASTERY PROBLEM (continued)

[f]

<table>
<tr><td colspan="6" align="center">Zylar, Inc.
Budgeted Income Statement
For Year Ended December 31, 20X3</td></tr>
<tr><td></td><td rowspan="2">Annual Budget</td><td colspan="4" align="center">Quarter</td></tr>
<tr><td></td><td>1st</td><td>2d</td><td>3d</td><td>4th</td></tr>
<tr><td>Operating Revenue:
  Net Sales (Schedule 1)..........</td><td></td><td></td><td></td><td></td><td></td></tr>
<tr><td>Cost of Merchandise Sold:
  Beginning Inventory...........</td><td></td><td></td><td></td><td></td><td></td></tr>
<tr><td> Purchases (Schedule 2).........</td><td></td><td></td><td></td><td></td><td></td></tr>
<tr><td> Total Merchandise Available.....</td><td></td><td></td><td></td><td></td><td></td></tr>
<tr><td> Less Ending Inventory..........</td><td></td><td></td><td></td><td></td><td></td></tr>
<tr><td> Cost of Merchandise Sold.......</td><td></td><td></td><td></td><td></td><td></td></tr>
<tr><td>Gross Profit on Operations........</td><td></td><td></td><td></td><td></td><td></td></tr>
<tr><td>Operating Expenses:
  Selling Expenses (Schedule 3)....</td><td></td><td></td><td></td><td></td><td></td></tr>
<tr><td> Administrative Expenses
  (Schedule 4)..................</td><td></td><td></td><td></td><td></td><td></td></tr>
<tr><td> Total Operating Expenses.......</td><td></td><td></td><td></td><td></td><td></td></tr>
<tr><td>Income from Operations..........</td><td></td><td></td><td></td><td></td><td></td></tr>
<tr><td>Other Expense Deduction
(Schedule 5)...................</td><td></td><td></td><td></td><td></td><td></td></tr>
<tr><td>Net Income before Federal Income Tax.........................</td><td></td><td></td><td></td><td></td><td></td></tr>
<tr><td> Federal Income Tax Expense.....</td><td></td><td></td><td></td><td></td><td></td></tr>
<tr><td>Net Income after Federal Income Tax.........................</td><td></td><td></td><td></td><td></td><td></td></tr>
</table>

[g]

<table>
<tr><td colspan="5" align="center">Zylar, Inc.
Cash Receipts Budget Schedule
For Year Ended December 31, 20X3   Schedule A</td></tr>
<tr><td></td><td colspan="4" align="center">Quarter</td></tr>
<tr><td></td><td>1st</td><td>2d</td><td>3d</td><td>4th</td></tr>
<tr><td>From Sales:
  Prior Year's 4th Quarter ($161,280)............</td><td></td><td></td><td></td><td></td></tr>
<tr><td> 1st Quarter Sales ($142,800)..................</td><td></td><td></td><td></td><td></td></tr>
<tr><td> 2d Quarter Sales ($223,800)..................</td><td></td><td></td><td></td><td></td></tr>
<tr><td> 3d Quarter Sales ($226,200)..................</td><td></td><td></td><td></td><td></td></tr>
<tr><td> 4th Quarter Sales ($187,200).................</td><td></td><td></td><td></td><td></td></tr>
<tr><td> Total Receipts from Sales....................</td><td></td><td></td><td></td><td></td></tr>
<tr><td>From Other Sources:
  Note Payable to Bank.......................</td><td></td><td></td><td></td><td></td></tr>
<tr><td>Total Cash Receipts...........................</td><td></td><td></td><td></td><td></td></tr>
</table>

14-4 MASTERY PROBLEM (concluded)

[h]

Zylar, Inc.
Cash Payments Budget Schedule
For Year Ended December 31, 20X3

Schedule B

	Quarter			
	1st	2d	3d	4th
For Merchandise:				
Prior Year's 4th Quarter Purchases ($105,600) . . .				
1st Quarter Purchases ($111,350)				
2d Quarter Purchases ($159,380)				
3d Quarter Purchases ($149,180)				
4th Quarter Purchases ($120,280)				
Total Cash Payments for Purchases				
For Operating Expenses:				
Cash Selling Expenses				
Cash Administrative Expenses				
Total Cash Operating Expenses				
For Other Cash Payments:				
Federal Income Tax Expense				
Equipment Purchases				
Cash Dividend				
Note Payable and Interest				
Total Other Cash Payments				
Total Cash Payments				

[i]

Zylar, Inc.
Cash Budget
For Year Ended December 31, 20X3

	Quarter			
	1st	2d	3d	4th
Cash Balance—Beginning				
Cash Receipts (Schedule A)				
Cash Available				
Less Cash Payments (Schedule B)				
Cash Balance—Ending				

14-5 CHALLENGE PROBLEM, p. 413

Preparing a performance report [1, 2]

Quasar Robotics, Inc.
Performance Report
For Quarter Ended March 31, 20X3

	Budget 1st Qtr.	Actual 1st Qtr.	Increase (Decrease) Amount	Increase (Decrease) Percentage
Unit Sales	80,000	82,400	2,400	3.00%
Operating Revenue:				
Net Sales	$336,000	$346,080	$10,080	3.00%
Cost of Merchandise Sold	184,000	192,520	8,520	4.63%
Gross Profit on Operations	$152,000	$153,560	$1,560	1.03%
Operating Expenses:				
Selling Expenses:				
Advertising Expense	$2,500	$2,650	$150	6.00%
Delivery Expense	4,320	4,380	60	1.39%
Depr. Expense—Delivery Equipment	4,260	4,260	0	0.00%
Depr. Expense—Warehouse Equipment	3,450	3,450	0	0.00%
Miscellaneous Expense—Sales	1,670	1,650	(20)	(1.20)%
Salary Expense—Commissions	10,080	10,382	302	3.00%
Salary Expense—Regular	25,680	25,680	0	0.00%
Supplies Expense—Sales	2,450	2,630	180	7.35%
Total Selling Expenses	$54,410	$55,082	$672	1.23%
Administrative Expenses:				
Depr. Expense—Office Equipment	$4,200	$4,200	0	0.00%
Insurance Expense	900	900	0	0.00%
Miscellaneous Expense—Administrative	6,500	6,580	80	1.23%
Payroll Taxes Expense	8,470	8,500	30	0.35%
Rent Expense	2,500	2,500	0	0.00%
Salary Expense—Administrative	34,800	34,800	0	0.00%
Supplies Expense—Administrative	4,400	4,160	(240)	(5.45)%
Uncollectible Accounts Expense	3,360	3,380	20	0.60%
Utilities Expense	5,400	5,490	90	1.67%
Total Administrative Expenses	$70,530	$70,510	$(20)	(0.03)%
Total Operating Expenses	$124,940	$125,592	$652	0.52%
Income from Operations	$27,060	$27,968	$908	3.36%
Other Expenses:				
Interest Expense	$1,200	$1,200	0	0.00%
Net Income before Federal Income Tax	$25,860	$26,768	$908	3.51%
Federal Income Tax Expense	5,170	5,350	180	3.48%
Net Income after Federal Income Tax	$20,690	$21,418	$728	3.52%

14-5 CHALLENGE PROBLEM

Extra form

	Budget 1st Qtr.	Actual 1st Qtr.	Increase (Decrease) Amount	Percentage
Unit Sales				
Operating Revenue:				
Net Sales				
Cost of Merchandise Sold				
Gross Profit on Operations				
Operating Expenses:				
Selling Expenses:				
Advertising Expense				
Delivery Expense				
Depr. Expense—Delivery Equipment				
Depr. Expense—Warehouse Equipment				
Miscellaneous Expense—Sales				
Salary Expense—Commissions				
Salary Expense—Regular				
Supplies Expense—Sales				
Total Selling Expenses				
Administrative Expenses:				
Depr. Expense—Office Equipment				
Insurance Expense				
Miscellaneous Expense—Adminstrative				
Payroll Taxes Expense				
Rent Expense				
Salary Expense—Administrative				
Supplies Expense—Administrative				
Uncollectible Accounts Expense				
Utilities Expense				
Total Administrative Expenses				
Total Operating Expenses				
Income from Operations				
Other Expenses:				
Interest Expense				
Net Income before Federal Income Tax				
Federal Income Tax Expense				
Net Income after Federal Income Tax				

15-1 WORK TOGETHER, p. 422

Preparing an income statement with contribution margin [3]

Wightman's Lumber
Income Statement
For Month Ended January 31, 20--

Name _____ Date _____ Class _____

15-1 WORK TOGETHER

Extra form

15-1 ON YOUR OWN, p. 422

Preparing an income statement with contribution margin [4]

Wightman's Lumber
Income Statement
For Month Ended February 28, 20--

15-1 ON YOUR OWN

Extra form

15-2 WORK TOGETHER, p. 426

Calculating breakeven in sales dollars and unit sales and preparing a breakeven income statement

[4]

Breakeven point in sales dollars:

Unit sales breakeven point for July:

[5]

Cherie's Pizza
Breakeven Income Statement
For Month Ended July 31, 20--

15-2 WORK TOGETHER

Extra form

15-2 ON YOUR OWN, p. 426

Calculating breakeven in sales dollars and unit sales and preparing a breakeven income statement

[6]

Breakeven point in sales dollars:

Unit sales breakeven point for August:

[7]

	Cherie's Pizza		
	Breakeven Income Statement		
	For Month Ended August 31, 20--		

15-2 ON YOUR OWN

Extra form

15-3 WORK TOGETHER, p. 434

Calculating sales to earn a planned net income, calculating the effect of volume changes on net income, and calculating the effect of changes in selling price

[3]

Sales dollars needed to achieve $3,000 planned net income for July:

[4]

	Per Unit	Number of Units		
		4,000	5,000	6,000
Net Sales				
Variable Costs				
Contribution Margin				
Fixed Costs				
Net Income (Loss)				

[5]

	Per Unit	Units at Normal Price	Per Unit	Units at Reduced Price
		7,500		9,000
Net Sales				
Variable Costs				
Contribution Margin				
Fixed Costs				
Net Income (Loss)				

15-3 WORK TOGETHER

Extra space for calculations

Name _____ Date _____ Class _____

15-3 ON YOUR OWN, p. 434

Calculating sales to earn a planned net income, calculating the effect of volume changes on net income, and calculating the effect of changes in selling price [6]

Sales dollars needed to achieve $3,000 planned net income for August:

[7]

	Per Unit	Number of Units		
		7,000	8,000	9,000
Net Sales				
Variable Costs				
Contribution Margin				
Fixed Costs				
Net Income (Loss)				

[8]

	Per Unit	Units at Normal Price	Per Unit	Units at Increased Price
		10,000		9,500
Net Sales				
Variable Costs				
Contribution Margin				
Fixed Costs				
Net Income (Loss)				

15-3 ON YOUR OWN

Extra space for calculations

15-1 APPLICATION PROBLEM, p. 436

Preparing an income statement reporting contribution margin [1]

Milford Pump Company
Income Statement
For Month Ended November 30, 20--

Operating Revenue:		
Net Sales		
Variable Costs:		
Cost of Merchandise Sold		
Sales Commissions		
Delivery Costs		
Other Selling Costs		
Other Administrative Costs		
Total Variable Costs		
Contribution Margin		
Fixed Costs:		
Rent		
Insurance		
Other Selling Costs		
Other Administrative Costs		
Other Expenses		
Total Fixed Costs		
Net Income		

Extra space for calculations

15-1 APPLICATION PROBLEM (concluded)

[2]

Contribution margin per unit:

[3]

Variable cost per unit:

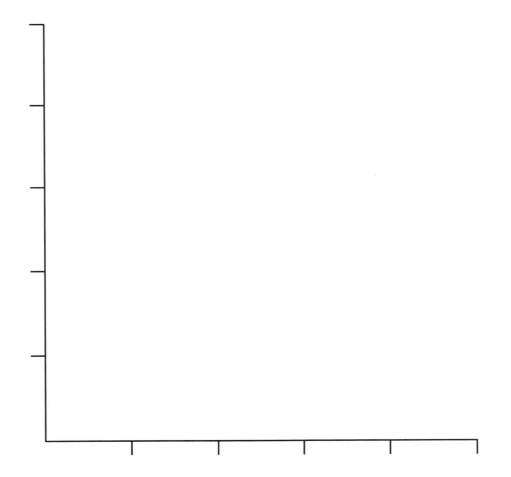

15-2 APPLICATION PROBLEM, p. 436

Calculating contribution margin and breakeven point [4]

Calculate the contribution margin per unit:

Calculate the unit sales breakeven point:

Calculate the sales dollar breakeven point:

_____
_____
_____
_____
_____

15-2 APPLICATION PROBLEM

Extra space for calculations

15-3 APPLICATION PROBLEM, p. 437

Calculating plans for net income [1]

Calculate the contribution margin per unit

a. Calculate the unit sales breakeven point:

b. Calculate the sales dollar breakeven point:

[2]

Calculate the contribution margin per unit:

Calculate the required contribution margin

a. Calculate unit sales

b. Calculate sales dollars

15-3 APPLICATION PROBLEM (concluded)

[3]

Calculate the contribution margin per unit:

a. Calculate the unit sales breakeven point

b. Calculate the sales dollar breakeven point

_____
_____
_____
_____
_____
_____

15-4 APPLICATION PROBLEM, p. 437

Calculating the effects on net income of changes in unit sales price, variable costs, fixed costs, and volume

[1]

	Per Unit	Number of Units		
		17,000	20,000	23,000
Net Sales...............				
Variable Costs...........				
Contribution Margin......				
Fixed Costs.............				
Net Income (Loss).......				

[2a]

	Alternative 1			Alternative 2		
	Per Unit	Units Sold	Total	Per Unit	Units Sold	Total
Net Sales.............						
Variable Costs........						
Contribution Margin...						
Fixed Costs..........						
Net Income (Loss)....						

[2b]

	Alternative 1			Alternative 2		
	Per Unit	Units Sold	Total	Per Unit	Units Sold	Total
Net Sales.............						
Variable Costs........						
Contribution Margin...						
Fixed Costs..........						
Net Income (Loss)....						

Name _____ Date _____ Class _____

15-4 APPLICATION PROBLEM (concluded)

[3]

	Current Price			Price Reduction and Sales Volume Increase		
	Per Unit	Units Sold	Total	Per Unit	Units Sold	Total
Net Sales						
Variable Costs						
Contribution Margin						
Fixed Costs						
Net Income (Loss)						

Extra forms

	Per Unit	Number of Units		
Net Sales				
Variable Costs				
Contribution Margin				
Fixed Costs				
Net Income (Loss)				

	Alternative 1			Alternative 2		
	Per Unit	Units Sold	Total	Per Unit	Units Sold	Total
Net Sales						
Variable Costs						
Contribution Margin						
Fixed Costs						
Net Income (Loss)						

15-5 APPLICATION PROBLEM, p. 438

Calculating sales mix

Calculate the sales mix: [a]

Calculate the contribution margin rate: [b]

Calculate total sales dollars: [c]

15-5 APPLICATION PROBLEM (concluded)

Calculate product sales dollars:

[d]

Calculate product unit sales:

[e]

15-6 MASTERY PROBLEM, p. 438

Calculating contribution margins and breakeven point, calculating sales dollars [1] and unit sales for planned net income

Ratliff Corporation
Income Statement
For Month Ended August 31, 20--

Operating Revenue:		
Net Sales		
Variable Costs:		
Cost of Merchandise Sold		
Sales Commission		
Delivery Costs		
Other Selling Costs		
Other Administrative Costs		
Total Variable Costs		
Contribution Margin		
Fixed Costs:		
Rent		
Insurance		
Other Selling Costs		
Other Administrative Costs		
Other Expenses		
Total Fixed Costs		
Net Income		

[2]

Calculate the contribution margin rate:

[3]

Calculate the sales dollar breakeven point:

15-6 MASTERY PROBLEM (concluded)

[4]

Calculate the unit sales breakeven point:

[5]

Calculate the required contribution margin:

a. Calculate sales dollars

b. Calculate unit sales

[6]

	Alternative 1 Current Machines			Alternative 2 Computer-Based Machines		
	Per Unit	Units Sold	Total	Per Unit	Units Sold	Total
Net Sales.............						
Variable Costs.........						
Contribution Margin.....						
Fixed Costs...........						
Net Income (Loss)......						

15-7 CHALLENGE PROBLEM, p. 439

Calculating the effects on net income of changes in unit sales price, variable costs, and fixed costs [1]

	Alternative 1 Current Unit Sales Price			Alternative 2 Decreased Unit Sales Price		
	Per Unit	Units Sold	Total	Per Unit	Units Sold	Total
Net Sales...............						
Variable Costs............						
Contribution Margin.......						
Fixed Costs...............						
Net Income (Loss)..........						

Space for calculations

15-7 CHALLENGE PROBLEM (concluded)

[2]

	Alternative 1 Purchase Power Cable			Alternative 2 Produce Power Cable		
	Per Unit	Units Sold	Total	Per Unit	Units Sold	Total
Net Sales...............						
Variable Costs...........						
Contribution Margin......						
Fixed Costs.............						
Net Income (Loss)........						

Space for calculations

16-1 WORK TOGETHER / ON YOUR OWN, p. 451

Analyzing comparative financial statements

[5]

	Current Year	Prior Year	Increase (Decrease) Amount	Increase (Decrease) Percentage
Operating Revenue: Net Sales...............	$865,000.00	$740,000.00		
Cost of Merchandise Sold: Merchandise Inv., Jan. 1	145,800.00	147,600.00		
Net Purchases.......................	372,000.00	358,300.00		
Total Cost of Mdse. Avail. for Sale......	$517,800.00	$505,900.00		
Less Mdse. Inventory, Dec. 31	188,700.00	145,800.00		
Cost of Merchandise Sold	329,100.00	360,100.00		
Gross Profit on Operations.............	$535,900.00	$379,900.00		

[6]

	Current Year Amount	Current Year Percentage	Prior Year Amount	Prior Year Percentage
Operating Revenue: Net Sales...............	$865,000.00		$740,000.00	
Cost of Merchandise Sold: Merchandise Inv., Jan. 1	145,800.00		147,600.00	
Net Purchases.......................	372,000.00		358,300.00	
Total Cost of Mdse. Avail. for Sale......	$517,800.00		$505,900.00	
Less Mdse. Inventory, Dec. 31	188,700.00		145,800.00	
Cost of Merchandise Sold	329,100.00		360,100.00	
Gross Profit on Operations.............	$535,900.00		$379,900.00	

16-1 WORK TOGETHER

Extra space for calculations

16-1 ON YOUR OWN, p. 451

Analyzing comparative financial statements [7]

Baycom Corporation Comparative Balance Sheet December 31, 20-- and 20--				
	Current Year	Prior Year	Increase (Decrease)	
			Amount	Percentage
ASSETS				
Current Assets:				
Cash	$ 246,300	$ 204,900	41,400	20.2
Accounts Receivable (net)	574,000	469,200	104,800	22.3
Merchandise Inventory	597,000	623,800	(26,800)	(4.3)
Other Current Assets	16,100	11,300	4,800	42.5
Total Current Assets	$1,433,400	$1,309,200	124,200	9.5
Total Plant Assets (net)	713,600	681,100	32,500	4.8
Total Assets	$2,147,000	$1,990,300	156,700	7.9
LIABILITIES				
Current Liabilities:				
Notes Payable	$ 261,200	$ 281,600	(20,400)	(7.2)
Interest Payable	8,900	10,700	(1,800)	(16.8)
Accounts Payable	344,900	393,300	(48,400)	(12.3)
Federal Income Tax Payable	7,300	3,300	4,000	121.2
Other Current Liabilities	5,400	6,500	(1,100)	(16.9)
Total Current Liabilities	$ 627,700	$ 695,400	(67,700)	(9.7)
Long-Term Liability:				
Mortgage Payable	$ 480,000	$ 325,000	155,000	47.7
Total Liabilities	$1,107,700	$1,020,400	87,300	8.6
STOCKHOLDERS' EQUITY				
Capital Stock	$ 500,000	$ 450,000	50,000	11.1
Retained Earnings	539,300	519,900	19,400	3.7
Total Stockholders' Equity	$1,039,300	$ 969,900	69,400	7.2
Total Liabilities and Stockholders' Equity	$2,147,000	$1,990,300	156,700	7.9

16-1 ON YOUR OWN (concluded)

[8]

Baycom Corporation
Comparative Balance Sheet
December 31, 20-- and 20--

	Current Year		Prior Year	
	Amount	Percentage	Amount	Percentage
ASSETS				
Current Assets:				
Cash	$ 246,300		$ 204,900	
Accounts Receivable (book value)	574,000		469,200	
Merchandise Inventory	597,000		623,800	
Other Current Assets	16,100		11,300	
Total Current Assets	$1,433,400		$1,309,200	
Total Plant Assets (book value)	713,600		681,100	
Total Assets	$2,147,000		$1,990,300	
LIABILITIES				
Current Liabilities:				
Notes Payable	$ 261,200		$ 281,600	
Interest Payable	8,900		10,700	
Accounts Payable	344,900		393,300	
Federal Income Tax Payable	7,300		3,300	
Other Current Liabilities	5,400		6,500	
Total Current Liabilities	$ 627,700		$ 695,400	
Long-Term Liability:				
Mortgage Payable	$ 480,000		$ 325,000	
Total Liabilities	$1,107,700		$1,020,400	
STOCKHOLDERS' EQUITY				
Capital Stock	$ 500,000		$ 450,000	
Retained Earnings	539,300		519,900	
Total Stockholders' Equity	$1,039,300		$ 969,900	
Total Liabilities and Stockholders' Equity	$2,147,000		$1,990,300	

16-2 WORK TOGETHER, p. 460

Calculating earnings performance and efficiency analysis ratios [4]

	January 1	December 31
Total Assets	$4,600,000.00	$5,300,000.00
Book Value of Accounts Receivable	630,000.00	710,000.00
Merchandise Inventory	500,000.00	550,000.00
Stockholders' Equity	$2,500,000.00	$2,900,000.00
Net Sales (all sales on account)		5,760,000.00
Cost of Merchandise Sold		3,810,000.00
Net Income after Federal Income Tax		530,000.00
Shares of Capital Stock Outstanding		100,000
Market Price per Share		$ 52.50

[4a]

Rate earned on average total assets:

[4b]

Rate earned on average stockholders' equity:

[4c]

Rate earned on net sales:

[4d]

Earnings per share:

16-2 WORK TOGETHER (concluded)

[4e]

Price earnings ratio:

[4f]

Accounts receivable turnover ratio:

[4g]

Average number of days for accounts receivable payment:

[4h]

Merchandise inventory turnover ratio:

[4i]

Average number of days' sales in merchandise inventory:

16-2 ON YOUR OWN, p. 460

Calculating earnings performance and efficiency analysis ratios [5]

	January 1	December 31
Total Assets	$3,400,000.00	$4,000,000.00
Book Value of Accounts Receivable	475,000.00	525,000.00
Merchandise Inventory	300,000.00	280,000.00
Stockholders' Equity	$1,900,000.00	$3,000,000.00
Net Sales (all sales on account)		4,320,000.00
Cost of Merchandise Sold		2,800,000.00
Net Income after Federal Income Tax		392,000.00
Shares of Capital Stock Outstanding		100,000
Market Price per Share		$ 48.00

[5a]

Rate earned on average total assets:

[5b]

Rate earned on average stockholders' equity:

[5c]

Rate earned on net sales:

[5d]

Earnings per share:

16-2 ON YOUR OWN (concluded)

[5e]

Price earnings ratio:

[5f]

Accounts receivable turnover ratio:

[5g]

Average number of days for accounts receivable payment:

[5h]

Merchandise inventory turnover ratio:

[5i]

Average number of days' sales in merchandise inventory:

16-3 WORK TOGETHER, p. 465

Analyzing short-term and long-term financial strength [8]

	Current Year	Prior Year
Total Current Assets	$2,150,000.00	$1,900,000.00
Total Quick Assets (cash + accounts receivable)	664,000.00	1,176,500.00
Total Assets	3,210,000.00	2,960,000.00
Total Current Liabilities	830,000.00	905,000.00
Total Liabilities	1,340,000.00	1,325,000.00
Total Stockholders' Equity	1,870,000.00	1,635,000.00
Shares of Capital Stock Outstanding	120,000	113,000

[8a]

Working capital:

[8b]

Current ratio:

[8c]

Acid-test ratio:

16-3 WORK TOGETHER (concluded)

[8d]

Debt ratio:

[8e]

Equity ratio:

[8f]

Equity per share:

Extra space for calculations

16-3 ON YOUR OWN, p. 465

Analyzing short-term and long-term financial strength [9]

	Current Year	Prior Year
Total Current Assets	$1,612,000.00	$1,400,000.00
Total Quick Assets (cash + accounts receivable)	805,000.00	725,000.00
Total Assets	2,450,000.00	2,050,000.00
Total Current Liabilities	620,000.00	410,000.00
Total Liabilities	1,580,000.00	975,000.00
Total Stockholders' Equity	870,000.00	1,075,000.00
Shares of Capital Stock Outstanding	70,000	65,000

[9a]

Working capital:

[9b]

Current ratio:

[9c]

Acid-test ratio:

16-3 ON YOUR OWN (concluded)

[9d]

Debt ratio:

[9e]

Equity ratio:

[9f]

Equity per share:

Extra space for calculations

16-1 APPLICATION PROBLEM, p. 467

Analyzing comparative financial statements using trend analysis [1]

The comparative statements prepared in this problem are needed to complete Application Problems 16-3, 16-4, 16-5, and 16-6.

CyberOptic Corporation
Comparative Income Statement
For Years Ended December 31, 20-- and 20--

	CURRENT YEAR	PRIOR YEAR	INCREASE (DECREASE) AMOUNT	%
Operating Revenue:				
Net Sales	1041 980 00	914 560 00		
Cost of Merchandise Sold:				
Merchandise Inventory, Jan. 1	220 380 00	125 010 00		
Net Purchases	827 450 00	789 480 00		
Total Cost of Merchandise Available for Sale	1047 830 00	914 490 00		
Less Merchandise Inventory, Dec. 31	318 840 00	220 380 00		
Cost of Merchandise Sold	728 990 00	694 110 00		
Gross Profit on Operations	312 990 00	220 450 00		
Operating Expenses:				
Selling Expenses:				
Advertising Expense	7 360 00	5 800 00		
Delivery Expense	13 800 00	12 430 00		
Salary Expense—Sales	59 800 00	49 730 00		
Supplies Expense	2 760 00	2 490 00		
Other Selling Expenses	3 680 00	3 310 00		
Total Selling Expenses	87 400 00	73 760 00		
Administrative Expenses:				
Salary Expense—Administrative	22 080 00	20 720 00		
Uncollectible Accounts Expense	9 200 00	4 140 00		
Other Administrative Expenses	11 040 00	9 950 00		
Total Administrative Expenses	42 320 00	34 810 00		
Total Operating Expenses	129 720 00	108 570 00		
Income from Operations	183 270 00	111 880 00		
Other Expenses:				
Interest Expense	18 400 00	15 750 00		
Net Income before Federal Income Tax	164 870 00	96 130 00		
Less Federal Income Tax Expense	47 550 00	20 930 00		
Net Income after Federal Income Tax	117 320 00	75 200 00		

16-1 APPLICATION PROBLEM (continued)

[1]

CyberOptic Corporation
Comparative Balance Sheet
December 31, 20-- and 20--

	CURRENT YEAR	PRIOR YEAR	INCREASE (DECREASE) AMOUNT	%
ASSETS				
Current Assets:				
Cash	137 490 00	138 530 00		
Accounts Receivable (book value)	78 820 00	76 820 00		
Merchandise Inventory	318 840 00	220 380 00		
Other Current Assets	10 800 00	10 570 00		
Total Current Assets	545 950 00	446 300 00		
Plant Assets (book value)	252 980 00	224 370 00		
Total Assets	798 930 00	670 670 00		
LIABILITIES				
Current Liabilities:				
Notes Payable	86 250 00	57 530 00		
Interest Payable	5 460 00	4 720 00		
Accounts Payable	143 560 00	139 980 00		
Federal Income Tax Payable	4 220 00	1 130 00		
Other Current Liabilities	22 080 00	17 270 00		
Total Current Liabilities	261 570 00	220 630 00		
Long-Term Liability:				
Mortgage Payable	80 000 00	100 000 00		
Total Liabilities	341 570 00	320 630 00		
STOCKHOLDERS' EQUITY				
Capital Stock	250 000 00	200 000 00		
Retained Earnings	207 360 00	150 040 00		
Total Stockholders' Equity	457 360 00	350 040 00		
Total Liabilities and Stockholders' Equity	798 930 00	670 670 00		

16-1 APPLICATION PROBLEM (continued)

[1]

CyberOptic Corporation
Comparative Statement of Stockholders' Equity
For Years Ended December 31, 20-- and 20--

	CURRENT YEAR	PRIOR YEAR	INCREASE (DECREASE) AMOUNT	%
Capital Stock:				
$5 Per Share				
Balance, January 1	200 000 00	200 000 00		
Additional Capital Stock Issued	50 000 00	- 0 -		
Balance, December 31	250 000 00	200 000 00		
Retained Earnings:				
Balance, January 1	150 040 00	114 840 00		
Net Income after Federal Income Tax	117 320 00	75 200 00		
Total	267 360 00	190 040 00		
Less Dividends Declared	60 000 00	40 000 00		
Balance, December 31	207 360 00	150 040 00		
Total Stockholders' Equity, December 31	457 360 00	350 040 00		
Capital Stock Shares Outstanding	50 000	40 000		

16-1 APPLICATION PROBLEM (concluded)

[2]

[a]	Net sales:	Trend: Reason:
[b]	Net income:	Trend: Reason:
[c]	Net stockholders' equity:	Trend: Reason:
[d]	Total assets:	Trend: Reason:

16-2 APPLICATION PROBLEM, p. 467

Analyzing comparative financial statements using component percentage analysis [1]

CyberOptic Corporation

Comparative Income Statement

For Years Ended December 31, 20-- and 20--

	CURRENT YEAR AMOUNT	%	PRIOR YEAR AMOUNT	%
Operating Revenue:				
Net Sales	1041 9 8 0 00		914 5 6 0 00	
Cost of Merchandise Sold:				
Merchandise Inventory, Jan. 1	220 3 8 0 00		125 0 1 0 00	
Net Purchases	827 4 5 0 00		789 4 8 0 00	
Total Cost of Merchandise Available for Sale	1047 8 3 0 00		914 4 9 0 00	
Less Merchandise Inventory, Dec. 31	318 8 4 0 00		220 3 8 0 00	
Cost of Merchandise Sold	728 9 9 0 00		694 1 1 0 00	
Gross Profit on Operations	312 9 9 0 00		220 4 5 0 00	
Operating Expenses:				
Selling Expenses:				
Advertising Expense	7 3 6 0 00		5 8 0 0 00	
Delivery Expense	13 8 0 0 00		12 4 3 0 00	
Salary Expense—Sales	59 8 0 0 00		49 7 3 0 00	
Supplies Expense	2 7 6 0 00		2 4 9 0 00	
Other Selling Expenses	3 6 8 0 00		3 3 1 0 00	
Total Selling Expenses	87 4 0 0 00		73 7 6 0 00	
Administrative Expenses:				
Salary Expense—Administrative	22 0 8 0 00		20 7 2 0 00	
Uncollectible Accounts Expense	9 2 0 0 00		4 1 4 0 00	
Other Administrative Expenses	11 0 4 0 00		9 9 5 0 00	
Total Administrative Expenses	42 3 2 0 00		34 8 1 0 00	
Total Operating Expenses	129 7 2 0 00		108 5 7 0 00	
Income from Operations	183 2 7 0 00		111 8 8 0 00	
Other Expenses:				
Interest Expense	18 4 0 0 00		15 7 5 0 00	
Net Income before Federal Income Tax	164 8 7 0 00		96 1 3 0 00	
Less Federal Income Tax	47 5 5 0 00		20 9 3 0 00	
Net Income after Federal Income Tax	117 3 2 0 00		75 2 0 0 00	

16-2 APPLICATION PROBLEM (continued)

[1]

CyberOptic Corporation
Comparative Statement of Stockholders' Equity
For Years Ended December 31, 20-- and 20--

	Current Year Amount	%	Prior Year Amount	%
Capital Stock:				
$5 Per Share				
Balance, January 1	200 000 00		200 000 00	
Additional Capital Stock Issued	50 000 00		- 0 -	
Balance, December 31	250 000 00		200 000 00	
Retained Earnings:				
Balance, January 1	150 040 00		114 840 00	
Net Income after Federal Income Tax	117 320 00		75 200 00	
Total	267 360 00		190 040 00	
Less Dividends Declared	60 000 00		40 000 00	
Balance, December 31	207 360 00		150 040 00	
Total Stockholders' Equity, December 31	457 360 00		350 040 00	
Capital Stock Shares Outstanding	50 000		40 000	

16-2 APPLICATION PROBLEM (continued)

[1]

CyberOptic Corporation
Comparative Balance Sheet
December 31, 20-- and 20--

	Current Year Amount	%	Prior Year Amount	%
ASSETS				
Current Assets:				
Cash	137 490 00		138 530 00	
Accounts Receivable (book value)	78 820 00		76 820 00	
Merchandise Inventory	318 840 00		220 380 00	
Other Current Assets	10 800 00		10 570 00	
Total Current Assets	545 950 00		446 300 00	
Plant Assets (book value)	252 980 00		224 370 00	
Total Assets	798 930 00		670 670 00	
LIABILITIES				
Current Liabilities:				
Notes Payable	86 250 00		57 530 00	
Interest Payable	5 460 00		4 720 00	
Accounts Payable	143 560 00		139 980 00	
Federal Income Tax Payable	4 220 00		1 130 00	
Other Current Liabilities	22 080 00		17 270 00	
Total Current Liabilities	261 570 00		220 630 00	
Long-Term Liability:				
Mortgage Payable	80 000 00		100 000 00	
Total Liabilities	341 570 00		320 630 00	
STOCKHOLDERS' EQUITY				
Capital Stock	250 000 00		200 000 00	
Retained Earnings	207 360 00		150 040 00	
Total Stockholders' Equity	457 360 00		350 040 00	
Total Liabilities and Stockholders' Equity	798 930 00		670 670 00	

16-2 APPLICATION PROBLEM (continued)

[2]

[a] **(1)** As a Percentage of Net Sales: Cost of merchandise sold: Current year: Prior year:	Trend: Reason:
(2) Gross profit on operations: Current year: Prior year:	Trend: Reason:
(3) Total operating expenses: Current year: Prior year:	Trend: Reason:
(4) Net income after federal income tax: Current year: Prior year:	Trend: Reason:

16-2 APPLICATION PROBLEM (concluded)

[2]

[b] (1)	As a Percentage of Total Stockholders' Equity: Retained earnings: Current year: Prior year:	Trend: Reason:
(2)	Capital stock: Current year: Prior year:	Trend: Reason:
[c] (1)	As a Percentage of Total Assets or Total Liabilities and Stockholders' Equity: Current assets: Current year: Prior year:	Trend: Reason:
(2)	Current liabilities: Current year: Prior year:	Trend: Reason:

16-2 APPLICATION PROBLEM

Extra form

	CURRENT YEAR	PRIOR YEAR	INCREASE (DECREASE)	
			AMOUNT	%

Name _____ Date _____ Class _____

16-3 APPLICATION PROBLEM, p. 468

Analyzing earnings performance from comparative financial statements [1, 2]

The comparative statements from Application Problem 16-1 are needed to complete this problem.

[a]	Rate earned on average total assets: Current year: Prior year:	Trend: Reason:
[b]	Rate earned on average stockholders' equity: Current year: Prior year:	Trend: Reason:
[c]	Rate earned on net sales: Current year: Prior year:	Trend: Reason:
[d]	Earnings per share: Current year: Prior year:	Trend: Reason:
[e]	Price earnings ratio: Current year: Prior year:	Trend: Reason:

16-3 APPLICATION PROBLEM

Extra form

	CURRENT YEAR	PRIOR YEAR	INCREASE (DECREASE)	
			AMOUNT	%

Name _____ Date _____ Class _____

16-4 APPLICATION PROBLEM, p. 468

Analyzing efficiency from comparative financial statements [1, 2]

The comparative statements from Application Problem 16-1 are needed to complete this problem.

[a]	Accounts receivable turnover ratio: Current year: Prior year:	Trend: Reason:
[b]	Average number of days for payment: Current year: Prior year:	Trend: Reason:
[c]	Merchandise inventory turnover ratio: Current year: Prior year:	Trend: Reason:
[d]	Number of days' sales in merchandise inventory: Current year: Prior year:	Trend: Reason:

16-4 APPLICATION PROBLEM

Extra form

	CURRENT YEAR	PRIOR YEAR	INCREASE (DECREASE)	
			AMOUNT	%

Name _____ Date _____ Class _____

16-5 APPLICATION PROBLEM, p. 468

The comparative balance sheet from Application Problem 16-1 is needed to complete this problem.

Analyzing short-term financial strength from a comparative balance sheet [1, 2]

[a]	Working capital: Current year: Prior year:	Trend: Reason:
[b]	Current ratio: Current year: Prior year:	Trend: Reason:
[c]	Acid-test ratio: Current year: Prior year:	Trend: Reason:

16-6 APPLICATION PROBLEM, p. 469

The comparative balance sheet from Application Problem 16-1 is needed to complete this problem.

Analyzing long-term financial strength from a comparative balance sheet [1, 2]

[a]	Debt ratio: Current year: Prior year:	Trend: Reason:
[b]	Equity ratio: Current year: Prior year:	Trend: Reason:
[c]	Equity per share: Current year: Prior year:	Trend: Reason:

Chapter 16 Financial Statement Analysis • **195**

16-6 APPLICATION PROBLEM

Extra form

	CURRENT YEAR	PRIOR YEAR	INCREASE (DECREASE) AMOUNT	%

16-7 MASTERY PROBLEM, p. 469

Analyzing comparative financial statements [1]

Advanced Auto Technology, Inc.

Comparative Income Statement

For Years Ended December 31, 20-- and 20--

	CURRENT YEAR	PRIOR YEAR	INCREASE (DECREASE) AMOUNT	%
Operating Revenue:				
Net Sales	2064 000 00	1563 900 00		
Cost of Merchandise Sold:				
Merchandise Inventory, Jan. 1	172 890 00	53 760 00		
Net Purchases	1255 600 00	1109 660 00		
Total Cost of Merchandise Available for Sale	1428 490 00	1163 420 00		
Less Merchandise Inventory, Dec. 31	194 230 00	172 890 00		
Cost of Merchandise Sold	1234 260 00	990 530 00		
Gross Profit on Operations	829 740 00	573 370 00		
Operating Expenses:				
Selling Expenses:				
Advertising Expense	15 260 00	10 170 00		
Delivery Expense	22 880 00	17 440 00		
Salary Expense—Sales	286 050 00	216 500 00		
Supplies Expense	13 350 00	10 170 00		
Other Selling Expenses	38 140 00	30 510 00		
Total Selling Expenses	375 680 00	284 790 00		
Administrative Expenses:				
Salary Expense—Administrative	80 090 00	63 930 00		
Uncollectible Accounts Expense	11 440 00	7 270 00		
Other Administrative Expenses	57 210 00	47 950 00		
Total Administrative Expenses	148 740 00	119 150 00		
Total Operating Expenses	524 420 00	403 940 00		
Income from Operations	305 320 00	169 430 00		
Other Expenses:				
Interest Expense	25 560 00	22 500 00		
Net Income before Federal Income Tax	279 760 00	146 930 00		
Less Federal Income Tax Expense	92 360 00	40 550 00		
Net Income after Federal Income Tax	187 400 00	106 380 00		

16-7 MASTERY PROBLEM (continued)

[1]

Advanced Auto Technology, Inc.
Comparative Statement of Stockholders' Equity
For Years Ended December 31, 20-- and 20--

	CURRENT YEAR	PRIOR YEAR	INCREASE (DECREASE) AMOUNT	%
Capital Stock:				
$5 Per Share				
Balance, January 1	200 000 00	200 000 00		
Additional Capital Stock Issued	40 000 00	- 0 -		
Balance, December 31	240 000 00	200 000 00		
Retained Earnings:				
Balance, January 1	173 160 00	106 780 00		
Net Income after Federal Income Tax	187 400 00	106 380 00		
Total	360 560 00	213 160 00		
Less Dividends Declared	62 500 00	40 000 00		
Balance, December 31	298 060 00	173 160 00		
Total Stockholders' Equity, December 31	538 060 00	373 160 00		
Capital Stock Shares Outstanding	48 000	40 000		

16-7 MASTERY PROBLEM (continued)

[1]

Advanced Auto Technology, Inc.
Comparative Balance Sheet
December 31, 20-- and 20--

	CURRENT YEAR	PRIOR YEAR	INCREASE (DECREASE) AMOUNT	%
ASSETS				
Current Assets:				
Cash	75 400 00	32 560 00		
Accounts Receivable (book value)	201 640 00	242 890 00		
Merchandise Inventory	194 230 00	172 890 00		
Other Current Assets	10 920 00	8 520 00		
Total Current Assets	482 190 00	456 860 00		
Plant Assets (book value)	422 000 00	306 000 00		
Total Assets	904 190 00	762 860 00		
LIABILITIES				
Current Liabilities:				
Notes Payable	64 860 00	83 410 00		
Interest Payable	5 160 00	8 040 00		
Accounts Payable	113 450 00	154 470 00		
Federal Income Tax Payable	5 500 00	1 280 00		
Other Current Liabilities	2 160 00	2 500 00		
Total Current Liabilities	191 130 00	249 700 00		
Long-Term Liability:				
Mortgage Payable	175 000 00	140 000 00		
Total Liabilities	366 130 00	389 700 00		
STOCKHOLDERS' EQUITY				
Capital Stock	240 000 00	200 000 00		
Retained Earnings	298 060 00	173 160 00		
Total Stockholders' Equity	538 060 00	373 160 00		
Total Liabilities and Stockholders' Equity	904 190 00	762 860 00		

16-7 MASTERY PROBLEM (continued)

[2]

[a] Net sales:

Trend:

Reason:

[b] Net income:

Trend:

Reason:

[c] Net stockholders' equity:

Trend:

Reason:

[d] Total assets:

Trend:

Reason:

16-7 MASTERY PROBLEM (continued)

[3]

Advanced Auto Technology, Inc.
Comparative Income Statement
For Years Ended December 31, 20-- and 20--

	CURRENT YEAR AMOUNT	%	PRIOR YEAR AMOUNT	%
Operating Revenue:				
Net Sales	2064 000 00		1563 900 00	
Cost of Merchandise Sold:				
Merchandise Inventory, Jan. 1	172 890 00		53 760 00	
Net Purchases	1255 600 00		1109 660 00	
Total Cost of Merchandise Available for Sale	1428 490 00		1163 420 00	
Less Merchandise Inventory, Dec. 31	194 230 00		172 890 00	
Cost of Merchandise Sold	1234 260 00		990 530 00	
Gross Profit on Operations	829 740 00		573 370 00	
Operating Expenses:				
Selling Expenses:				
Advertising Expense	15 260 00		10 170 00	
Delivery Expense	22 880 00		17 440 00	
Salary Expense—Sales	286 050 00		216 500 00	
Supplies Expense	13 350 00		10 170 00	
Other Selling Expenses	38 140 00		30 510 00	
Total Selling Expenses	375 680 00		284 790 00	
Administrative Expenses:				
Salary Expense—Administrative	80 090 00		63 930 00	
Uncollectible Accounts Expense	11 440 00		7 270 00	
Other Administrative Expenses	57 210 00		47 950 00	
Total Administrative Expenses	148 740 00		119 150 00	
Total Operating Expenses	524 420 00		403 940 00	
Income from Operations	305 320 00		169 430 00	
Other Expenses:				
Interest Expense	25 560 00		22 500 00	
Net Income before Federal Income Tax	279 760 00		146 930 00	
Less Federal Income Tax Expense	92 360 00		40 550 00	
Net Income after Federal Income Tax	187 400 00		106 380 00	

16-7 MASTERY PROBLEM (continued)

[4]

[a]

(1) As a Percentage of Net Sales:

Cost of merchandise sold:

Current year:

Prior year:

Trend:

Reason:

(2) Gross profit on operations:

Current year:

Prior year:

Trend:

Reason:

(3) Total operating expenses:

Current year:

Prior year:

Trend:

Reason:

(4) Net income after federal income tax:

Current year:

Prior year:

Trend:

Reason:

16-7 MASTERY PROBLEM (continued)

[4]

[b] **(1)**	As a Percentage of Total Stockholders' Equity: Retained earnings: Current year: Prior year:	Trend: Reason:
(2)	Capital stock: Current year: Prior year:	Trend: Reason:
[c] **(1)**	As a Percentage of Total Assets or Total Liabilities and Stockholders' Equity: Current assets: Current year: Prior year:	Trend: Reason:
(2)	Current liabilities: Current year: Prior year:	Trend: Reason:

16-7 MASTERY PROBLEM (continued)

[5, 6]

[a]

(1) Profitability ratios:
Rate earned on average total assets:
Current year:

Prior year:

Trend:

Reason:

(2) Rate earned on average stockholders' equity:
Current year:

Prior year:

Trend:

Reason:

(3) Rate earned on net sales:
Current year:

Prior year:

Trend:

Reason:

(4) Earnings per share:
Current year:

Prior year:

Trend:

Reason:

(5) Price earnings ratio:
Current year:

Prior year:

Trend:

Reason:

Name _____ Date _____ Class _____

16-7 MASTERY PROBLEM (continued)

[5, 6]

[b] (1)	Efficiency ratios: Accounts receivable turnover ratio: Current year: Prior year:	Trend: Reason:
(2)	Merchandise inventory turnover ratio: Current year: Prior year:	Trend: Reason:
[c] (1)	Short-term financial strength ratios: Working capital: Current year: Prior year:	Trend: Reason:
(2)	Current ratio: Current year: Prior year:	Trend: Reason:
(3)	Acid-test ratio: Current year: Prior year:	Trend: Reason:

16-7 MASTERY PROBLEM (concluded)

[5, 6]

[d] Long-term financial strength ratios:

(1) Debt ratio:

Current year:

Prior year:

Trend:

Reason:

(2) Equity ratio:

Current year:

Prior year:

Trend:

Reason:

(3) Equity per share:

Current year:

Prior year:

Trend:

Reason:

16-8 CHALLENGE PROBLEM, p. 470

Analyzing comparative financial statements [1]

CompuCircuit Corporation
Comparative Income Statement
For Years Ended December 31, 20-- and 20--

	CURRENT YEAR	PRIOR YEAR	INCREASE (DECREASE) AMOUNT	%
Operating Revenue:				
Net Sales	1287 900 00	1532 330 00		
Cost of Merchandise Sold:				
Merchandise Inventory, Jan. 1	324 560 00	293 500 00		
Net Purchases	924 350 00	1049 740 00		
Total Cost of Merchandise Available for Sale	1248 910 00	1343 240 00		
Less Merchandise Inventory, Dec. 31	335 780 00	324 560 00		
Cost of Merchandise Sold	913 130 00	1018 680 00		
Gross Profit on Operations	374 770 00	513 650 00		
Operating Expenses:				
Selling Expenses:				
Advertising Expense	20 330 00	26 400 00		
Delivery Expense	33 170 00	40 920 00		
Salary Expense—Sales	86 670 00	116 160 00		
Supplies Expense	8 560 00	10 560 00		
Other Selling Expenses	37 450 00	46 200 00		
Total Selling Expenses	186 180 00	240 240 00		
Administrative Expenses:				
Salary Expense—Administrative	64 200 00	77 880 00		
Uncollectible Accounts Expense	4 280 00	9 240 00		
Other Administrative Expenses	55 640 00	66 000 00		
Total Administrative Expenses	124 120 00	153 120 00		
Total Operating Expenses	310 300 00	393 360 00		
Income from Operations	64 470 00	120 290 00		
Other Expenses:				
Interest Expense	31 030 00	26 400 00		
Net Income before Federal Income Tax	33 440 00	93 890 00		
Less Federal Income Tax Expense	5 020 00	20 170 00		
Net Income after Federal Income Tax	28 420 00	73 720 00		

16-8 CHALLENGE PROBLEM (continued)

[1]

CompuCircuit Corporation
Comparative Statement of Stockholders' Equity
For Years Ended December 31, 20-- and 20--

	CURRENT YEAR	PRIOR YEAR	INCREASE (DECREASE) AMOUNT	%
Capital Stock:				
$5 Per Share				
Balance, January 1	400 000 00	400 000 00		
Additional Capital Stock Issued	-0-	-0-		
Balance, December 31	400 000 00	400 000 00		
Retained Earnings:				
Balance, January 1	67 060 00	43 340 00		
Net Income after Federal income Tax	28 420 00	73 720 00		
Total	95 480 00	117 060 00		
Less Dividends Declared	50 000 00	50 000 00		
Balance, December 31	45 480 00	67 060 00		
Total Stockholders' Equity, December 31	445 480 00	467 060 00		
Capital Stock Shares Outstanding	20 000	20 000		

16-8 CHALLENGE PROBLEM (continued)

[1]

CompuCircuit Corporation
Comparative Balance Sheet
December 31, 20-- and 20--

	CURRENT YEAR	PRIOR YEAR	INCREASE (DECREASE) AMOUNT	%
ASSETS				
Current Assets:				
Cash	33 650 00	98 770 00		
Accounts Receivable (book value)	88 490 00	105 500 00		
Merchandise Inventory	335 780 00	324 560 00		
Other Current Assets	145 830 00	125 130 00		
Total Current Assets	603 750 00	653 960 00		
Plant Assets (book value)	312 700 00	325 700 00		
Total Assets	916 450 00	979 660 00		
LIABILITIES				
Current Liabilities:				
Notes Payable	142 000 00	112 200 00		
Interest Payable	3 100 00	2 600 00		
Accounts Payable	72 040 00	135 920 00		
Federal Income Tax Payable	500 00	2 000 00		
Other Current Liabilities	28 330 00	27 880 00		
Total Current Liabilities	245 970 00	280 600 00		
Long-Term Liability:				
Mortgage Payable	225 000 00	232 000 00		
Total Liabilities	470 970 00	512 600 00		
STOCKHOLDERS' EQUITY				
Capital Stock	400 000 00	400 000 00		
Retained Earnings	45 480 00	67 060 00		
Total Stockholders' Equity	445 480 00	467 060 00		
Total Liabilities and Stockholders' Equity	916 450 00	979 660 00		

16-8 CHALLENGE PROBLEM (continued)

[2]

[a]	Net sales:	Trend: Reason:
[b]	Net income:	Trend: Reason:
[c]	Net stockholders' equity:	Trend: Reason:
[d]	Total assets:	Trend: Reason:

16-8 CHALLENGE PROBLEM (continued)

[3]

CompuCircuit Corporation
Comparative Income Statement
For Years Ended December 31, 20-- and 20--

	CURRENT YEAR AMOUNT	%	PRIOR YEAR AMOUNT	%
Operating Revenue:				
Net Sales	1287 900 00		1532 330 00	
Cost of Merchandise Sold:				
Merchandise Inventory, Jan. 1	324 560 00		293 500 00	
Net Purchases	924 350 00		1049 740 00	
Total Cost of Merchandise Available for Sale	1248 910 00		1343 240 00	
Less Merchandise Inventory, Dec. 31	335 780 00		324 560 00	
Cost of Merchandise Sold	913 130 00		1018 680 00	
Gross Profit on Operations	374 770 00		513 650 00	
Operating Expenses:				
Selling Expenses:				
Advertising Expense	20 330 00		26 400 00	
Delivery Expense	33 170 00		40 920 00	
Salary Expense—Sales	86 670 00		116 160 00	
Supplies Expense	8 560 00		10 560 00	
Other Selling Expenses	37 450 00		46 200 00	
Total Selling Expenses	186 180 00		240 240 00	
Administrative Expenses:				
Salary Expense—Administrative	64 200 00		77 880 00	
Uncollectible Accounts Expense	4 280 00		9 240 00	
Other Administrative Expenses	55 640 00		66 000 00	
Total Administrative Expenses	124 120 00		153 120 00	
Total Operating Expenses	310 300 00		393 360 00	
Income from Operations	64 470 00		120 290 00	
Other Expenses:				
Interest Expense	31 030 00		26 400 00	
Net Income before Federal Income Tax	33 440 00		93 890 00	
Less Federal Income Tax	5 020 00		20 170 00	
Net Income after Federal Income Tax	28 420 00		73 720 00	

16-8 CHALLENGE PROBLEM (continued)

[4]

[a] **(1)**	As a Percentage of Net Sales: Cost of merchandise sold: Current year: Prior year:	Trend: Reason:
(2)	Gross profit on operations: Current year: Prior year:	Trend: Reason:
(3)	Total operating expenses: Current year: Prior year:	Trend: Reason:
(4)	Net income after federal income tax: Current year: Prior year:	Trend: Reason:

16-8 CHALLENGE PROBLEM (continued)

[4]

[b] **(1)**	As a Percentage of Total Stockholders' Equity: Retained earnings: Current year: Prior year:	Trend: Reason:
(2)	Capital stock: Current year: Prior year:	Trend: Reason:
[c] **(1)**	As a Percentage of Total Assets or Total Liabilities and Stockholders' Equity: Current assets: Current year: Prior year:	Trend: Reason:
(2)	Current liabilities: Current year: Prior year:	Trend: Reason:

16-8 CHALLENGE PROBLEM (continued)

[5, 6]

[a]

(1) Profitability ratios:
Rate earned on average total assets:

Current year:

Prior year:

Trend:
Reason:

(2) Rate earned on average stockholders' equity:

Current year:

Prior year:

Trend:
Reason:

(3) Rate earned on net sales:
Current year:

Prior year:

Trend:
Reason:

(4) Earnings per share:
Current year:

Prior year:

Trend:
Reason:

(5) Price earnings ratio:
Current year:

Prior year:

Trend:
Reason:

[b]

(1) Efficiency ratios:
Accounts receivable turnover ratio:

Current year:

Prior year:

Trend:
Reason:

Name _____ Date _____ Class _____

16-8 CHALLENGE PROBLEM (continued)

[5, 6]

[b] (2)	Efficiency ratios: Merchandise inventory turnover ratio: Current year: Prior year:	Trend: Reason:
[c] (1)	Short-term financial strength ratios: Working capital: Current year: Prior year:	Trend: Reason:
(2)	Current ratio: Current year: Prior year:	Trend: Reason:
(3)	Acid-test ratio: Current year: Prior year:	Trend: Reason:
[d] (1)	Long-term financial strength ratios: Debt ratio: Current year: Prior year:	Trend: Reason:
(2)	Equity ratio: Current year: Prior year:	Trend: Reason:
(3)	Equity per share: Current year: Prior year:	Trend: Reason:

16-8 CHALLENGE PROBLEM

Extra form

	CURRENT YEAR	PRIOR YEAR	INCREASE (DECREASE) AMOUNT	%

17-1 WORK TOGETHER, p. 481

Classifying cash flows [4]

Transaction	Cash Inflow	Cash Outflow	Operating Activity	Investing Activity	Financing Activity
a. Receipts from the issue of capital stock					
b. Cash purchase of office furniture					
c. Dividend payment					
d. Advertising expense					
e. Receipts from the sale of merchandise					
f. Cash received from the issue of a mortgage					
g. Repayment of loan principal					
h. Purchase of another company's stock					

17-1 ON YOUR OWN, p. 481

Classifying cash flows [5]

Transaction	Cash Inflow	Cash Outflow	Operating Activity	Investing Activity	Financing Activity
a. Receipts from the issue of bonds					
b. Cash purchase of office furniture					
c. Salary expense					
d. Receipts from tuxedo rentals					
e. Receipts from the issue of a mortgage					
f. Cash receipt from sale of equipment					
g. Cash purchase of treasury stock					
h. Payment of property taxes					

17-1 WORK TOGETHER / ON YOUR OWN

Extra form

17-2 WORK TOGETHER, p. 487

Preparing the operating activity section for a statement of cash flows

	Zephyr Corporation Comparative Balance Sheet December 31, 20X1 and 20X2		
	Current Year	Prior Year	Increase (Decrease)
ASSETS			
Current Assets:			
Cash	$ 98,760.00	$ 41,000.00	$ 57,760.00
Accounts Receivable (book value)	155,000.00	160,000.00	(5,000.00)
Supplies	6,000.00	5,500.00	500.00
Merchandise Inventory	98,000.00	92,000.00	6,000.00
Total Current Assets	$357,760.00	$298,500.00	$ 59,260.00
Plant Assets:			
Office Equipment	$ 45,000.00	$ 39,000.00	$ 6,000.00
Store Furniture	98,000.00	92,000.00	6,000.00
Building	140,000.00	140,000.00	0.00
Land	0.00	25,000.00	(25,000.00)
Less Accum. Depr.—Equipment, Furniture & Bldg.	40,900.00	13,600.00	27,300.00
Total Plant Assets (book value)	$242,100.00	$282,400.00	$ (40,300.00)
Total Assets	$599,860.00	$580,900.00	$ 18,960.00
LIABILITIES			
Current Liabilities:			
Notes Payable	$ 23,000.00	$ 21,000.00	$ 2,000.00
Accounts Payable	47,000.00	45,000.00	2,000.00
Sales Tax Payable	600.00	800.00	(200.00)
Total Current Liabilities	$ 70,600.00	$ 66,800.00	$ 3,800.00
Long-Term Liabilities:			
Mortgage Payable	$125,000.00	$140,000.00	$ (15,000.00)
Bonds Payable	80,000.00	70,000.00	10,000.00
Total Long-Term Liabilities	$205,000.00	$210,000.00	$ (5,000.00)
Total Liabilities	$275,600.00	$276,800.00	$ (1,200.00)
STOCKHOLDERS' EQUITY			
Total Stockholders' Equity	324,260.00	304,100.00	20,160.00
Total Liabilities and Stockholders' Equity	$599,860.00	$580,900.00	$ 18,960.00

[5–8]

Account	Current Year	Prior Year	Current Asset Current Liability	Increase (Decrease)	Source of Cash Use of Cash
Accounts Receivable (book value)					
Notes Payable					
Merchandise Inventory					
Supplies					
Accounts Payable					
Sales Tax Payable					

17-2/17-3 WORK TOGETHER (concluded)

Zephyr Corporation
Statement of Cash Flows
For Year Ended December 31, 20--

17-2 ON YOUR OWN, p. 487

Preparing the operating activity section for a statement of cash flows

Cirrus Corporation
Comparative Balance Sheet
December 31, 20X1 and 20X2

	Current Year	Prior Year	Increase (Decrease)
ASSETS			
Current Assets:			
Cash	$ 66,300.00	$ 70,000.00	$ (3,700.00)
Accounts Receivable (book value)	94,000.00	90,000.00	4,000.00
Prepaid Insurance	2,000.00	3,000.00	(1,000.00)
Merchandise Inventory	92,000.00	110,000.00	(18,000.00)
Total Current Assets	$254,300.00	$273,000.00	$(18,700.00)
Plant Assets:			
Office Equipment	$ 46,000.00	$ 26,000.00	$ 20,000.00
Office Furniture	18,000.00	12,000.00	6,000.00
Building	235,000.00	210,000.00	25,000.00
Land	0.00	12,000.00	(12,000.00)
Less Accum. Depr.—Equipment, Furniture & Bldg.	24,500.00	19,600.00	4,900.00
Total Plant Assets (book value)	$274,500.00	$240,400.00	$ 34,100.00
Total Assets	$528,800.00	$513,400.00	$ 15,400.00
LIABILITIES			
Current Liabilities:			
Notes Payable	$ 16,500.00	$ 18,000.00	$ (1,500.00)
Accounts Payable	38,000.00	34,000.00	4,000.00
Total Current Liabilities	$ 54,500.00	$ 52,000.00	$ 2,500.00
Long-Term Liabilities:			
Mortgage Payable	$178,000.00	$186,000.00	$ (8,000.00)
Bonds Payable	40,000.00	50,000.00	(10,000.00)
Total Long-Term Liabilities	$218,000.00	$236,000.00	$(18,000.00)
Total Liabilities	$272,500.00	$288,000.00	$(15,500.00)
STOCKHOLDERS' EQUITY			
Total Stockholders' Equity	$256,300.00	$225,400.00	$ 30,900.00
Total Liabilities and Stockholders' Equity	$528,800.00	$513,400.00	$ 15,400.00

[10–13]

Account	Current Year	Prior Year	Current Asset Current Liability	Increase (Decrease)	Source of Cash Use of Cash
Accounts Receivable (book value)					
Prepaid Insurance					
Merchandise Inventory					
Notes Payable					
Accounts Payable					

17-2/17-3 ON YOUR OWN (continued)

Cirrus Corporation
Statement of Cash Flows
For Year Ended December 31, 20--

17-3 WORK TOGETHER, p. 493

The comparative balance sheet from Work Together 17-2 is needed to complete this problem.

Preparing the investing and financing activities sections for the statement of cash flows; completing the statement of cash flows [5]

Account	Current Year	Prior Year	Long-Term Asset Long-Term Liability	Increase (Decrease)	Source of Cash Use of Cash
Mortgage Payable					
Office Equipment					
Store Furniture					
Building					
Bonds Payable					
Land (no gain on sale)					

[7]

Activity	Amount	Source of Cash Use of Cash
Sale of additional common stock	$20,000.00	
Payment of cash dividend	10,000.00	

17-3 ON YOUR OWN, p. 493

The comparative balance sheet from On Your Own 17-2 is needed to complete this problem.

Preparing the investing and financing activities sections for the statement of cash flows; completing the statement of cash flows [10]

Account	Current Year	Prior Year	Long-Term Asset Long-Term Liability	Increase (Decrease)	Source of Cash Use of Cash
Office Equipment	$ 46,000.00	$ 26,000.00			
Office Furniture	18,000.00	12,000.00			
Building	235,000.00	210,000.00			
Land (no gain on sale)	0.00	12,000.00			
Mortgage Payable	178,000.00	186,000.00			
Bonds Payable	40,000.00	50,000.00			

[12]

Activity	Amount	Source of Cash Use of Cash
Sale of additional common stock	$20,000.00	
Payment of cash dividend	10,000.00	

17-3 WORK TOGETHER / ON YOUR OWN

Extra form

17-1 APPLICATION PROBLEM, p. 495

Classifying cash flows [a–g]

Transaction	Cash Inflow	Cash Outflow	Operating Activity	Investing Activity	Financing Activity
a. Dividend payment					
b. Payment of insurance premium					
c. Receipts from signing of a note payable					
d. Payment of payroll taxes					
e. Cash purchase of computer equipment					
f. Sale of treasury stock					
g. Receipts from consulting services					

17-2 APPLICATION PROBLEM, p. 495

Calculating the cash flows from operating activities

Use the statement of cash flows on page 224.

[1]

Item	Amount	Source of Cash Use of Cash
Net income		

[2]

Item	Amount	Source of Cash Use of Cash
Depreciation expense		

[3]

Account	Current Year	Prior Year	Current Asset Current Liability	Increase (Decrease)	Source of Cash Use of Cash
Accounts Receivable (book value)	$ 55,515	$ 48,000			
Merchandise Inventory	118,316	121,000			
Supplies	6,148	5,500			
Accounts Payable	49,762	44,000			

17-2/17-3/17-4 APPLICATION PROBLEM, pp. 495–496

Completing a statement of cash flows

Flexcor Corporation
Statement of Cash Flows
For Year Ended December 31, 20--

Name _____ Date _____ Class _____

17-3 APPLICATION PROBLEM, p. 496

Calculating the cash flows from investing activities [1, 2]

Use the statement of cash flows on page 226.

Account	Current Year	Prior Year	Long-Term Asset Long-Term Liability	Increase (Decrease)	Source of Cash Use of Cash
Office Equipment	$ 22,800	$ 12,500			
Office Furniture	12,210	9,000			
Land	100,000	140,000			

17-4 APPLICATION PROBLEM, p. 496

Calculating the cash flows from financing activities and completing a statement of cash flows [1]

Use the statement of cash flows started on page 226.

Account	Current Year	Prior Year	Long-Term Asset Long-Term Liability	Increase (Decrease)	Source of Cash Use of Cash
Mortgage Payable					

[2]

Activity	Amount	Source of Cash Use of Cash
Sale of additional common stock		
Payment of cash dividend		

[4]

Item	Amount
Net increase in Cash	

[5]

Item	Amount
Cash balance, beginning of period	

[6]

Item	Amount
Cash balance, end of period	

Complete the statement of cash flows on page 226.

17-4 APPLICATION PROBLEM

Extra form

17-5 MASTERY PROBLEM, p. 497

Preparing a statement of cash flows

West Coast Construction, Inc.
Comparative Income Statement
For Years Ended December 31, 20-- and 20--

	Current Year	Prior Year	Increase (Decrease)
Operating Revenue:			
Net Sales	$712,655.00	$745,220.00	$(32,565.00)
Cost of Merchandise Sold	292,035.00	301,124.00	(9,089.00)
Gross Profit on Operations	$420,620.00	$444,096.00	$(23,476.00)
Operating Expenses:			
Depreciation Expense—Equipment	$15,071.00	$14,261.00	$810.00
Other Operating Expenses	366,979.00	352,975.00	14,004.00
Total Operating Expenses	$382,050.00	$367,236.00	$14,814.00
Net Income before Federal Income Tax	$38,570.00	$76,860.00	$(38,290.00)
Less Federal Income Tax Expense	11,571.00	23,058.00	(11,487.00)
Net Income after Federal Income Tax	$26,999.00	$53,802.00	$(26,803.00)

West Coast Construction, Inc.
Comparative Statement of Stockholders' Equity
For Years Ended December 31, 20-- and 20--

	Current Year	Prior Year	Increase (Decrease)
Capital Stock:			
$15.00 Per Share			
Balance, January 1	$150,000.00	$150,000.00	$0.00
Additional Capital Stock Issued	15,000.00	0.00	15,000.00
Balance, December 31	$165,000.00	$150,000.00	$15,000.00
Retained Earnings:			
Balance, January 1	$92,986.00	$59,184.00	$33,802.00
Net Income after Federal Income Tax	26,999.00	53,802.00	(26,803.00)
Total	$119,985.00	$112,986.00	$6,999.00
Less Dividend Payment	$27,500.00	$20,000.00	7,500.00
Balance, December 31	92,485.00	92,986.00	$(501.00)
Total Stockholders' Equity, December 31	$257,485.00	$242,986.00	$14,499.00

17-5 MASTERY PROBLEM (continued)

West Coast Construction, Inc.
Comparative Balance Sheet
December 31, 20-- and 20--

	Current Year	Prior Year	Increase (Decrease)
ASSETS			
Current Assets:			
Cash	$ 63,768.00	$ 31,524.00	$ 32,244.00
Accounts Receivable (book value)	258,967.00	288,763.00	(29,796.00)
Supplies	1,251.00	1,577.00	(326.00)
Merchandise Inventory	89,545.00	93,450.00	(3,905.00)
Total Current Assets	$413,531.00	$415,314.00	$ (1,783.00)
Plant Assets:			
Equipment	$ 72,320.00	$ 62,320.00	$ 10,000.00
Less Accumulated Depr.—Equipment	32,750.00	17,679.00	15,071.00
Total Plant Assets (book value)	$ 39,570.00	$ 44,641.00	$ (5,071.00)
Total Assets	$453,101.00	$459,955.00	$ (6,854.00)
LIABILITIES			
Current Liabilities:			
Notes Payable	$ 14,003.00	$ 15,575.00	$ (1,572.00)
Accounts Payable	111,624.00	129,064.00	(17,440.00)
Total Current Liabilities	$125,627.00	$144,639.00	$ (19,012.00)
Long-Term Liability:			
Mortgage Payable	$ 69,989.00	$ 72,330.00	$ (2,341.00)
Total Liabilities	$195,616.00	$216,969.00	$ (21,353.00)
STOCKHOLDERS' EQUITY			
Total Stockholders' Equity	$257,485.00	$242,986.00	$ 14,499.00
Total Liabilities and Stockholders' Equity	$453,101.00	$459,955.00	$ (6,854.00)

17-5 MASTERY PROBLEM (continued)

[1]

Item	Amount	Source of Cash / Use of Cash
Net income		
Depreciation expense		

[2]

Account	Current Year	Prior Year	Current Asset Current Liability	Increase (Decrease)	Source of Cash Use of Cash
Accounts Receivable					
Supplies					
Merchandise Inventory					
Notes Payable					
Accounts Payable					

[3, 4]

Account	Current Year	Prior Year	Long-Term Asset Long-Term Liability	Increase (Decrease)	Source of Cash Use of Cash
Equipment					
Mortgage Payable					

[5]

Activity	Amount	Source of Cash Use of Cash
Sale of additional common stock		
Payment of cash dividend		

17-5 MASTERY PROBLEM (concluded)

[6–9]

West Coast Construction, Inc.
Statement of Cash Flows
For Year Ended December 31, 20--

Name _____ Date _____ Class _____

17-6 CHALLENGE PROBLEM, p. 498

Preparing a statement of cash flows

Pacific Digital Corporation
Comparative Income Statement
For Years Ended December 31, 20-- and 20--

	Current Year	Prior Year	Increase (Decrease)
Operating Revenue:			
Net Sales	$ 673,194.00	$ 640,220.00	$ 32,974.00
Cost of Merchandise Sold	308,436.00	271,074.00	37,362.00
Gross Profit on Operations	$ 364,758.00	$ 369,146.00	$ (4,388.00)
Operating Expenses:			
Depr. Expense—Equipment, Furniture & Bldg.	$ 27,300.00	$ 9,400.00	$ 17,900.00
Other Operating Expenses	337,488.00	344,356.00	(6,868.00)
Amortized Patent	9,420.00	9,420.00	0.00
Total Expenses	$ 374,208.00	$ 363,176.00	$ 11,032.00
Net Income (Net Loss)	$ (9,450.00)	$ 5,970.00	$(15,420.00)

Pacific Digital Corporation
Comparative Statement of Stockholders' Equity
For Years Ended December 31, 20-- and 20--

	Current Year	Prior Year	Increase (Decrease)
Capital Stock:			
$10.00 Per Share			
Balance, January 1	$ 307,130.00	$ 307,130.00	$ 0.00
Additional Capital Stock Issued (1,400 shares)	14,000.00	0.00	14,000.00
Balance, December 31	$ 321,130.00	$ 307,130.00	$ 14,000.00
Retained Earnings:			
Balance, January 1	$ 15,970.00	$ 10,000.00	$ 5,970.00
Net Income (Net Loss)	(9,450.00)	5,970.00	(15,420.00)
Balance, December 31	$ 6,520.00	$ 15,970.00	$ 21,390.00
Total Stockholders' Equity, December 31	$ 327,650.00	$ 323,100.00	35,390.00

17-6 CHALLENGE PROBLEM (continued)

Pacific Digital Corporation
Comparative Balance Sheet
December 31, 20-- and 20--

	Current Year	Prior Year	Increase (Decrease)
ASSETS			
Current Assets:			
Cash	$ 46,710.00	$ 40,770.00	$ 5,940.00
Notes Receivable	20,260.00	12,650.00	7,610.00
Accounts Receivable (book value)	113,100.00	135,000.00	(21,900.00)
Supplies	5,000.00	1,600.00	3,400.00
Merchandise Inventory	182,100.00	93,200.00	88,900.00
Total Current Assets	$367,170.00	$283,220.00	$ 83,950.00
Plant Assets:			
Office Equipment	$ 55,620.00	$ 45,320.00	$ 10,300.00
Office Furniture	13,210.00	10,000.00	3,210.00
Building	65,000.00	0.00	65,000.00
Land	100,000.00	150,000.00	(50,000.00)
Less Accum. Depr.—Equipment, Furniture & Bldg.	40,900.00	13,600.00	27,300.00
Total Plant Assets (book value)	$192,930.00	$191,720.00	$ 1,210.00
Intangible Assets:			
Patents	28,260.00	37,680.00	(9,420.00)
Total Assets	$588,360.00	$512,620.00	$ 75,740.00
LIABILITIES			
Current Liabilities:			
Notes Payable	$ 15,560.00	$ 22,410.00	$ (6,850.00)
Accounts Payable	114,850.00	105,900.00	8,950.00
Salaries Payable	9,700.00	10,700.00	(1,000.00)
Total Current Liabilities	$140,110.00	$139,010.00	$ 1,100.00
Long-Term Liability:			
Mortgage Payable	120,600.00	50,510.00	70,090.00
Total Liabilities	$260,710.00	$189,520.00	$ 71,190.00
STOCKHOLDERS' EQUITY			
Total Stockholders' Equity	$327,650.00	$323,100.00	$ 4,550.00
Total Liabilities and Stockholders' Equity	$588,360.00	$512,620.00	$ 75,740.00

17-6 CHALLENGE PROBLEM (concluded)

Pacific Digital Corporation
Statement of Cash Flows
For Year Ended December 31, 20--

17-6 CHALLENGE PROBLEM

Extra form

18-1 WORK TOGETHER (concluded)

[4, 5]

Begin this problem on pages 238 and 239. Use this page with page 240.

Co. _____
(continued)
March 31, 20--

	5	6	7	8	9	10	11	12	
	\multicolumn{4}{c}{DEPARTMENTAL MARGIN STATEMENTS}	\multicolumn{2}{c}{INCOME STATEMENT}	\multicolumn{2}{c}{BALANCE SHEET}	
	BOOKS		MUSIC						
	DEBIT	CREDIT	DEBIT	CREDIT	DEBIT	CREDIT	DEBIT	CREDIT	

18-1 WORK TOGETHER, p. 511

Prepare a work sheet with departmental margins [4, 5]

Adjustment information is listed on page 241.

Callostay
Work
For Month Ended

	ACCOUNT TITLE	TRIAL BALANCE DEBIT	TRIAL BALANCE CREDIT	ADJUSTMENTS DEBIT	ADJUSTMENTS CREDIT	
1	Cash	46 213 30				1
2	Accounts Receivable	26 935 70				2
3	Allowance for Uncollectible Accounts		1 33 90			3
4	Merchandise Inventory—Books	52 360 80				4
5	Merchandise Inventory—Music	58 921 20				5
6	Supplies	2 400 00				6
7	Prepaid Insurance	528 40				7
8	Office Equipment	12 500 00				8
9	Accum. Depr.—Office Equipment		2 800 00			9
10	Store Equipment—Books	11 580 20				10
11	Accum. Depr.—Store Equip., Books		925 40			11
12	Store Equipment—Music	27 602 80				12
13	Accum. Depr.—Store Equip., Music		5 612 30			13
14	Accounts Payable		27 823 50			14
15	Employee Income Tax Payable		1 110 90			15
16	Federal Income Tax Payable					16
17	Social Security Tax Payable		1 603 14			17
18	Medicare Tax Payable		369 96			18
19	Salaries Payable					19
20	Unemployment Tax Payable—Federal		49 00			20
21	Unemployment Tax Payable—State		330 75			21
22	Dividends Payable					22
23	Capital Stock		115 000 00			23
24	Retained Earnings		49 116 55			24
25	Dividends	5 000 00				25
26	Income Summary—Books					26
27	Income Summary—Music					27
28	Income Summary—General					28
29	Sales—Books		77 253 40			29
30	Sales Discount—Books	201 52				30
31	Sales Returns and Allowances—Books	142 08				31
32	Sales—Music		66 952 50			32
33	Sales Discount—Music	186 92				33
34	Sales Returns and Allowances—Music	94 18				34
35	Purchases—Books	26 218 20				35
36	Purchases Discount—Books		158 30			36
37	Purchases Returns and Allowances—Books		214 60			37
38	Purchases—Music	22 480 50				38
39	Purchases Discounts—Music		255 38			39

18-1 WORK TOGETHER (continued)

[4, 5]

Co.
Sheet
March 31, 20--

	DEPARTMENTAL MARGIN STATEMENTS				INCOME STATEMENT		BALANCE SHEET	
	BOOKS		MUSIC					
	DEBIT	CREDIT	DEBIT	CREDIT	DEBIT	CREDIT	DEBIT	CREDIT

18-1 WORK TOGETHER (continued)

[4, 5]

Callostay
Work Sheet
For Month Ended

	ACCOUNT TITLE	TRIAL BALANCE DEBIT	TRIAL BALANCE CREDIT	ADJUSTMENTS DEBIT	ADJUSTMENTS CREDIT	
40	Purchases Returns and Allow.—Music		3 6 92			40
41	Advertising Expense—Books	2 3 1 0 80				41
42	Depreciation Expense—Store Equip., Books					42
43	Insurance Expense—Books					43
44	Payroll Taxes Expense—Books	3 9 5 60				44
45	Salary Expense—Books	13 5 6 2 30				45
46	Supplies Expense—Books					46
47	Advertising Expense—Music	1 5 3 8 20				47
48	Delivery Expense—Music	1 6 0 4 90				48
49	Depr. Expense—Store Equip., Music					49
50	Insurance Expense—Music					50
51	Payroll Taxes Expense—Music	4 3 5 30				51
52	Salary Expense—Music	11 9 2 6 10				52
53	Supplies Expense—Music					53
54	Uncollectible Accounts Expense—Music					54
55	Credit Card Fee Expense	1 5 8 6 30				55
56	Depreciation Expense—Office Equipment					56
57	Insurance Expense—Administrative					57
58	Miscellaneous Expense	1 2 4 5 20				58
59	Payroll Taxes Expense—Administrative	5 3 7 10				59
60	Rent Expense	4 5 6 0 00				60
61	Salary Expense—Administrative	12 8 4 5 60				61
62	Supplies Expense—Administrative					62
63	Utilities Expense	1 8 3 3 30				63
64						64
65						65
66						66
67						67
68	Federal Income Tax Expense	2 0 0 0 00				68
69		349 7 4 6 50	349 7 4 6 50			69
70						70
71						71
72						72
73						73
74						74
75						75
76						76
77						77
78						78

18-1 WORK TOGETHER (continued)

[4, 5]

Adjustment Information, March 31

Uncollectible Accounts Expense—Music Estimated at 1.0% of Sales on Account	
Sales on Account for the Month	$25,500.00
Merchandise Inventory—Books	51,200.80
Merchandise Inventory—Music	62,578.00
Supplies Used—Books	420.00
Supplies Used—Music	205.00
Supplies Used—Administrative	348.50
Insurance Expired—Books	90.80
Insurance Expired—Music	136.00
Insurance Expired—Administrative	88.00
Depreciation Expense—Office Equipment	1,400.00
Depreciation Expense—Store Equipment, Books	450.00
Depreciation Expense—Store Equipment, Music	3,780.00
Federal Income Tax for the Month	1,000.00

Extra form

18-1 WORK TOGETHER

Extra form

						% OF NET SALES

18-2 ON YOUR OWN, p. 511

Journalizing direct and indirect expenses [6]

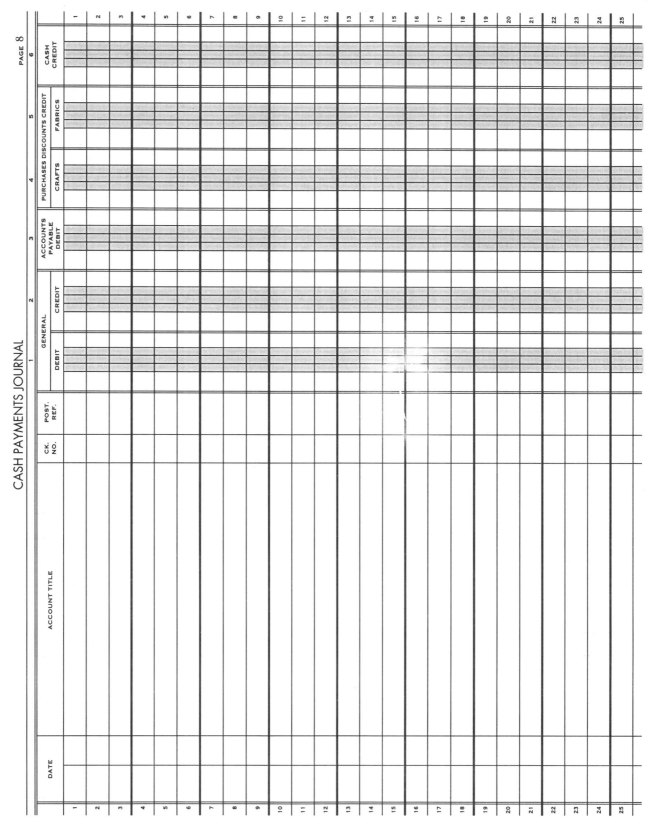

Chapter 18 Cost Accounting for a Merchandising Business • 243

Name _____ Date _____ Class _____

18-1 ON YOUR OWN

Extra form

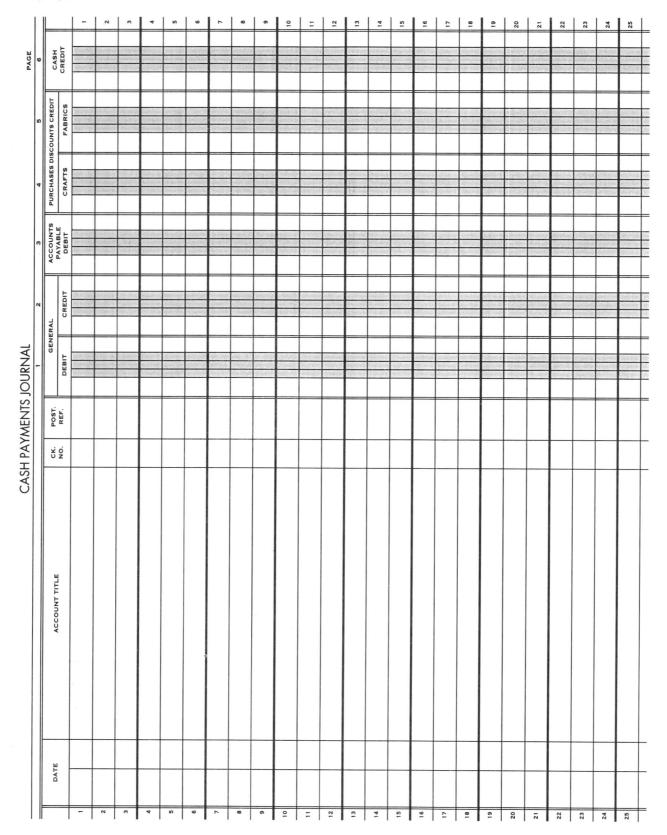

18-2 WORK TOGETHER, p. 516

Departmental margin statement [5]

The work sheet from Work Together 18-1 is needed to complete this problem.

Callostay Co.
Departmental Margin Statement—Books
For Month Ended March 31, 20--

					% OF NET SALES
Operating Revenue:					
Sales					
Less: Sales Discount					
Sales Returns & Allow.					
Net Sales					
Cost of Merchandise Sold					
Mdse. Inv., Mar. 1, 20--					
Purchases					
Less: Purchases Discount					
Purchases Returns & Allow.					
Net Purchases					
Total Cost of Mdse. Avail. for Sale					
Less Mdse. Inv., Mar. 31, 20--					
Cost of Merchandise Sold					
Gross Profit on Operations					
Direct Expenses:					
Advertising Expense					
Depr. Exp.—Store Equipment					
Insurance Expense					
Payroll Taxes Expense					
Salary Expense					
Supplies Expense					
Total Direct Expenses					
Departmental Margin					

18-2 ON YOUR OWN, p. 516

Departmental margin statement [6]

The work sheet from Work Together 18-1 is needed to complete this problem.

Callostay Co.
Departmental Margin Statement—Music
For Month Ended March 31, 20--

					% OF NET SALES
Operating Revenue:					
Sales					
Less: Sales Discount					
Sales Returns & Allow.					
Net Sales					
Cost of Merchandise Sold					
Mdse. Inv., Mar. 1, 20--					
Purchases					
Less: Purchases Discount					
Purchases Returns & Allow.					
Net Purchases					
Total Cost of Mdse. Avail. for Sale					
Less Mdse. Inv., Mar. 31, 20--					
Cost of Merchandise Sold					
Gross Profit on Operations					
Direct Expenses:					
Advertising Expense					
Delivery Expense					
Depr. Exp.—Store Equipment					
Insurance Expense					
Payroll Taxes Expense					
Salary Expense					
Supplies Expense					
Uncollectible Accounts Expense					
Total Direct Expenses					
Departmental Margin					

18-1 APPLICATION PROBLEM, p. 518

Journalizing direct and indirect expenses

CASH PAYMENTS JOURNAL PAGE 5

DATE	ACCOUNT TITLE	CK. NO.	POST. REF.	GENERAL DEBIT	GENERAL CREDIT	ACCOUNTS PAYABLE DEBIT	PURCHASES DISCOUNTS CREDIT PAINT	PURCHASES DISCOUNTS CREDIT WALLPAPER	CASH CREDIT

18-1 APPLICATION PROBLEM

Extra form

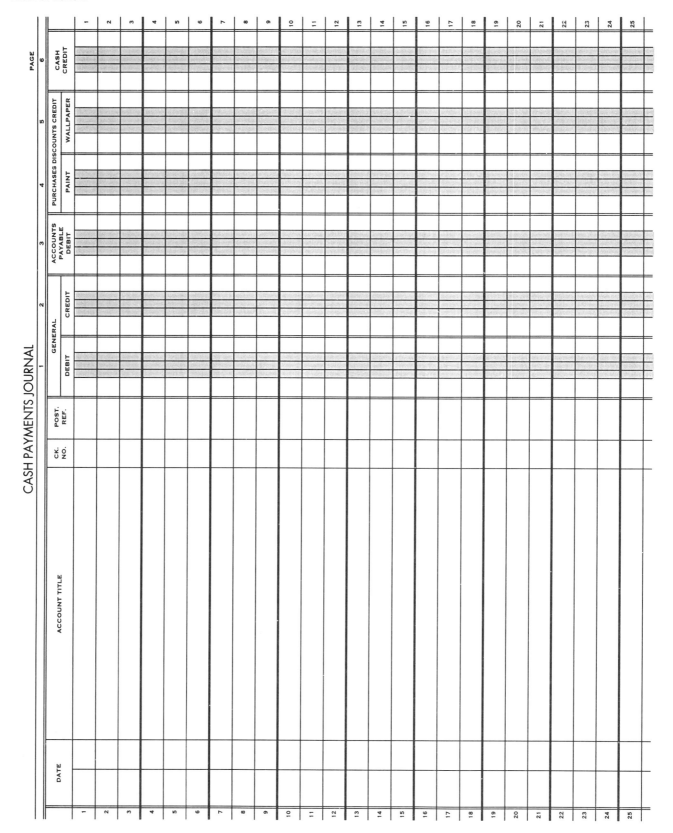

18-2 APPLICATION PROBLEM (concluded)

[1, 2]

Begin this problem on pages 250 and 251. Use this page with page 252.

Center
(continued)
July 31, 20--

| | Departmental Margin Statements | | | | Income Statement | | Balance Sheet | |
| | Clothing | | Equipment | | | | | |
	Debit	Credit	Debit	Credit	Debit	Credit	Debit	Credit

18-2 APPLICATION PROBLEM, p. 518

Preparing a work sheet with departmental margins [1, 2]

The work sheet prepared in this problem is needed to complete Application Problems 18-3 and 18-4.

AllSports
Work
For Month Ended

	ACCOUNT TITLE	TRIAL BALANCE DEBIT	TRIAL BALANCE CREDIT	ADJUSTMENTS DEBIT	ADJUSTMENTS CREDIT	
1	Cash	38 2 1 3 30				1
2	Accounts Receivable	16 9 3 5 70				2
3	Allowance for Uncollectible Accounts		3 3 90			3
4	Merchandise Inventory—Clothing	32 3 6 0 80				4
5	Merchandise Inventory—Equip.	48 9 2 1 20				5
6	Supplies	1 6 4 9 00				6
7	Prepaid Insurance	6 2 4 30				7
8	Delivery Equipment—Equip.	11 5 3 1 80				8
9	Accum. Depr.—Deliver Equipment, Equip.		3 5 5 7 00			9
10	Office Equipment	1 4 2 6 00				10
11	Accum. Depr.—Office Equipment		1 8 4 90			11
12	Store Equipment—Clothing	1 5 8 0 20				12
13	Accum. Depr.—Store Equip., Clothing		5 2 5 40			13
14	Store Equipment—Equip.	7 6 0 2 80				14
15	Accum. Depr.—Store Equipment, Equip.		2 6 1 2 30			15
16	Accounts Payable		20 8 2 3 50			16
17	Employee Income Tax Payable		1 1 1 0 90			17
18	Federal Income Tax Payable					18
19	Social Security Tax Payable		1 6 0 3 14			19
20	Medicare Tax Payable		3 6 9 96			20
21	Salaries Payable					21
22	Sales Tax Payable		3 4 7 2 50			22
23	Unemployment Tax Payable—Federal		4 9 00			23
24	Unemployment Tax Payable—State		3 3 0 75			24
25	Dividends Payable					25
26	Capital Stock		85 0 0 0 00			26
27	Retained Earnings		47 9 0 4 85			27
28	Dividends	5 0 0 0 00				28
29	Income Summary—Clothing					29
30	Income Summary—Equip.					30
31	Income Summary—General					31
32	Sales—Clothing		27 2 5 3 40			32
33	Sales Discount—Clothing	1 0 1 52				33
34	Sales Returns and Allowances—Clothing	4 2 08				34
35	Sales—Equip.		30 9 5 2 50			35
36	Sales Discount—Equip.	8 6 92				36
37	Sales Returns and Allowances—Equip.	9 4 18				37
38	Purchases—Clothing	16 2 1 8 20				38
39	Purchases Discount—Clothing		5 8 30			39

250 • Working Papers

18-2 APPLICATION PROBLEM (continued)

[1, 2]

Center
Sheet
July 31, 20--

	DEPARTMENTAL MARGIN STATEMENTS				INCOME STATEMENT		BALANCE SHEET	
	CLOTHING		EQUIPMENT		DEBIT	CREDIT	DEBIT	CREDIT
	DEBIT	CREDIT	DEBIT	CREDIT				

18-2 APPLICATION PROBLEM (continued)

[1, 2]

AllSports
Work Sheet
For Month Ended

	ACCOUNT TITLE	TRIAL BALANCE		ADJUSTMENTS	
		DEBIT	CREDIT	DEBIT	CREDIT
40	Purchases Returns and Allowances—Clothing		1 4 60		
41	Purchases—Equip.	19 4 8 0 50			
42	Purchases Discount—Equip.		5 5 38		
43	Purchases Returns and Allowances—Equip.		3 6 92		
44	Advertising Expense—Clothing	3 1 0 80			
45	Depreciation Expense—Store Equip., Clothing				
46	Insurance Expense—Clothing				
47	Payroll Taxes Expense—Clothing	3 9 5 60			
48	Salary Expense—Clothing	3 5 6 2 30			
49	Supplies Expense—Clothing				
50	Advertising Expense—Equip.	5 3 8 20			
51	Delivery Expense—Equip.	1 3 0 4 90			
52	Depreciation Expense—Del. Equip., Equip.				
53	Depreciation Expense—Store Equip., Equip.				
54	Insurance Expense—Equip.				
55	Payroll Taxes Expense—Equip.	4 3 5 30			
56	Salary Expense—Equip.	3 9 2 6 10			
57	Supplies Expense—Equip.				
58	Uncollectible Accounts Expense—Equip.				
59	Credit Card Fee Expense	5 8 6 30			
60	Depreciation Expense—Office Equipment				
61	Insurance Expense—Administrative				
62	Miscellaneous Expense	1 2 4 5 20			
63	Payroll Taxes Expense—Administrative	5 3 7 10			
64	Rent Expense	4 5 6 0 00			
65	Salary Expense—Administrative	4 8 4 5 60			
66	Supplies Expense—Administrative				
67	Utilities Expense	1 8 3 3 30			
73		225 9 4 9 20	225 9 4 9 20		

252 • Working Papers

18-3 APPLICATION PROBLEM, p. 519

Preparing departmental margin statements

The work sheet prepared in Application Problem 18-2 is needed to complete this problem. The statements prepared in this problem are needed to complete Application Problem 18-4.

AllSports Center
Departmental Margin Statement—Clothing
For Month Ended July 31, 20--

				% OF NET SALES
Operating Revenue:				
Sales				
Less: Sales Discount				
Sales Returns & Allow.				
Net Sales				
Cost of Merchandise Sold				
Mdse. Inv., July 1, 20--				
Purchases				
Less: Purchases Discount				
Purchases Returns & Allow.				
Net Purchases				
Total Cost of Mdse. Avail. for Sale				
Less Mdse. Inv., July 31, 20--				
Cost of Merchandise Sold				
Gross Profit on Operations				
Direct Expenses:				
Advertising Expense				
Depr. Exp.—Store Equipment				
Insurance Expense				
Payroll Taxes Expense				
Salary Expense				
Supplies Expense				
Total Direct Expenses				
Departmental Margin				

18-3 APPLICATION PROBLEM (concluded)

The work sheet prepared in Application Problem 18-2 is needed to complete this problem. The statements prepared in this problem are needed to complete Application Problem 18-4.

AllSports Center
Departmental Margin Statement—Equipment
For Month Ended July 31, 20--

						% OF NET SALES
Operating Revenue:						
Sales						
Less: Sales Discount						
Sales Returns & Allow.						
Net Sales						
Cost of Merchandise Sold						
Mdse. Inv., July 1, 20--						
Purchases						
Less: Purchases Discount						
Purchases Returns & Allow.						
Net Purchases						
Total Cost of Mdse. Avail. for Sale						
Less Mdse. Inv., July 31, 20--						
Cost of Merchandise Sold						
Gross Profit on Operations						
Direct Expenses:						
Advertising Expense						
Delivery Expense						
Depr. Exp.—Delivery Equipment						
Depr. Exp.—Store Equipment						
Insurance Expense						
Payroll Taxes Expense						
Salary Expense						
Supplies Expense						
Uncollectible Accounts Expense						
Total Direct Expenses						
Departmental Margin						

18-4 APPLICATION PROBLEM, p. 519

Preparing an income statement with departmental margins

The work sheet prepared in Application Problem 18-2 and statements prepared in Application Problem 18-3 are needed to complete Application Problem 18-4.

AllSports Center
Income Statement
For Month Ended July 31, 20--

	DEPARTMENTAL		COMPANY	
	CLOTHING	EQUIPMENT	AMOUNTS	% OF NET SALES
Net Sales				
Cost of Merchandise Sold				
Gross Profit on Operations				
Direct Expenses				
Departmental Margin				
Indirect Expenses:				
Credit Card Fee Expense				
Depr. Exp.—Office Equip.				
Insurance Expense—Admin.				
Miscellaneous Expense				
Payroll Taxes Expense—Admin.				
Rent Expense				
Salary Expense—Admin.				
Supplies Expense—Admin.				
Utilities Expense				
Total Indirect Expenses				
Net Income before Fed. Inc. Tax				
Less Federal Income Tax Expense				
Net Income after Fed. Inc. Tax				

18-4 APPLICATION PROBLEM

Extra form

| | DEPARTMENTAL || COMPANY || % OF NET SALES |
	CLOTHING	EQUIPMENT	AMOUNTS		

18-5 MASTERY PROBLEM (continued)

[1, 2]

Begin this problem on pages 258 and 259. Use this page with page 260.

DeCor, Inc.
(continued)
December 31, 20--

	DEPARTMENTAL MARGIN STATEMENTS				INCOME STATEMENT		BALANCE SHEET	
	FURNITURE		ACCESSORIES					
	DEBIT	CREDIT	DEBIT	CREDIT	DEBIT	CREDIT	DEBIT	CREDIT

18-5 MASTERY PROBLEM, p. 519

Begin Mastery Problem 18-5 on this page.

Completing end-of-fiscal period work for a merchandising business using departmental margins [1, 2]

Furniture
Work
For Year Ended

	ACCOUNT TITLE	TRIAL BALANCE		ADJUSTMENTS	
		DEBIT	CREDIT	DEBIT	CREDIT
1	Cash	52 1 2 6 50			
2	Accounts Receivable	2 7 6 8 40			
3	Allowance for Uncollectible Accounts		5 4 20		
4	Merchandise Inventory—Furniture	103 8 3 6 30			
5	Merchandise Inventory—Accessories	35 3 9 4 70			
6	Supplies	3 3 7 8 30			
7	Prepaid Insurance	6 7 1 5 20			
8	Office Equipment	5 4 5 7 00			
9	Accum. Depr.—Office Equipment		8 6 0 60		
10	Store Equipment—Furniture	19 0 4 0 00			
11	Accum. Depr.—Store Equip., Furniture		5 8 3 2 10		
12	Store Equipment—Accessories	8 9 1 0 00			
13	Accum. Depr.—Store Equip., Accessories		2 5 6 8 30		
14	Accounts Payable		26 1 3 1 60		
15	Employee Income Tax Payable		9 3 6 90		
16	Federal Income Tax Payable				
17	Social Security Tax Payable		1 0 7 3 15		
18	Medicare Tax Payable		2 47 65		
19	Salaries Payable				
20	Sales Tax Payable		2 1 5 6 10		
21	Unemployment Tax Payable—Federal		6 80		
22	Unemployment Tax Payable—State		4 5 90		
23	Dividends Payable				
24	Capital Stock		110 0 0 0 00		
25	Retained Earnings		85 9 7 4 80		
26	Dividends	5 0 0 0 00			
27	Income Summary—Furniture				
28	Income Summary—Accessories				
29	Income Summary—General				
30	Sales—Furniture		357 5 7 3 50		
31	Sales Discount—Furniture	8 9 3 20			
32	Sales Returns and Allowances—Furniture	8 4 1 30			
33	Sales—Accessories		112 1 9 7 30		
34	Sales Discount—Accessories	3 7 2 60			
35	Sales Returns and Allowances—Accessories	1 5 9 80			
36	Purchases—Furniture	233 5 2 1 60			
37	Purchases Discount—Furniture		1 5 5 8 40		
38	Purchases Returns and Allowances—Furniture		1 0 3 8 90		
39	Purchases—Accessories	81 6 7 9 30			

258 • Working Papers

18-5 MASTERY PROBLEM (continued)

[1, 2]

DeCor, Inc.
Sheet
December 31, 20--

	DEPARTMENTAL MARGIN STATEMENTS				INCOME STATEMENT		BALANCE SHEET	
	FURNITURE		ACCESSORIES					
	DEBIT	CREDIT	DEBIT	CREDIT	DEBIT	CREDIT	DEBIT	CREDIT

18-5 MASTERY PROBLEM (continued)

[1, 2]

Use this page with page 257.

Furniture
Work Sheet
For Year Ended

	ACCOUNT TITLE	TRIAL BALANCE DEBIT	TRIAL BALANCE CREDIT	ADJUSTMENTS DEBIT	ADJUSTMENTS CREDIT	
40	Purchases Discount—Accessories		277 40			40
41	Purchases Returns and Allow.—Accessories		118 90			41
42	Advertising Expense—Furniture	2838 40				42
43	Depreciation Expense—Store Equip., Furniture					43
44	Insurance Expense—Furniture					44
45	Payroll Taxes Expense—Furniture	5568 00				45
46	Salary Expense—Furniture	56240 00				46
47	Supplies Expense—Furniture					47
48	Uncollectible Accounts Expense—Furniture					48
49	Advertising Expense—Accessories	715 60				49
50	Depr. Expense—Store Equip., Accessories					50
51	Insurance Expense—Accessories					51
52	Payroll Taxes Expense—Accessories	2365 00				52
53	Salary Expense—Accessories	23890 00				53
54	Supplies Expense—Accessories					54
55	Credit Card Fee Expense	6255 30				55
56	Depreciation Expense—Office Equipment					56
57	Insurance Expense—Administrative					57
58	Miscellaneous Expense	8076 80				58
59	Payroll Taxes Expense—Administrative	1873 00				59
60	Rent Expense	15000 00				60
61	Salary Expense—Administrative	18920 00				61
62	Supplies Expense—Administrative					62
63	Utilities Expense	4016 20				63
64						64
65						65
66						66
67						67
68	Federal Income Tax Expense	2800 00				68
69		708652 50	708652 50			69

18-5 MASTERY PROBLEM (continued)

[3]

Furniture DeCor, Inc.
Departmental Margin Statement—Furniture
For Year Ended December 31, 20--

					% OF NET SALES
Operating Revenue:					
Sales					
Less: Sales Discount					
Sales Returns & Allow.					
Net Sales					
Cost of Merchandise Sold					
Mdse. Inv., Jan. 1, 20--					
Purchases					
Less: Purchases Discount					
Purchases Returns & Allow.					
Net Purchases					
Total Cost of Mdse. Avail. for Sale					
Less Mdse. Inv., Dec. 31, 20--					
Cost of Merchandise Sold					
Gross Profit on Operations					
Direct Expenses:					
Advertising Expense					
Depr. Exp.—Store Equipment					
Insurance Expense					
Payroll Taxes Expense					
Salary Expense					
Supplies Expense					
Uncollectible Accounts Expense					
Total Direct Expenses					
Departmental Margin					

18-5 MASTERY PROBLEM (continued)

[3]

Furniture DeCor, Inc.
Departmental Margin Statement—Accessories
For Year Ended December 31, 20--

				% OF NET SALES
Operating Revenue:				
Sales				
Less: Sales Discount				
Sales Returns & Allow.				
Net Sales				
Cost of Merchandise Sold				
Mdse. Inv., Jan. 1, 20--				
Purchases				
Less: Purchases Discount				
Purchases Returns & Allow.				
Net Purchases				
Total Cost of Mdse. Avail. for Sale				
Less Mdse. Inv., Dec. 31, 20--				
Cost of Merchandise Sold				
Gross Profit on Operations				
Direct Expenses:				
Advertising Expense				
Depr. Exp.—Store Equipment				
Insurance Expense				
Payroll Taxes Expense				
Salary Expense				
Supplies Expense				
Total Direct Expenses				
Departmental Margin				

18-5 MASTERY PROBLEM (continued)

[4]

Furniture DeCor, Inc.
Income Statement
For Year Ended December 31, 20--

	DEPARTMENTAL		COMPANY	
	FURNITURE	ACCESSORIES	AMOUNTS	% OF NET SALES
Net Sales				
Cost of Merchandise Sold				
Gross Profit on Operations				
Direct Expenses				
Departmental Margin				
Indirect Expenses:				
Credit Card Fee Expense				
Depr. Exp.—Office Equip.				
Insurance Expense—Admin.				
Miscellaneous Expense				
Payroll Taxes Expense—Admin.				
Rent Expense				
Salary Expense—Admin.				
Supplies Expense—Admin.				
Utilities Expense				
Total Indirect Expenses				
Net Income before Fed. Inc. Tax				
Less Federal Income Tax Expense				
Net Income after Fed. Inc. Tax				

18-5 MASTERY PROBLEM

Extra form

	DEPARTMENTAL		COMPANY		% OF NET SALES
	FURNITURE	ACCESSORIES	AMOUNTS		

18-6 CHALLENGE PROBLEM, p. 520

Analyzing a departmental margin statement [1]

Ultra Video, Inc.
Departmental Margin Statement—Camcorder
For Years Ended December 31, 20X7 and 20X6

	20X7 AMOUNTS		% OF NET SALES	20X6 AMOUNTS		% OF NET SALES
Operating Revenue:						
Sales		432 611 90			384 805 90	
Less Sales Returns and Allowances		1 718 80			1 533 10	
Net Sales		430 893 10			383 272 80	
Cost of Merchandise Sold:						
Merchandise Inventory, January 1, 20--	46 166 80			41 010 20		
Purchases	237 204 90			203 901 10		
Total Cost of Mdse. Available for Sale	283 371 70			244 911 30		
Less Mdse. Inventory, Dec. 31, 20--	42 048 50			45 609 50		
Cost of Merchandise Sold		241 323 20			199 301 80	
Gross Profit on Operations		189 569 90			183 971 00	
Direct Expenses:						
Advertising Expense	4 320 90			3 449 50		
Delivery Expense	10 237 20			8 432 00		
Depr. Expense—Delivery Equipment	5 960 10			4 599 30		
Depr. Expense—Store Equipment	3 901 60			3 432 60		
Insurance Expense	3 398 20			3 023 70		
Payroll Taxes Expense	5 265 30			4 360 40		
Salary Expense	50 243 70			42 960 00		
Supplies Expense	3 922 80			2 981 90		
Uncollectible Accounts Expense	4 899 60			3 827 90		
Total Direct Expenses		92 149 40			77 067 30	
Departmental Margin		97 420 50			106 903 70	

18-6 CHALLENGE PROBLEM (concluded)

[2]

Change in % of Net Sales	
a. Cost of Merchandise Sold	
b. Gross Profit	
c. Total Direct Departmental Expenses	
d. Departmental Margin	

[3]

a. Is the departmental margin for the camcorder department at a satisfactory percentage of sales? Explain why it is or is not satisfactory.

b. Is the trend of the cost of merchandise sold percentage favorable or unfavorable? Explain why it is or is not favorable. Can you suggest some possible reasons for the change in cost of merchandise sold from 20X6 to 20X7?

c. Is the trend of the total direct departmental expenses percentage favorable or unfavorable? Explain why the trend is or is not favorable.

19-1 WORK TOGETHER, p. 530

Classifying manufacturing costs; specifying the ledger used for initial recording [4, 5]

	Direct Materials	Direct Labor	Factory Overhead	Materials Ledger	Cost Ledger (Sheet)	Finished Goods Ledger
a. Wages earned by production employees		✓			✓	
b. Aluminum used to produce gutters	✓			✓		
c. Factory rent			✓			
d. Cleaning solvent used to clean production machinery			✓	✓		
e. Production employees' fringe benefits			✓			

19-1 ON YOUR OWN, p. 530

Classifying manufacturing costs; specifying the ledger used for initial recording [6, 7]

	Direct Materials	Direct Labor	Factory Overhead	Materials Ledger	Cost Ledger (Sheet)	Finished Goods Ledger
a. Rivets used in production of gutters			✓	✓		
b. Wages earned by maintenance employees			✓			
c. Factory property taxes			✓			
d. Fringe benefits of factory supervisor			✓			
e. Wages earned by gutter inspector			✓			

Name _____ Date _____ Class _____

19-1 WORK TOGETHER / ON YOUR OWN

Extra form

COST SHEET

Job No. _____ Date _____
Item _____ Date wanted _____
No. of items _____ Date completed _____
Ordered for _____

DIRECT MATERIALS		DIRECT LABOR				SUMMARY	
REQ. NO.	AMOUNT	DATE	AMOUNT	DATE	AMOUNT	ITEM	AMOUNT

19-2 WORK TOGETHER, p. 538

Determining total cost and unit cost for a job and determining total cost for a finished item [6]

COST SHEET

Job No. __657__
Item __K-39 Sofa__
No. of items __70__
Ordered for __Stock__

Date __July 18, 20--__
Date wanted __July 25, 20--__
Date completed __July 25, 20--__

DIRECT MATERIALS		DIRECT LABOR				SUMMARY	
REQ. NO.	AMOUNT	DATE	AMOUNT	DATE	AMOUNT	ITEM	AMOUNT
147	$1,105.58	July 18	$1,378.65				
149	1,264.79	20	1,195.03				
152	963.02	21	979.84				
154	586.98	22	1,036.01				
155	1,435.76	24	1,378.41				
159	1,088.52						

Space for calculations:

[7]

FINISHED GOODS LEDGER CARD

Description __Sofa__
Minimum __80__
Stock No. __K-39__
Location __S-9__

MANUFACTURED/RECEIVED					SHIPPED/ISSUED					BALANCE			
DATE	JOB NO.	QUAN-TITY	UNIT COST	TOTAL COST	DATE	SALES INVOICE NO.	QUAN-TITY	UNIT COST	TOTAL COST	DATE	QUAN-TITY	UNIT COST	TOTAL COST
										July 23	150	$285.00	$42,750.00

19-2 WORK TOGETHER

Extra form

COST SHEET

Job No. _____   Date _____

Item _____   Date wanted _____

No. of items _____   Date completed _____

Ordered for _____

DIRECT MATERIALS		DIRECT LABOR				SUMMARY	
REQ. NO.	AMOUNT	DATE	AMOUNT	DATE	AMOUNT	ITEM	AMOUNT

19-2 ON YOUR OWN, p. 538

Determining total cost and unit cost for a job and determining total cost for a finished item [8]

COST SHEET

Job No. __711__   Date __August 3, 20--__

Item __S-68 Chair__   Date wanted __August 10, 20--__

No. of items __80__   Date completed __August 10, 20--__

Ordered for __Stock__

DIRECT MATERIALS		DIRECT LABOR				SUMMARY	
REQ. NO.	AMOUNT	DATE	AMOUNT	DATE	AMOUNT	ITEM	AMOUNT
211	$ 2,106.44	Aug. 3	$1,286.90				
212	1,865.22	5	843.62				
215	1,954.57	6	1,140.74				
217	2,284.05	8	971.20				
218	1,372.91	9	1,362.75				
221	1,883.54						

Space for calculations:

[9]

FINISHED GOODS LEDGER CARD

Description __Chair__   Stock No. __S-68__

Minimum __100__   Location __L-7__

MANUFACTURED/RECEIVED					SHIPPED/ISSUED					BALANCE			
DATE	JOB NO.	QUAN-TITY	UNIT COST	TOTAL COST	DATE	SALES INVOICE NO.	QUAN-TITY	UNIT COST	TOTAL COST	DATE	QUAN-TITY	UNIT COST	TOTAL COST
										Aug. 9	185	$374.00	$69,190.00

Name _____ Date _____ Class _____

19-2 ON YOUR OWN

Extra form

COST SHEET

Job No. _____ Date _____

Item _____ Date wanted _____

No. of items _____ Date completed _____

Ordered for _____

DIRECT MATERIALS		DIRECT LABOR				SUMMARY	
REQ. NO.	AMOUNT	DATE	AMOUNT	DATE	AMOUNT	ITEM	AMOUNT

19-1 APPLICATION PROBLEM, p. 540

Classifying manufacturing costs and determining which ledger to use for initial recording [1, 2]

	Direct Materials	Direct Labor	Factory Overhead	None	Materials Ledger	Cost Ledger (Sheet)	Finished Goods Ledger
a. Wages of factory supervisor							
b. Fringe benefits of factory supervisor							
c. Rent of company headquarters							
d. Rubber to produce tires							
e. Factory property taxes							
f. Wages of production employees							
g. Glue used in tire production							
h. Cleaning solvent used to clean factory equipment							
i. Inspector's wages							
j. Wages of marketing manager							

19-1 APPLICATION PROBLEM

Extra form

COST SHEET

Job No. _____ Date _____

Item _____ Date wanted _____

No. of items _____ Date completed _____

Ordered for _____

DIRECT MATERIALS		DIRECT LABOR				SUMMARY	
REQ. NO.	AMOUNT	DATE	AMOUNT	DATE	AMOUNT	ITEM	AMOUNT

Name _____ Date _____ Class _____

19-2 APPLICATION PROBLEM, p. 540

Classifying manufacturing costs and determining which ledger to use [1–3]
for initial recording

					MATERIALS LEDGER CARD									

Article _____ Acct. No. _____

Reorder _____ Minimum _____ Location _____

ORDERED			RECEIVED					ISSUED				BALANCE		
DATE	PUR- CHASE ORDER NO.	QUAN- TITY	DATE	PUR- CHASE ORDER NO.	QUAN- TITY	UNIT PRICE	VALUE	DATE	REQUI- SITION NO.	QUAN- TITY	UNIT PRICE	VALUE	DATE	QUAN- TITY	UNIT PRICE	VALUE

19-3 APPLICATION PROBLEM, p. 541

Calculating factory overhead applied rate

Chapter 19 Cost Accounting for a Manufacturing Business • 275

Name _____ Date _____ Class _____

19-2 APPLICATION PROBLEM

Extra form

							MATERIALS LEDGER CARD								

Article _____ Acct. No. _____

Reorder _____ Minimum _____ Location _____

ORDERED			RECEIVED					ISSUED					BALANCE		
DATE	PUR-CHASE ORDER NO.	QUAN-TITY	DATE	PUR-CHASE ORDER NO.	QUAN-TITY	UNIT PRICE	VALUE	DATE	REQUI-SITION NO.	QUAN-TITY	UNIT PRICE	VALUE	DATE	QUAN-TITY	UNIT PRICE	VALUE

276 • Working Papers

Name _____ Date _____ Class _____

19-4 APPLICATION PROBLEM, p. 541

Preparing a cost sheet [1, 2]

COST SHEET

Job No. _____   Date _____
Item _____   Date wanted _____
No. of items _____ Date completed _____
Ordered for _____

DIRECT MATERIALS		DIRECT LABOR				SUMMARY	
REQ. NO.	AMOUNT	DATE	AMOUNT	DATE	AMOUNT	ITEM	AMOUNT

19-4 APPLICATION PROBLEM

Extra form

COST SHEET

Job No. _____ Date _____

Item _____ Date wanted _____

No. of items _____ Date completed _____

Ordered for _____

DIRECT MATERIALS		DIRECT LABOR				SUMMARY	
REQ. NO.	AMOUNT	DATE	AMOUNT	DATE	AMOUNT	ITEM	AMOUNT

19-5 APPLICATION PROBLEM, p. 541

Recording entries in a finished goods ledger [1–3]

FINISHED GOODS LEDGER CARD

Description _____   Stock No. _____

Minimum _____   Location _____

MANUFACTURED/RECEIVED					SHIPPED/ISSUED					BALANCE			
DATE	JOB NO.	QUAN-TITY	UNIT COST	TOTAL COST	DATE	SALES INVOICE NO.	QUAN-TITY	UNIT COST	TOTAL COST	DATE	QUAN-TITY	UNIT COST	TOTAL COST

19-5 APPLICATION PROBLEM

Extra form

FINISHED GOODS LEDGER CARD

Description _____ Stock No. _____

Minimum _____ Location _____

MANUFACTURED/RECEIVED					SHIPPED/ISSUED					BALANCE			
DATE	JOB NO.	QUAN-TITY	UNIT COST	TOTAL COST	DATE	SALES INVOICE NO.	QUAN-TITY	UNIT COST	TOTAL COST	DATE	QUAN-TITY	UNIT COST	TOTAL COST

19-6 MASTERY PROBLEM, p. 542

Preparing cost records

[1]

[2, 3]

COST SHEET

Job No. _____ Date _____

Item _____ Date wanted _____

No. of items _____ Date completed _____

Ordered for _____

DIRECT MATERIALS		DIRECT LABOR				SUMMARY	
REQ. NO.	AMOUNT	DATE	AMOUNT	DATE	AMOUNT	ITEM	AMOUNT

19-6 MASTERY PROBLEM (concluded)

[4–6]

FINISHED GOODS LEDGER CARD

Description _____ Stock No. _____

Minimum _____ Location _____

MANUFACTURED/RECEIVED					SHIPPED/ISSUED					BALANCE			
DATE	JOB NO.	QUAN-TITY	UNIT COST	TOTAL COST	DATE	SALES INVOICE NO.	QUAN-TITY	UNIT COST	TOTAL COST	DATE	QUAN-TITY	UNIT COST	TOTAL COST

Extra form

FINISHED GOODS LEDGER CARD

Description _____ Stock No. _____

Minimum _____ Location _____

MANUFACTURED/RECEIVED					SHIPPED/ISSUED					BALANCE			
DATE	JOB NO.	QUAN-TITY	UNIT COST	TOTAL COST	DATE	SALES INVOICE NO.	QUAN-TITY	UNIT COST	TOTAL COST	DATE	QUAN-TITY	UNIT COST	TOTAL COST

Name _____ Date _____ Class _____

19-7 CHALLENGE PROBLEM, p. 543

Preparing cost records [1]

a. Direct materials cost

b. Direct labor cost

c. Direct labor hours

[2, 3]

COST SHEET						
Job No. _____				Date _____			
Item _____				Date wanted _____			
No. of items _____				Date completed _____			
Ordered for _____						
DIRECT MATERIALS		DIRECT LABOR				SUMMARY	
REQ. NO.	AMOUNT	DATE	AMOUNT	DATE	AMOUNT	ITEM	AMOUNT

Chapter 19 Cost Accounting for a Manufacturing Business • **283**

19-7 CHALLENGE PROBLEM (concluded)

[4–6]

FINISHED GOODS LEDGER CARD

Description _____ Stock No. _____

Minimum _____ Location _____

MANUFACTURED/RECEIVED					SHIPPED/ISSUED					BALANCE			
DATE	JOB NO.	QUAN-TITY	UNIT COST	TOTAL COST	DATE	SALES INVOICE NO.	QUAN-TITY	UNIT COST	TOTAL COST	DATE	QUAN-TITY	UNIT COST	TOTAL COST

20-1 WORK TOGETHER, p. 555

Preparing manufacturing journal entries [4]

MATERIALS PURCHASES JOURNAL — PAGE 12

	DATE	ACCOUNT CREDITED	PURCH. NO.	POST. REF.	MATERIALS DR. ACCTS. PAY. CR.	
1						1
2						2

GENERAL JOURNAL — PAGE 18

	DATE	ACCOUNT TITLE	DOC. NO.	POST. REF.	DEBIT	CREDIT	
1							1
2							2
3							3
4							4
5							5
6							6
7							7
8							8
9							9
10							10
11							11
12							12
13							13
14							14
15							15
16							16
17							17
18							18
19							19
20							20
21							21
22							22
23							23
24							24
25							25
26							26

20-1 WORK TOGETHER (concluded)

[4]

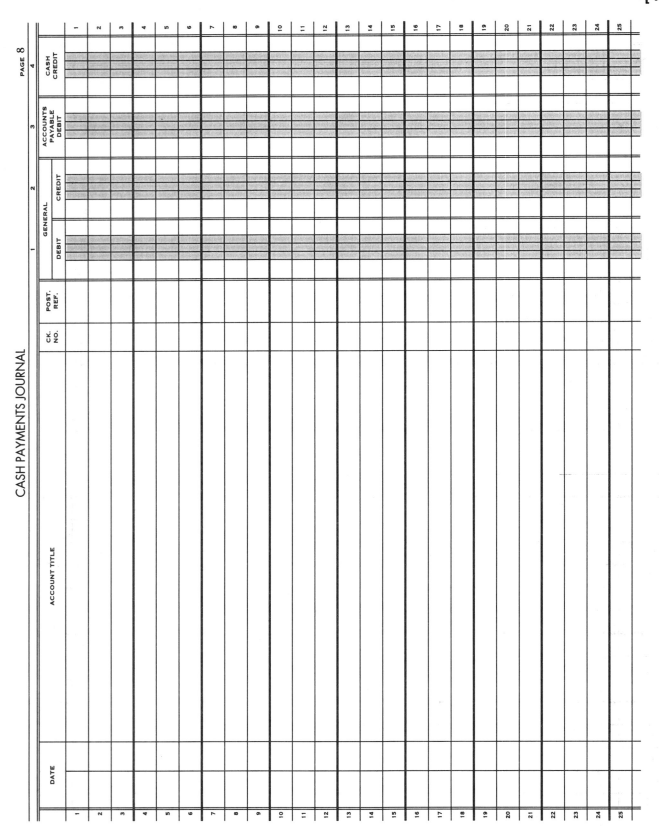

20-1 ON YOUR OWN, p. 556

Preparing manufacturing journal entries [5]

MATERIALS PURCHASES JOURNAL
PAGE 18

	DATE	ACCOUNT CREDITED	PURCH. NO.	POST. REF.	MATERIALS DR. ACCTS. PAY. CR.	
1						1
2						2

GENERAL JOURNAL
PAGE 23

	DATE	ACCOUNT TITLE	DOC. NO.	POST. REF.	DEBIT	CREDIT	
1							1
2							2
3							3
4							4
5							5
6							6
7							7
8							8
9							9
10							10
11							11
12							12
13							13
14							14
15							15
16							16
17							17
18							18
19							19
20							20
21							21
22							22
23							23
24							24
25							25
26							26

20-1 ON YOUR OWN (concluded)

[5]

CASH PAYMENTS JOURNAL PAGE 22

DATE	ACCOUNT TITLE	CK. NO.	POST. REF.	GENERAL DEBIT	GENERAL CREDIT	ACCOUNTS PAYABLE DEBIT	CASH CREDIT

20-2 WORK TOGETHER, p. 563

Preparing statement of cost of goods manufactured, income statement, and balance sheet [4]

Work sheet begins on page 290.

Bedthings, Inc.
Statement of Cost of Goods Manufactured
For Month Ended April 30, 20--

Extra form

20-2 WORK TOGETHER (continued)

Bedthings, Inc.
Work Sheet
For Month Ended March 31, 20--

#	ACCOUNT TITLE	TRIAL BALANCE DEBIT	TRIAL BALANCE CREDIT	ADJUSTMENTS DEBIT	ADJUSTMENTS CREDIT	INCOME STATEMENT DEBIT	INCOME STATEMENT CREDIT	BALANCE SHEET DEBIT	BALANCE SHEET CREDIT
1	Cash	2570000						2570000	
2	Accounts Receivable	1618750 0						16187500	
3	Allowance for Uncollectible Accounts		304000		(a) 120000				424000
4	Materials	9222000						9222000	
5	Work in Process	7836000						7836000	
6	Finished Goods	11852000						11852000	
7	Supplies—Factory	262000			(b) 82000			262000	
8	Supplies—Sales	240000						158000	
9	Factory Equipment	17550000						17550000	
10	Accum. Depr.—Factory Equipment		3218000						3218000
11	Office Equipment	1990000						1990000	
12	Accum. Depr.—Office Equipment		826000		(c) 60000				886000
13	Building	28800000						28800000	
14	Accum. Depr.—Building		1307100 0						1307100 0
15	Land	12564000						12564000	
16	Accounts Payable		14785000						14785000
17	Employee Income Tax Payable		843000						843000
18	Federal Income Tax Payable		1207000		(d) 1207000				1207000
19	Social Security Tax Payable		834400						834400
20	Medicare Tax Payable		192600						192600
21	Mortgage Payable		8500000						8500000
22	Capital Stock		43000000						43000000
23	Retained Earnings		19603000						19603000
24	Income Summary		1116000				1116000		
25	Sales		32870000				32870000		
26	Cost of Goods Sold	23949000				23949000			
27	Factory Overhead								
28	Depr. Expense—Factory Equipment								
29	Depr. Expense—Building								
30	Utilities Expense—Factory								

20-2 WORK TOGETHER (continued)

	ACCOUNT TITLE	TRIAL BALANCE DEBIT	TRIAL BALANCE CREDIT	ADJUSTMENTS DEBIT	ADJUSTMENTS CREDIT	INCOME STATEMENT DEBIT	INCOME STATEMENT CREDIT	BALANCE SHEET DEBIT	BALANCE SHEET CREDIT	
31	Insurance Expense—Factory									31
32	Payroll Taxes Expense—Factory									32
33	Property Tax Expense—Factory									33
34	Supplies Expense—Factory									34
35	Advertising Expense	5 3 3 0 00				5 3 3 0 00				35
36	Salary Expense—Sales	22 6 5 0 00				22 6 5 0 00				36
37	Supplies Expense—Sales			(b) 8 2 0 00		8 2 0 00				37
38	Depr. Expense—Office Equipment			(c) 6 0 0 00		6 0 0 00				38
39	Payroll Taxes Expense—Admin.	5 3 8 0 00				5 3 8 0 00				39
40	Property Tax Expense—Admin.	2 5 5 00				2 5 5 00				40
41	Salary Expense—Admin.	17 0 0 0 00				17 0 0 0 00				41
42	Uncollectible Accounts Expense			(a) 1 2 0 0 00		1 2 0 0 00				42
43	Utilities Expense—Admin.	7 9 0 00				7 9 0 00				43
44	Federal Income Tax Expense			(d) 12 0 7 0 00		12 0 7 0 00				44
45		1381 6 3 0 00	1381 6 3 0 00	14 6 9 0 00	14 6 9 0 00	305 5 8 5 00	329 8 6 0 00	1089 9 1 5 00	1065 6 4 0 00	45
46	Net Income after Federal Income Tax					24 2 7 5 00			24 2 7 5 00	46
47						329 8 6 0 00	329 8 6 0 00	1089 9 1 5 00	1089 9 1 5 00	47
48										48

20-2 WORK TOGETHER (continued)

[5]

Bedthings, Inc.
Income Statement
For Month Ended March 31, 20--

20-2 WORK TOGETHER (continued)

[6]

Bedthings, Inc.
Balance Sheet
March 31, 20--

20-2 WORK TOGETHER (concluded)

[6]

Bedthings, Inc.
Balance Sheet (continued)
March 31, 20--

20-2 ON YOUR OWN, p. 563

Preparing statement of cost of goods manufactured, income statement, and balance sheet [7]

Work sheet begins on page 296.

Bedthings, Inc.
Statement of Cost of Goods Manufactured
For Month Ended April 31, 20--

Extra form

20-2 ON YOUR OWN (continued)

Bedthings, Inc.
Work Sheet
For Month Ended April 30, 20--

#	ACCOUNT TITLE	TRIAL BALANCE DEBIT	TRIAL BALANCE CREDIT	ADJUSTMENTS DEBIT	ADJUSTMENTS CREDIT	INCOME STATEMENT DEBIT	INCOME STATEMENT CREDIT	BALANCE SHEET DEBIT	BALANCE SHEET CREDIT
1	Cash	3128000						3128000	
2	Accounts Receivable	1551900						1551900	
3	Allowance for Uncollectible Accounts		4240 00		(a) 40000				464000
4	Materials	1085600						1085600	
5	Work in Process	854600						854600	
6	Finished Goods	1205200						1205200	
7	Supplies—Factory	262000						262000	
8	Supplies—Sales	217000			(b) 78000			139000	
9	Factory Equipment	1755000						1755000	
10	Accum. Depr.—Factory Equipment		3218000						3218000
11	Office Equipment	199000						199000	
12	Accum. Depr.—Office Equipment		886000		(c) 60000				946000
13	Building	2880000						2880000	
14	Accum. Depr.—Building		1307100						1307100
15	Land	1354050						1354050	
16	Accounts Payable		1514400						1514400
17	Employee Income Tax Payable		113800						113800
18	Federal Income Tax Payable		1037000		(d) 1037000				1037000
19	Social Security Tax Payable		1205000						1205000
20	Medicare Tax Payable		278000						278000
21	Mortgage Payable		8500000						8500000
22	Capital Stock		4300000						4300000
23	Retained Earnings		2203050						2203050
24	Income Summary	59000				59000			
25	Sales		3623750				3623750		
26	Cost of Goods Sold	2663250				2663250			
27	Factory Overhead								
28	Depr. Expense—Factory Equipment								
29	Depr. Expense—Building								
30	Utilities Expense—Factory								

20-2 ON YOUR OWN (continued)

	ACCOUNT TITLE	TRIAL BALANCE		ADJUSTMENTS		INCOME STATEMENT		BALANCE SHEET	
		DEBIT	CREDIT	DEBIT	CREDIT	DEBIT	CREDIT	DEBIT	CREDIT
31	Insurance Expense—Factory								
32	Payroll Taxes Expense—Factory								
33	Property Tax Expense—Factory								
34	Supplies Expense—Factory								
35	Advertising Expense	6 0 5 0 00				6 0 5 0 00			
36	Salary Expense—Sales	27 9 4 0 00				27 9 4 0 00			
37	Supplies Expense—Sales			(b) 7 8 0 00		7 8 0 00			
38	Depr. Expense—Office Equipment			(c) 6 0 0 00		6 0 0 00			
39	Payroll Taxes Expense—Admin.	5 8 9 0 00				5 8 9 0 00			
40	Property Tax Expense—Admin.	2 5 5 00				2 5 5 00			
41	Salary Expense—Admin.	18 8 0 0 00				18 8 0 0 00			
42	Uncollectible Accounts Expense			(a) 4 0 0 00		4 0 0 00			
43	Utilities Expense—Admin.	8 6 5 00				8 6 5 00			
44	Federal Income Tax Expense			(d) 10 3 7 0 00		10 3 7 0 00			
45		1451 3 2 0 00	1451 3 2 0 00	12 1 5 0 00	12 1 5 0 00	338 8 6 5 00	362 3 7 5 00	1123 8 2 5 00	1100 3 1 5 00
46	Net Income after Federal Income Tax					23 5 1 0 00			23 5 1 0 00
47						362 3 7 5 00	362 3 7 5 00	1123 8 2 5 00	1123 8 2 5 00

20-2 ON YOUR OWN (continued)

[8]

Bedthings, Inc.
Income Statement
For Month Ended April 30, 20--

20-2 ON YOUR OWN (continued)

Bedthings, Inc.
Balance Sheet
April 30, 20--

20-2 ON YOUR OWN (concluded)

[9]

Bedthings, Inc.
Balance Sheet (continued)
April 30, 20--

20-1 APPLICATION PROBLEM, p. 565

Journalizing cost accounting transactions for a manufacturing company [1, 2]

MATERIALS PURCHASES JOURNAL

PAGE 4

DATE	ACCOUNT CREDITED	PURCH. NO.	POST. REF.	MATERIALS DR. ACCTS. PAY. CR.

20-1 APPLICATION PROBLEM (concluded)

[1, 3]

CASH PAYMENTS JOURNAL — PAGE 8

DATE	ACCOUNT TITLE	CK. NO.	POST. REF.	GENERAL DEBIT	GENERAL CREDIT	ACCOUNTS PAYABLE DEBIT	PURCHASES DISCOUNT CREDIT	CASH CREDIT

20-2 APPLICATION PROBLEM, p. 565

Journalizing and posting entries that summarize cost records at the end of a fiscal period [1–5]

The ledger and journals prepared in this problem are needed to complete Application Problem 20-3.

CASH PAYMENTS JOURNAL PAGE 6

DATE	ACCOUNT TITLE	CK. NO.	POST. REF.	GENERAL DEBIT	GENERAL CREDIT	ACCOUNTS PAYABLE DEBIT	PURCHASES DISCOUNT CREDIT	CASH CREDIT

Chapter 20 Accounting Transactions and Financial Reporting for a Manufacturing Business

20-2 APPLICATION PROBLEM (continued)

[2, 3]

GENERAL JOURNAL

PAGE 3

	DATE	ACCOUNT TITLE	DOC. NO.	POST. REF.	DEBIT	CREDIT	
1							1
2							2
3							3
4							4
5							5
6							6
7							7
8							8
9							9
10							10
11							11
12							12
13							13
14							14
15							15
16							16
17							17
18							18
19							19
20							20
21							21
22							22
23							23
24							24
25							25
26							26
27							27
28							28
29							29
30							30
31							31

20-2 APPLICATION PROBLEM (continued)

[1–5]

GENERAL LEDGER

ACCOUNT Materials   **ACCOUNT NO.** 1125

DATE		ITEM	POST. REF.	DEBIT	CREDIT	BALANCE DEBIT	BALANCE CREDIT
20-- Mar.	1	Balance	✓			138 419 00	
	31		MP3	51 524 00		189 943 00	

ACCOUNT Work in Process   **ACCOUNT NO.** 1130

DATE		ITEM	POST. REF.	DEBIT	CREDIT	BALANCE DEBIT	BALANCE CREDIT
20-- Mar.	1	Balance	✓			17 781 00	

ACCOUNT Finished Goods   **ACCOUNT NO.** 1135

DATE		ITEM	POST. REF.	DEBIT	CREDIT	BALANCE DEBIT	BALANCE CREDIT
20-- Mar.	1	Balance	✓			156 196 00	

ACCOUNT Employee Income Tax Payable   **ACCOUNT NO.** 2110

DATE	ITEM	POST. REF.	DEBIT	CREDIT	BALANCE DEBIT	BALANCE CREDIT

20-2 APPLICATION PROBLEM (continued)

[1–5]

GENERAL LEDGER

ACCOUNT Social Security Tax Payable   ACCOUNT NO. 2120

DATE	ITEM	POST. REF.	DEBIT	CREDIT	BALANCE DEBIT	BALANCE CREDIT

ACCOUNT Medicare Tax Payable   ACCOUNT NO. 2130

DATE	ITEM	POST. REF.	DEBIT	CREDIT	BALANCE DEBIT	BALANCE CREDIT

ACCOUNT Income Summary   ACCOUNT NO. 3120

DATE	ITEM	POST. REF.	DEBIT	CREDIT	BALANCE DEBIT	BALANCE CREDIT

ACCOUNT Cost of Goods Sold   ACCOUNT NO. 5105

DATE	ITEM	POST. REF.	DEBIT	CREDIT	BALANCE DEBIT	BALANCE CREDIT

20-2 APPLICATION PROBLEM (continued)

[1–5]

GENERAL LEDGER

ACCOUNT Factory Overhead ACCOUNT NO. 5505

DATE	ITEM	POST. REF.	DEBIT	CREDIT	BALANCE DEBIT	BALANCE CREDIT

ACCOUNT Depreciation Expense—Factory Equipment ACCOUNT NO. 5510

DATE	ITEM	POST. REF.	DEBIT	CREDIT	BALANCE DEBIT	BALANCE CREDIT
20-- Mar. 31	Balance	✓			7 6 2 8 40	

ACCOUNT Depreciation Expense—Building ACCOUNT NO. 5515

DATE	ITEM	POST. REF.	DEBIT	CREDIT	BALANCE DEBIT	BALANCE CREDIT
20-- Mar. 31	Balance	✓			2 0 8 1 30	

ACCOUNT Heat, Light, and Power Expense ACCOUNT NO. 5520

DATE	ITEM	POST. REF.	DEBIT	CREDIT	BALANCE DEBIT	BALANCE CREDIT
20-- Mar. 31	Balance	✓			5 7 7 8 50	

20-2 APPLICATION PROBLEM (concluded)

[1–5]

GENERAL LEDGER

ACCOUNT Insurance Expense—Factory ACCOUNT NO. 5525

DATE	ITEM	POST. REF.	DEBIT	CREDIT	BALANCE DEBIT	BALANCE CREDIT
20-- Mar. 31	Balance	✓			973 70	

ACCOUNT Miscellaneous Expense—Factory ACCOUNT NO. 5530

DATE	ITEM	POST. REF.	DEBIT	CREDIT	BALANCE DEBIT	BALANCE CREDIT
20-- Mar. 31	Balance	✓			609 50	

ACCOUNT Payroll Taxes Expense—Factory ACCOUNT NO. 5535

DATE	ITEM	POST. REF.	DEBIT	CREDIT	BALANCE DEBIT	BALANCE CREDIT
20-- Mar. 31	Balance	✓			17 154 20	

ACCOUNT Property Tax Expense—Factory ACCOUNT NO. 5540

DATE	ITEM	POST. REF.	DEBIT	CREDIT	BALANCE DEBIT	BALANCE CREDIT
20-- Mar. 31	Balance	✓			3 781 70	

ACCOUNT Supplies Expense—Factory ACCOUNT NO. 5545

DATE	ITEM	POST. REF.	DEBIT	CREDIT	BALANCE DEBIT	BALANCE CREDIT
20-- Mar. 31	Balance	✓			8 043 10	

20-3 APPLICATION PROBLEM, p. 566

Preparing a statement of cost of goods manufactured

The ledger and journals prepared in Application Problem 20-2 are needed to complete this problem.

Cramer Corporation

Statement of Cost of Goods Manufactured

For Month Ended March 31, 20--

Direct Materials		
Direct Labor		
Factory Overhead Applied		
Total Cost of Work Placed in Process		
Work in Process Inventory, March 1, 20--		
Total Cost of Work in Process During March		
Less Work in Process Inventory, March 31, 20--		
Cost of Goods Manufactured		

20-3 APPLICATION PROBLEM

Extra form

20-4 MASTERY PROBLEM, p. 566

Journalizing entries that summarize cost records at the end of a fiscal period [1]

CASH PAYMENTS JOURNAL PAGE 10

DATE	ACCOUNT TITLE	CK. NO.	POST. REF.	GENERAL DEBIT	GENERAL CREDIT	ACCOUNTS PAYABLE DEBIT	PURCHASES DISCOUNT CREDIT	CASH CREDIT

20-4 MASTERY PROBLEM (continued)

[2-5]

GENERAL JOURNAL
PAGE 5

	DATE	ACCOUNT TITLE	DOC. NO.	POST. REF.	DEBIT	CREDIT	
1							1
2							2
3							3
4							4
5							5
6							6
7							7
8							8
9							9
10							10
11							11
12							12
13							13
14							14
15							15
16							16
17							17
18							18
19							19
20							20
21							21
22							22
23							23
24							24
25							25
26							26
27							27
28							28
29							29
30							30
31							31

20-4 MASTERY PROBLEM (continued)

[1–5]

GENERAL LEDGER

ACCOUNT Materials ACCOUNT NO. 1125

DATE		ITEM	POST. REF.	DEBIT	CREDIT	BALANCE DEBIT	BALANCE CREDIT
20-- May	1	Balance	✓			77 316 00	
	31		MP5	67 589 00		144 905 00	

ACCOUNT Work in Process ACCOUNT NO. 1130

DATE		ITEM	POST. REF.	DEBIT	CREDIT	BALANCE DEBIT	BALANCE CREDIT
20-- May	1	Balance	✓			48 960 00	

ACCOUNT Finished Goods ACCOUNT NO. 1135

DATE		ITEM	POST. REF.	DEBIT	CREDIT	BALANCE DEBIT	BALANCE CREDIT
20-- May	1	Balance	✓			120 750 00	

ACCOUNT Employee Income Tax Payable ACCOUNT NO. 2110

DATE	ITEM	POST. REF.	DEBIT	CREDIT	BALANCE DEBIT	BALANCE CREDIT

ACCOUNT Social Security Tax Payable ACCOUNT NO. 2120

DATE	ITEM	POST. REF.	DEBIT	CREDIT	BALANCE DEBIT	BALANCE CREDIT

ACCOUNT Medicare Tax Payable ACCOUNT NO. 2125

DATE	ITEM	POST. REF.	DEBIT	CREDIT	BALANCE DEBIT	BALANCE CREDIT

20-4 MASTERY PROBLEM (continued)

[1–5]

GENERAL LEDGER

ACCOUNT Income Summary   ACCOUNT NO. 3120

DATE	ITEM	POST. REF.	DEBIT	CREDIT	BALANCE DEBIT	BALANCE CREDIT

ACCOUNT Cost of Goods Sold   ACCOUNT NO. 5105

DATE	ITEM	POST. REF.	DEBIT	CREDIT	BALANCE DEBIT	BALANCE CREDIT

ACCOUNT Factory Overhead   ACCOUNT NO. 5505

DATE	ITEM	POST. REF.	DEBIT	CREDIT	BALANCE DEBIT	BALANCE CREDIT

ACCOUNT Depreciation Expense—Factory Equipment   ACCOUNT NO. 5510

DATE	ITEM	POST. REF.	DEBIT	CREDIT	BALANCE DEBIT	BALANCE CREDIT
20-- May 31	Balance	✓			1 4 7 3 60	

ACCOUNT Depreciation Expense—Building   ACCOUNT NO. 5515

DATE	ITEM	POST. REF.	DEBIT	CREDIT	BALANCE DEBIT	BALANCE CREDIT
20-- May 31	Balance	✓			7 2 0 00	

ACCOUNT Heat, Light, and Power Expense   ACCOUNT NO. 5520

DATE	ITEM	POST. REF.	DEBIT	CREDIT	BALANCE DEBIT	BALANCE CREDIT
20-- May 31	Balance	✓			2 3 1 0 00	

20-4 MASTERY PROBLEM (continued)

[1–5]

GENERAL LEDGER

ACCOUNT Insurance Expense—Factory   ACCOUNT NO. 5525

DATE	ITEM	POST. REF.	DEBIT	CREDIT	BALANCE DEBIT	BALANCE CREDIT
20-- May 31	Balance	✓			384 00	

ACCOUNT Miscellaneous Expense—Factory   ACCOUNT NO. 5530

DATE	ITEM	POST. REF.	DEBIT	CREDIT	BALANCE DEBIT	BALANCE CREDIT
20-- May 31	Balance	✓			32 00	

ACCOUNT Payroll Taxes Expense—Factory   ACCOUNT NO. 5535

DATE	ITEM	POST. REF.	DEBIT	CREDIT	BALANCE DEBIT	BALANCE CREDIT
20-- May 31	Balance	✓			10 840 20	

ACCOUNT Property Tax Expense—Factory   ACCOUNT NO. 5540

DATE	ITEM	POST. REF.	DEBIT	CREDIT	BALANCE DEBIT	BALANCE CREDIT
20-- May 31	Balance	✓			1 812 00	

ACCOUNT Supplies Expense—Factory   ACCOUNT NO. 5545

DATE	ITEM	POST. REF.	DEBIT	CREDIT	BALANCE DEBIT	BALANCE CREDIT
20-- May 31	Balance	✓			4 008 00	

20-4 MASTERY PROBLEM (concluded)

[6]

Simmons Corporation
Statement of Cost of Goods Manufactured
For Month Ended May 31, 20--

Direct Materials		
Direct Labor		
Factory Overhead Applied		
Total Cost of Work Placed in Process		
Work in Process Inventory, May 1, 20--		
Total Cost of Work in Process During May		
Less Work in Process Inventory, May 31, 20--		
Cost of Goods Manufactured		

20-5 CHALLENGE PROBLEM, p. 567

Journalizing entries that summarize cost records at the end of a fiscal period; preparing financial statements [1]

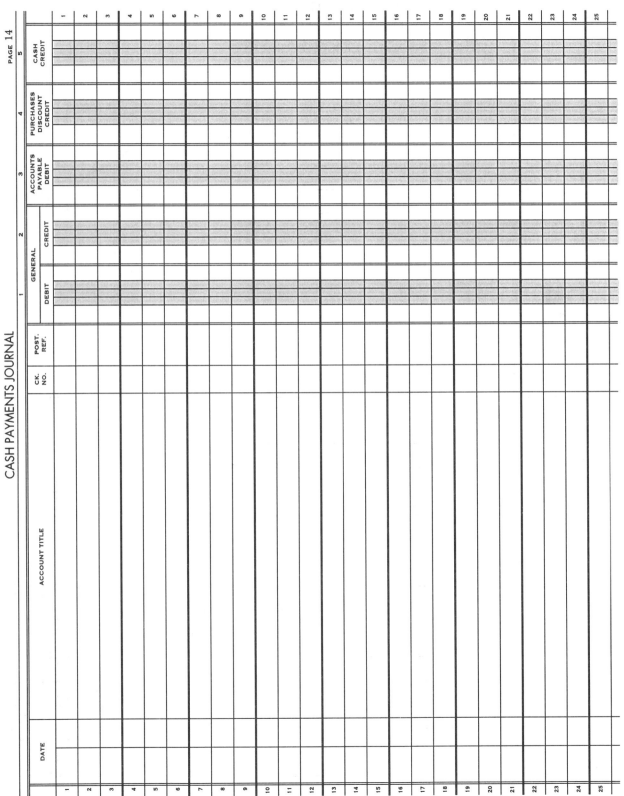

20-5 CHALLENGE PROBLEM (continued)

[2-5]

GENERAL JOURNAL PAGE 7

DATE	ACCOUNT TITLE	DOC. NO.	POST. REF.	DEBIT	CREDIT

20-5 CHALLENGE PROBLEM (continued)

[1–5]

GENERAL LEDGER

ACCOUNT Materials　　　　　　　　　　　　　　　　　　ACCOUNT NO. 1125

DATE		ITEM	POST. REF.	DEBIT	CREDIT	BALANCE DEBIT	BALANCE CREDIT
20-- July	1	Balance	✓			35 612 28	
	31		MP7	83 250 00		118 862 28	

ACCOUNT Work in Process　　　　　　　　　　　　　　　ACCOUNT NO. 1130

DATE		ITEM	POST. REF.	DEBIT	CREDIT	BALANCE DEBIT	BALANCE CREDIT
20-- July	1	Balance	✓			20 214 00	

ACCOUNT Finished Goods　　　　　　　　　　　　　　　ACCOUNT NO. 1135

DATE		ITEM	POST. REF.	DEBIT	CREDIT	BALANCE DEBIT	BALANCE CREDIT
20-- July	1	Balance	✓			38 409 28	

ACCOUNT Employee Income Tax Payable　　　　　　　　　ACCOUNT NO. 2110

DATE	ITEM	POST. REF.	DEBIT	CREDIT	BALANCE DEBIT	BALANCE CREDIT

ACCOUNT Social Security Tax Payable　　　　　　　　　　ACCOUNT NO. 2120

DATE	ITEM	POST. REF.	DEBIT	CREDIT	BALANCE DEBIT	BALANCE CREDIT

ACCOUNT Medicare Tax Payable　　　　　　　　　　　　ACCOUNT NO. 2125

DATE	ITEM	POST. REF.	DEBIT	CREDIT	BALANCE DEBIT	BALANCE CREDIT

20-5 CHALLENGE PROBLEM (continued)

[1–5]

GENERAL LEDGER

ACCOUNT Income Summary   ACCOUNT NO. 3120

DATE	ITEM	POST. REF.	DEBIT	CREDIT	BALANCE DEBIT	BALANCE CREDIT

ACCOUNT Cost of Goods Sold   ACCOUNT NO. 5105

DATE	ITEM	POST. REF.	DEBIT	CREDIT	BALANCE DEBIT	BALANCE CREDIT

ACCOUNT Factory Overhead   ACCOUNT NO. 5505

DATE	ITEM	POST. REF.	DEBIT	CREDIT	BALANCE DEBIT	BALANCE CREDIT

ACCOUNT Depreciation Expense—Factory Equipment   ACCOUNT NO. 5510

DATE	ITEM	POST. REF.	DEBIT	CREDIT	BALANCE DEBIT	BALANCE CREDIT
20-- July 31	Balance	✓			2 179 34	

ACCOUNT Depreciation Expense—Building   ACCOUNT NO. 5515

DATE	ITEM	POST. REF.	DEBIT	CREDIT	BALANCE DEBIT	BALANCE CREDIT
20-- July 31	Balance	✓			1 618 75	

ACCOUNT Heat, Light, and Power Expense   ACCOUNT NO. 5520

DATE	ITEM	POST. REF.	DEBIT	CREDIT	BALANCE DEBIT	BALANCE CREDIT
20-- July 31	Balance	✓			3 822 24	

20-5 CHALLENGE PROBLEM (continued)

[1–6]

GENERAL LEDGER

ACCOUNT Insurance Expense—Factory   ACCOUNT NO. 5525

DATE	ITEM	POST. REF.	DEBIT	CREDIT	BALANCE DEBIT	BALANCE CREDIT
20-- July 31	Balance	✓			1 3 5 2 60	

ACCOUNT Miscellaneous Expense—Factory   ACCOUNT NO. 5530

DATE	ITEM	POST. REF.	DEBIT	CREDIT	BALANCE DEBIT	BALANCE CREDIT
20-- July 31	Balance	✓			1 5 6 6 65	

ACCOUNT Payroll Taxes Expense—Factory   ACCOUNT NO. 5535

DATE	ITEM	POST. REF.	DEBIT	CREDIT	BALANCE DEBIT	BALANCE CREDIT
20-- July 31	Balance	✓			6 9 9 3 00	

ACCOUNT Property Tax Expense—Factory   ACCOUNT NO. 5540

DATE	ITEM	POST. REF.	DEBIT	CREDIT	BALANCE DEBIT	BALANCE CREDIT
20-- July 31	Balance	✓			1 3 5 5 55	

ACCOUNT Supplies Expense—Factory   ACCOUNT NO. 5545

DATE	ITEM	POST. REF.	DEBIT	CREDIT	BALANCE DEBIT	BALANCE CREDIT
20-- July 31	Balance	✓			1 8 0 0 04	

Cozart Company

Statement of Cost of Goods Manufactured

For Month Ended July 31, 20--

Direct Materials	
Direct Labor	
Factory Overhead Applied	
Total Cost of Work Placed in Process	
Work in Process Inventory, July 1, 20--	
Total Cost of Work in Process During July	
Less Work in Process Inventory, July 31, 20--	
Cost of Goods Manufactured	

20-5 CHALLENGE PROBLEM (continued)

[7]

Cozart Company
Work Sheet
For Month Ended July 31, 20--

	ACCOUNT TITLE	TRIAL BALANCE DEBIT	TRIAL BALANCE CREDIT	ADJUSTMENTS DEBIT	ADJUSTMENTS CREDIT	INCOME STATEMENT DEBIT	INCOME STATEMENT CREDIT	BALANCE SHEET DEBIT	BALANCE SHEET CREDIT
1	Cash	6306156							
2	Petty Cash	37500							
3	Accounts Receivable	11530030							
4	Allowance for Uncollectible Accounts		281965						
5	Materials	4411228							
6	Work in Process	3786000							
7	Finished Goods	6721645							
8	Supplies—Factory	2474 55							
9	Supplies—Sales	3107 03							
10	Supplies—Administrative	79420							
11	Prepaid Insurance	142223							
12	Factory Equipment	10300500							
13	Accum. Depr.—Factory Equipment		2811600						
14	Office Equipment	861300							
15	Accum. Depr.—Office Equipment		276930						
16	Store Equipment	7777150							
17	Accum. Depr.—Store Equipment		288456						
18	Building	23760000							
19	Accum. Depr.—Building		2376000						
20	Land	9944589							
21	Accounts Payable		1653586						
22	Employee Income Tax Payable		989072						
23	Federal Income Tax Payable								
24	Social Security Tax Payable		1168885						
25	Medicare Tax Payable		269743						
26	Unemployment Tax Payable—Federal		107880						
27	Unemployment Tax Payable—State		728190						
28	Mortgage Payable		5625000						
29	Capital Stock		45000000						
30	Retained Earnings		14596058						
31	Income Summary		191 83						
32	Sales		18358000						
33	Cost of Goods Sold	11217683							

20-5 CHALLENGE PROBLEM (continued)

[7]

	ACCOUNT TITLE	TRIAL BALANCE DEBIT	TRIAL BALANCE CREDIT	ADJUSTMENTS DEBIT	ADJUSTMENTS CREDIT	INCOME STATEMENT DEBIT	INCOME STATEMENT CREDIT	BALANCE SHEET DEBIT	BALANCE SHEET CREDIT	
34	Factory Overhead									34
35	Depr. Expense—Factory Equipment									35
36	Depr. Expense—Building									36
37	Heat, Light, and Power Expense									37
38	Insurance Expense—Factory									38
39	Miscellaneous Expense—Factory									39
40	Payroll Taxes Expense—Factory									40
41	Property Tax Expense—Factory									41
42	Supplies Expense—Factory									42
43	Advertising Expense	2 4 1 6 05								43
44	Delivery Expense	5 8 4 2 24								44
45	Depr. Expense—Store Equipment									45
46	Miscellaneous Expense—Sales	1 5 0 0 33								46
47	Salary Expense—Sales	11 6 0 4 38								47
48	Supplies Expense—Sales									48
49	Depr. Expense—Office Equipment									49
50	Insurance Expense—Admin.									50
51	Miscellaneous Expense—Admin.	1 5 6 141								51
52	Payroll Taxes Expense—Admin.	2 5 2 9 95								52
53	Property Tax Expense—Admin.	9 2 59								53
54	Salary Expense—Admin.	15 3 0 9 90								54
55	Supplies Expense—Admin.									55
56	Uncollectible Accounts Expense									56
57	Gain on Plant Assets		1 5 5 93							57
58	Miscellaneous Revenue									58
59	Interest Expense	4 6 8 74								59
60	Loss on Plant Assets									60
61	Federal Income Tax Expense									61
62		945 6 6 1 41	945 6 6 1 41							62
63										63
64										64
65										65
66										66

20-5 CHALLENGE PROBLEM

Extra form [7]

20-5 CHALLENGE PROBLEM (continued)

[8]

Cozart Company
Income Statement
For Month Ended July 31, 20--

				% OF NET SALES
Operating Revenue:				
Sales				
Cost of Goods Sold:				
Finished Goods Inventory, July 1, 20--				
Cost of Goods Manufactured				
Total Cost of Finished Goods Available for Sale				
Less Finished Goods Inventory, July 31, 20--				
Cost of Goods Sold				
Overapplied Overhead				
Net Cost of Goods Sold				
Gross Profit on Operations				
Operating Expenses:				
Selling Expenses:				
Advertising Expense				
Delivery Expense				
Depreciation Expense—Store Equipment				
Miscellaneous Expense—Sales				
Salary Expense—Sales				
Supplies Expense—Sales				
Total Selling Expenses				
Administrative Expenses:				
Depreciation Expense—Office Equipment				
Insurance Expense—Administrative				
Miscellaneous Expense—Administrative				
Payroll Taxes Expense—Administrative				
Property Tax Expense—Administrative				
Salary Expense—Administrative				
Supplies Expense—Administrative				
Uncollectible Accounts Expense				
Total Administrative Expenses				

20-5 CHALLENGE PROBLEM (continued)

[8]

Cozart Company

Income Statement (continued)

For Month Ended July 31, 20--

				% OF NET SALES
Total Operating Expenses				
Net Income from Operations				
Other Revenue:				
Gain on Plant Assets				
Other Expense:				
Interest Expense				
Net Deduction				
Net Income before Federal Income Tax				
Less Federal Income Tax Expense				
Net Income after Federal Income Tax				

20-5 CHALLENGE PROBLEM (continued)

[9]

Cozart Company
Balance Sheet
July 31, 20--

ASSETS			
Current Assets:			
Cash			
Petty Cash			
Accounts Receivable			
Less Allowance for Uncollectible Accounts			
Materials			
Work in Process			
Finished Goods			
Supplies—Factory			
Supplies—Sales			
Supplies—Administrative			
Prepaid Insurance			
Total Current Assets			
Plant Assets:			
Factory Equipment			
Less Accumulated Depr.—Factory Equipment			
Office Equipment			
Less Accumulated Depr.—Office Equipment			
Store Equipment			
Less Accumulated Depr.—Store Equipment			
Building			
Less Accumulated Depr.—Building			
Land			
Total Plant Assets			
Total Assets			
LIABILITIES			
Current Liabilities:			
Accounts Payable			
Employee Income Tax Payable			
Federal Income Tax Payable			

20-5 CHALLENGE PROBLEM (concluded)

[9]

Cozart Company
Balance Sheet (continued)
July 31, 20--

Social Security Tax Payable			
Medicare Tax Payable			
Unemployment Tax Payable—Federal			
Unemployment Tax Payable—State			
Total Current Liabilities			
Long-Term Liability:			
Mortgage Payable			
Total Liabilities			
STOCKHOLDERS' EQUITY			
Capital Stock			
Retained Earnings			
Total Stockholders' Equity			
Total Liabilities and Stockholders' Equity			

3 REINFORCEMENT ACTIVITY, p. 570

Processing and reporting cost accounting data for a manufacturing business [1]

[2, 4]

MATERIALS PURCHASES JOURNAL
PAGE 1

	DATE	ACCOUNT CREDITED	PURCH. NO.	POST. REF.	MATERIALS DR. ACCTS. PAY. CR.	
1						1
2						2
3						3
4						4
5						5
6						6
7						7
8						8
9						9
10						10
11						11
12						12
13						13
14						14
15						15
16						16
17						17
18						18
19						19
20						20
21						21
22						22
23						23

3 REINFORCEMENT ACTIVITY (continued)

[2, 6–9]

GENERAL JOURNAL — PAGE 1

DATE	ACCOUNT TITLE	DOC. NO.	POST. REF.	DEBIT	CREDIT

3 REINFORCEMENT ACTIVITY (continued)

[2, 5]

CASH PAYMENTS JOURNAL — PAGE 1

DATE	ACCOUNT TITLE	CK. NO.	POST. REF.	GENERAL DEBIT (1)	GENERAL CREDIT (2)	ACCOUNTS PAYABLE DEBIT (3)	PURCHASES DISCOUNT CREDIT (4)	CASH CREDIT (5)

3 REINFORCEMENT ACTIVITY (continued)

[4, 6–9]

GENERAL LEDGER

ACCOUNT Materials **ACCOUNT NO.** 1125

DATE	ITEM	POST. REF.	DEBIT	CREDIT	BALANCE DEBIT	BALANCE CREDIT
20-- Jan. 1	Balance	✓			20 048 00	

ACCOUNT Work in Process **ACCOUNT NO.** 1130

DATE	ITEM	POST. REF.	DEBIT	CREDIT	BALANCE DEBIT	BALANCE CREDIT

ACCOUNT Finished Goods **ACCOUNT NO.** 1135

DATE	ITEM	POST. REF.	DEBIT	CREDIT	BALANCE DEBIT	BALANCE CREDIT
20-- Jan. 1	Balance	✓			43 190 00	

ACCOUNT Accounts Payable **ACCOUNT NO.** 2105

DATE	ITEM	POST. REF.	DEBIT	CREDIT	BALANCE DEBIT	BALANCE CREDIT
20-- Jan. 31	Balance	✓			11 772 40	

ACCOUNT Employee Income Tax Payable **ACCOUNT NO.** 2110

DATE	ITEM	POST. REF.	DEBIT	CREDIT	BALANCE DEBIT	BALANCE CREDIT
20-- Jan. 31	Balance	✓				1 624 10

ACCOUNT Social Security Tax Payable **ACCOUNT NO.** 2120

DATE	ITEM	POST. REF.	DEBIT	CREDIT	BALANCE DEBIT	BALANCE CREDIT
20-- Jan. 31	Balance	✓				1 854 21

3 REINFORCEMENT ACTIVITY (continued)

[4, 6–9]

GENERAL LEDGER

ACCOUNT Medicare Tax Payable   **ACCOUNT NO.** 2125

DATE	ITEM	POST. REF.	DEBIT	CREDIT	BALANCE DEBIT	BALANCE CREDIT
20-- Jan. 31	Balance	✓				427 89

ACCOUNT Unemployment Tax Payable—Federal   **ACCOUNT NO.** 2130

DATE	ITEM	POST. REF.	DEBIT	CREDIT	BALANCE DEBIT	BALANCE CREDIT
20-- Jan. 31	Balance	✓				114 05

ACCOUNT Unemployment Tax Payable—State   **ACCOUNT NO.** 2135

DATE	ITEM	POST. REF.	DEBIT	CREDIT	BALANCE DEBIT	BALANCE CREDIT
20-- Jan. 31	Balance	✓				770 21

ACCOUNT Income Summary   **ACCOUNT NO.** 3120

DATE	ITEM	POST. REF.	DEBIT	CREDIT	BALANCE DEBIT	BALANCE CREDIT

ACCOUNT Cost of Goods Sold   **ACCOUNT NO.** 5105

DATE	ITEM	POST. REF.	DEBIT	CREDIT	BALANCE DEBIT	BALANCE CREDIT

ACCOUNT Factory Overhead   **ACCOUNT NO.** 5505

DATE	ITEM	POST. REF.	DEBIT	CREDIT	BALANCE DEBIT	BALANCE CREDIT

3 REINFORCEMENT ACTIVITY (continued)

[4, 6–9]

GENERAL LEDGER

ACCOUNT Depreciation Expense—Factory Equipment   **ACCOUNT NO.** 5510

DATE	ITEM	POST. REF.	DEBIT	CREDIT	BALANCE DEBIT	BALANCE CREDIT
20-- Jan. 31	Balance	✓			2 1 9 6 00	

ACCOUNT Depreciation Expense—Building   **ACCOUNT NO.** 5515

DATE	ITEM	POST. REF.	DEBIT	CREDIT	BALANCE DEBIT	BALANCE CREDIT
20-- Jan. 31	Balance	✓			1 1 5 3 00	

ACCOUNT Heat, Light, and Power Expense   **ACCOUNT NO.** 5520

DATE	ITEM	POST. REF.	DEBIT	CREDIT	BALANCE DEBIT	BALANCE CREDIT
20-- Jan. 31	Balance	✓			5 2 4 4 20	

ACCOUNT Insurance Expense—Factory   **ACCOUNT NO.** 5525

DATE	ITEM	POST. REF.	DEBIT	CREDIT	BALANCE DEBIT	BALANCE CREDIT
20-- Jan. 31	Balance	✓			1 9 2 00	

ACCOUNT Miscellaneous Expense—Factory   **ACCOUNT NO.** 5530

DATE	ITEM	POST. REF.	DEBIT	CREDIT	BALANCE DEBIT	BALANCE CREDIT
20-- Jan. 31	Balance	✓			4 7 0 47	

ACCOUNT Payroll Taxes Expense—Factory   **ACCOUNT NO.** 5535

DATE	ITEM	POST. REF.	DEBIT	CREDIT	BALANCE DEBIT	BALANCE CREDIT

ACCOUNT Property Tax Expense—Factory   **ACCOUNT NO.** 5540

DATE	ITEM	POST. REF.	DEBIT	CREDIT	BALANCE DEBIT	BALANCE CREDIT
20-- Jan. 31	Balance	✓			6 5 9 80	

ACCOUNT Supplies Expense—Factory   **ACCOUNT NO.** 5545

DATE	ITEM	POST. REF.	DEBIT	CREDIT	BALANCE DEBIT	BALANCE CREDIT
20-- Jan. 31	Balance	✓			1 4 8 5 25	

3 REINFORCEMENT ACTIVITY (continued)

[2, 10]

MATERIALS LEDGER CARD

Article: Base Wood Acct. No. 110
Reorder: 30,000 Minimum: 10,000 Location: B10

ORDERED			RECEIVED					ISSUED					BALANCE		
DATE	PUR-CHASE ORDER NO.	QUAN-TITY	DATE	PUR-CHASE ORDER NO.	QUAN-TITY	UNIT PRICE	VALUE	DATE	REQUI-SITION NO.	QUAN-TITY	UNIT PRICE	VALUE	DATE	QUAN-TITY	UNIT PRICE	VALUE
													20-- Jan. 1	18,000	0.20	3,600.00

MATERIALS LEDGER CARD

Article: Laminate Acct. No. 120
Reorder: 20,000 Minimum: 10,000 Location: B20

ORDERED			RECEIVED					ISSUED					BALANCE		
DATE	PUR-CHASE ORDER NO.	QUAN-TITY	DATE	PUR-CHASE ORDER NO.	QUAN-TITY	UNIT PRICE	VALUE	DATE	REQUI-SITION NO.	QUAN-TITY	UNIT PRICE	VALUE	DATE	QUAN-TITY	UNIT PRICE	VALUE
													20-- Jan. 1	17,000	0.60	10,200.00

3 REINFORCEMENT ACTIVITY (continued)

[2, 10]

MATERIALS LEDGER CARD

Article: Adhesive Acct. No. 210
Reorder: 1,000 Minimum: 520 Location: C10

ORDERED			RECEIVED				ISSUED				BALANCE		
DATE	PURCHASE ORDER NO.	QUANTITY	DATE	PURCHASE ORDER NO.	QUANTITY	UNIT PRICE	VALUE	DATE	REQUISITION NO.	QUANTITY	UNIT PRICE	VALUE	DATE	QUANTITY	UNIT PRICE	VALUE
													20-- Jan. 1	830.0	1.60	1,328.00

MATERIALS LEDGER CARD

Article: Casters Acct. No. 310
Reorder: 1,600 Minimum: 800 Location: D10

ORDERED			RECEIVED				ISSUED				BALANCE		
DATE	PURCHASE ORDER NO.	QUANTITY	DATE	PURCHASE ORDER NO.	QUANTITY	UNIT PRICE	VALUE	DATE	REQUISITION NO.	QUANTITY	UNIT PRICE	VALUE	DATE	QUANTITY	UNIT PRICE	VALUE
													20-- Jan. 1	1,800	1.25	2,250.00

MATERIALS LEDGER CARD

Article: Metal Glides (set of 2) Acct. No. 320
Reorder: 300 Minimum: 100 Location: D20

ORDERED			RECEIVED				ISSUED				BALANCE		
DATE	PURCHASE ORDER NO.	QUANTITY	DATE	PURCHASE ORDER NO.	QUANTITY	UNIT PRICE	VALUE	DATE	REQUISITION NO.	QUANTITY	UNIT PRICE	VALUE	DATE	QUANTITY	UNIT PRICE	VALUE
													20-- Jan. 1	300	1.00	300.00

3 REINFORCEMENT ACTIVITY (continued)

[2, 10]

MATERIALS LEDGER CARD

Article: Hinges (set of 2)   Acct. No. 330

Reorder: 1,000   Minimum: 300   Location: D30

ORDERED			RECEIVED					ISSUED					BALANCE		
DATE	PURCHASE ORDER NO.	QUANTITY	DATE	PURCHASE ORDER NO.	QUANTITY	UNIT PRICE	VALUE	DATE	REQUISITION NO.	QUANTITY	UNIT PRICE	VALUE	DATE	QUANTITY	UNIT PRICE	VALUE
													20-- Jan. 1	600	1.00	600.00

MATERIALS LEDGER CARD

Article: Fasteners   Acct. No. 340

Reorder: 1,000   Minimum: 600   Location: D40

ORDERED			RECEIVED					ISSUED					BALANCE		
DATE	PURCHASE ORDER NO.	QUANTITY	DATE	PURCHASE ORDER NO.	QUANTITY	UNIT PRICE	VALUE	DATE	REQUISITION NO.	QUANTITY	UNIT PRICE	VALUE	DATE	QUANTITY	UNIT PRICE	VALUE
													20-- Jan. 1	560	0.75	420.00

3 REINFORCEMENT ACTIVITY (continued)

[2, 3, 10]

COST SHEET

Job No. 232
Item C200 Computer Desk
No. of items 250
Ordered for Stock

Date January 3, 20--
Date wanted January 12, 20--
Date completed January 11, 20--

DIRECT MATERIALS		DIRECT LABOR				SUMMARY	
REQ. NO.	AMOUNT	DATE	AMOUNT	DATE	AMOUNT	ITEM	AMOUNT

COST SHEET

Job No. 233
Item P150 Printer Table
No. of items 200
Ordered for Stock

Date January 5, 20--
Date wanted January 17, 20--
Date completed January 14, 20--

DIRECT MATERIALS		DIRECT LABOR				SUMMARY	
REQ. NO.	AMOUNT	DATE	AMOUNT	DATE	AMOUNT	ITEM	AMOUNT

Name _____ Date _____ Class _____

3 REINFORCEMENT ACTIVITY (continued)

[2, 3, 10]

COST SHEET

Job No. __234__
Item __E400 Entertainment Center__
No. of items __120__
Ordered for __Stock__

Date __January 12, 20--__
Date wanted __January 18, 20--__
Date completed __January 19, 20--__

DIRECT MATERIALS		DIRECT LABOR				SUMMARY	
REQ. NO.	AMOUNT	DATE	AMOUNT	DATE	AMOUNT	ITEM	AMOUNT

COST SHEET

Job No. __235__
Item __V110 Video Tape Cabinet__
No. of items __150__
Ordered for __Stock__

Date __January 14, 20--__
Date wanted __January 27, 20--__
Date completed __January 27, 20--__

DIRECT MATERIALS		DIRECT LABOR				SUMMARY	
REQ. NO.	AMOUNT	DATE	AMOUNT	DATE	AMOUNT	ITEM	AMOUNT

Name _____ Date _____ Class _____

3 REINFORCEMENT ACTIVITY (continued)

[2, 3, 10]

COST SHEET

Job No. 236 Date January 18, 20--
Item B160 Book Case Date wanted January 28, 20--
No. of items 200 Date completed January 28, 20--
Ordered for Stock

DIRECT MATERIALS		DIRECT LABOR				SUMMARY	
REQ. NO.	AMOUNT	DATE	AMOUNT	DATE	AMOUNT	ITEM	AMOUNT

COST SHEET

Job No. 237 Date January 25, 20--
Item T120 TV Cart Date wanted January 31, 20--
No. of items 160 Date completed January 31, 20--
Ordered for Stock

DIRECT MATERIALS		DIRECT LABOR				SUMMARY	
REQ. NO.	AMOUNT	DATE	AMOUNT	DATE	AMOUNT	ITEM	AMOUNT

3 REINFORCEMENT ACTIVITY (continued)

[2, 3, 10]

COST SHEET

Job No. 238
Item C200 Computer Desk
No. of items 200
Ordered for Stock

Date January 28, 20--
Date wanted February 8, 20--
Date completed _____

DIRECT MATERIALS		DIRECT LABOR				SUMMARY	
REQ. NO.	AMOUNT	DATE	AMOUNT	DATE	AMOUNT	ITEM	AMOUNT

FINISHED GOODS LEDGER CARD

Description Computer Desk
Minimum 100

Stock No. C200
Location J10

MANUFACTURED/RECEIVED					SHIPPED/ISSUED					BALANCE			
DATE	JOB NO.	QUAN-TITY	UNIT COST	TOTAL COST	DATE	SALES INVOICE NO.	QUAN-TITY	UNIT COST	TOTAL COST	DATE	QUAN-TITY	UNIT COST	TOTAL COST
										20-- Jan. 1	150	65.00	9,750.00

FINISHED GOODS LEDGER CARD

Description Printer Table
Minimum 50

Stock No. P150
Location J20

MANUFACTURED/RECEIVED					SHIPPED/ISSUED					BALANCE			
DATE	JOB NO.	QUAN-TITY	UNIT COST	TOTAL COST	DATE	SALES INVOICE NO.	QUAN-TITY	UNIT COST	TOTAL COST	DATE	QUAN-TITY	UNIT COST	TOTAL COST
										20-- Jan. 1	50	55.00	2,750.00

3 REINFORCEMENT ACTIVITY (continued)

[2, 10]

FINISHED GOODS LEDGER CARD

Description: Entertainment Center Stock No. E400
Minimum: 50 Location: K10

MANUFACTURED/RECEIVED					SHIPPED/ISSUED					BALANCE		
DATE	JOB NO.	QUAN-TITY	UNIT COST	TOTAL COST	DATE	SALES INVOICE NO.	QUAN-TITY	UNIT COST	TOTAL COST	DATE	QUAN-TITY	UNIT COST	TOTAL COST
										20-- Jan. 1	40	110.00	4,400.00

FINISHED GOODS LEDGER CARD

Description: Video Tape Cabinet Stock No. V110
Minimum: 200 Location: K20

MANUFACTURED/RECEIVED					SHIPPED/ISSUED					BALANCE		
DATE	JOB NO.	QUAN-TITY	UNIT COST	TOTAL COST	DATE	SALES INVOICE NO.	QUAN-TITY	UNIT COST	TOTAL COST	DATE	QUAN-TITY	UNIT COST	TOTAL COST
										20-- Jan. 1	350	51.00	17,850.00

FINISHED GOODS LEDGER CARD

Description: Book Case Stock No. B160
Minimum: 50 Location: L10

MANUFACTURED/RECEIVED					SHIPPED/ISSUED					BALANCE		
DATE	JOB NO.	QUAN-TITY	UNIT COST	TOTAL COST	DATE	SALES INVOICE NO.	QUAN-TITY	UNIT COST	TOTAL COST	DATE	QUAN-TITY	UNIT COST	TOTAL COST
										20-- Jan. 1	60	86.00	5,160.00

3 REINFORCEMENT ACTIVITY (continued)

[2, 10]

FINISHED GOODS LEDGER CARD

Description: TV Cart Stock No. T120
Minimum: 25 Location: L20

MANUFACTURED/RECEIVED					SHIPPED/ISSUED					BALANCE			
DATE	JOB NO.	QUAN-TITY	UNIT COST	TOTAL COST	DATE	SALES INVOICE NO.	QUAN-TITY	UNIT COST	TOTAL COST	DATE	QUAN-TITY	UNIT COST	TOTAL COST
										20--Jan. 1	80	41.00	3,280.00

[10]

Direct and Indirect Materials Ledger Proof

Cost Ledger Proof

Finished Goods Ledger Proof

[11]

Furniture Decor, Inc.
Statement of Cost of Goods Manufactured
For Month Ended January 31, 20--

Direct Materials			
Direct Labor			
Factory Overhead Applied			
Total Cost of Work Placed in Process			
Work in Process Inventory, January 1, 20--			
Total Cost of Work in Process During January			
Less Work in Process Inventory, January 31, 20--			
Cost of Goods Manufactured			

Reinforcement Activity 3 • 343

3 REINFORCEMENT ACTIVITY (continued)

[12, 13]

Cozart Company
Work Sheet
For Month Ended July 31, 20--

	ACCOUNT TITLE	TRIAL BALANCE DEBIT	TRIAL BALANCE CREDIT	ADJUSTMENTS DEBIT	ADJUSTMENTS CREDIT	INCOME STATEMENT DEBIT	INCOME STATEMENT CREDIT	BALANCE SHEET DEBIT	BALANCE SHEET CREDIT	
1	Cash	30 200 50								1
2	Petty Cash	250 00								2
3	Accounts Receivable	46 687 50								3
4	Allowance for Uncollectible Accounts		806 00							4
5	Materials									5
6	Work in Process									6
7	Finished Goods									7
8	Supplies—Factory	1 237 25								8
9	Supplies—Sales	1 553 50								9
10	Supplies—Administrative	397 10								10
11	Prepaid Insurance	2 808 0								11
12	Factory Equipment	113 100 00								12
13	Accum. Depr.—Factory Equipment		33 930 00							13
14	Office Equipment	4 320 00								14
15	Accum. Depr.—Office Equipment		1 296 00							15
16	Store Equipment	3 895 00								16
17	Accum. Depr.—Store Equipment		1 363 00							17
18	Building	150 000 00								18
19	Accum. Depr.—Building		22 500 00							19
20	Land	50 600 00								20
21	Accounts Payable									21
22	Employee Income Tax Payable									22
23	Federal Income Tax Payable									23
24	Social Security Tax Payable									24
25	Medicare Tax Payable									25
26	Salaries Payable									26
27	Unemployment Tax Payable—Federal									27
28	Unemployment Tax Payable—State									28
29	Dividends Payable									29
30	Mortgage Payable		30 000 00							30

REINFORCEMENT ACTIVITY 3 (continued)

[12, 13]

ACCOUNT TITLE	TRIAL BALANCE DEBIT	TRIAL BALANCE CREDIT	ADJUSTMENTS DEBIT	ADJUSTMENTS CREDIT	INCOME STATEMENT DEBIT	INCOME STATEMENT CREDIT	BALANCE SHEET DEBIT	BALANCE SHEET CREDIT	
Capital Stock		200 000 00							31
Retained Earnings		14316 56							32
Dividends									33
Income Summary									34
Sales		9575 00							35
Cost of Goods Sold									36
Factory Overhead									37
Depr. Expense—Factory Equipment									38
Depr. Expense—Building									39
Heat, Light, and Power Expense									40
Insurance Expense—Factory									41
Miscellaneous Expense—Factory									42
Payroll Taxes Expense—Factory									43
Property Tax Expense—Factory									44
Supplies Expense—Factory									45
Advertising Expense	835 95								46
Delivery Expense	2053 45								47
Depr. Expense—Store Equipment									48
Miscellaneous Expense—Sales	519 10								49
Salary Expense—Sales	6133 25								50
Supplies Expense—Sales									51
Depr. Expense—Office Equipment									52
Insurance Expense—Admin.									53
Miscellaneous Expense—Admin.	441 85								54
Payroll Taxes Expense—Admin.	2025 35								55
Property Tax Expense—Admin.	56 90								56
Salary Expense—Admin.	8130 00								57
Supplies Expense—Admin.									58
Uncollectible Accounts Expense									59
Utilities Expense—Admin.	98 40								60

3 REINFORCEMENT ACTIVITY (continued)

[12, 13]

	ACCOUNT TITLE	TRIAL BALANCE DEBIT	TRIAL BALANCE CREDIT	ADJUSTMENTS DEBIT	ADJUSTMENTS CREDIT	INCOME STATEMENT DEBIT	INCOME STATEMENT CREDIT	BALANCE SHEET DEBIT	BALANCE SHEET CREDIT
61	Gain on Plant Assets								
62	Miscellaneous Revenue								
63	Interest Expense	300 00							
64	Loss on Plant Assets								
65	Federal Income Tax Expense								
66									
67									
68									
69									
70									
71									
72									
73									
74									
75									
76									
77									
78									
79									
80									
81									
82									
83									
84									
85									
86									
87									
88									
89									
90									
91									

REINFORCEMENT ACTIVITY (continued)

[14]

Furniture Decor, Inc.
Income Statement
For Month Ended January 31, 20--

					% OF NET SALES
Operating Revenue:					
Sales					
Cost of Goods Sold:					
Finished Goods Inventory, Jan. 1, 20--					
Cost of Goods Manufactured					
Total Cost of Finished Goods Available for Sale					
Less Finished Goods Inventory, Jan. 31, 20--					
Cost of Goods Sold					
Underapplied Overhead					
Net Cost of Goods Sold					
Gross Profit on Operations					
Operating Expenses:					
Selling Expenses:					
Advertising Expense					
Delivery Expense					
Depreciation Expense—Store Equipment					
Miscellaneous Expense—Sales					
Salary Expense—Sales					
Supplies Expense—Sales					
Total Selling Expenses					
Administrative Expenses:					
Depreciation Expense—Office Equipment					
Insurance Expense—Administrative					
Miscellaneous Expense—Administrative					
Payroll Taxes Expense—Administrative					
Property Tax Expense—Administrative					
Salary Expense—Administrative					
Supplies Expense—Administrative					
Uncollectible Accounts Expense					
Utilities Expense—Administrative					
Total Administrative Expenses					

3 REINFORCEMENT ACTIVITY (continued)

[14]

Furniture Decor, Inc.
Income Statement (continued)
For Month Ended January 31, 20--

				% OF NET SALES
Total Operating Expenses				
Net Income from Operations				
Other Expense:				
Interest Expense				
Net Income before Federal Income Tax				
Less Federal Income Tax Expense				
Net Income after Federal Income Tax				

3 REINFORCEMENT ACTIVITY (continued)

[15]

Furniture Decor, Inc.
Balance Sheet
January 31, 20--

ASSETS					
Current Assets:					
Cash					
Petty Cash					
Accounts Receivable					
Less Allowance for Uncollectible Accounts					
Materials					
Work in Process					
Finished Goods					
Supplies—Factory					
Supplies—Sales					
Supplies—Administrative					
Prepaid Insurance					
Total Current Assets					
Plant Assets:					
Factory Equipment					
Less Accumulated Depr.—Factory Equipment					
Office Equipment					
Less Accumulated Depr.—Office Equipment					
Store Equipment					
Less Accumulated Depr.—Store Equipment					
Building					
Less Accumulated Depr.—Building					
Land					
Total Plant Assets					
Total Assets					
LIABILITIES					
Current Liabilities:					
Accounts Payable					
Employee Income Tax Payable					
Federal Income Tax Payable					
Social Security Tax Payable					
Medicare Tax Payable					

3 REINFORCEMENT ACTIVITY (concluded)

[15]

Furniture Decor, Inc.
Balance Sheet (continued)
January 31, 20--

Unemployment Tax Payable—Federal			
Unemployment Tax Payable—State			
Total Current Liabilities			
Long-Term Liability:			
Mortgage Payable			
Total Liabilities			
STOCKHOLDERS' EQUITY			
Capital Stock			
Retained Earnings			
Total Stockholders' Equity			
Total Liabilities and Stockholders' Equity			

21-1 WORK TOGETHER, p. 586

Forming a partnership

Jensen's Boutique Balance Sheet March 31, 20--			
ASSETS			
Current Assets:			
Cash		$ 11,371.85	
Accounts Receivable	$ 2,434.95		
Less Allowance for Uncollectible Accounts	73.45	2,361.50	
Merchandise Inventory		24,350.00	
Supplies		620.90	
Total Current Assets			$ 38,704.25
Plant Assets:			
Equipment			8,778.75
Total Assets			$ 47,483.00
LIABILITIES			
Accounts Payable			$ 5,483.00
OWNERS' EQUITY			
Betty Jensen, Capital			42,000.00
Total Liabilities and Owner's Equity			$ 47,483.00

21-1 WORK TOGETHER (concluded)

[4]

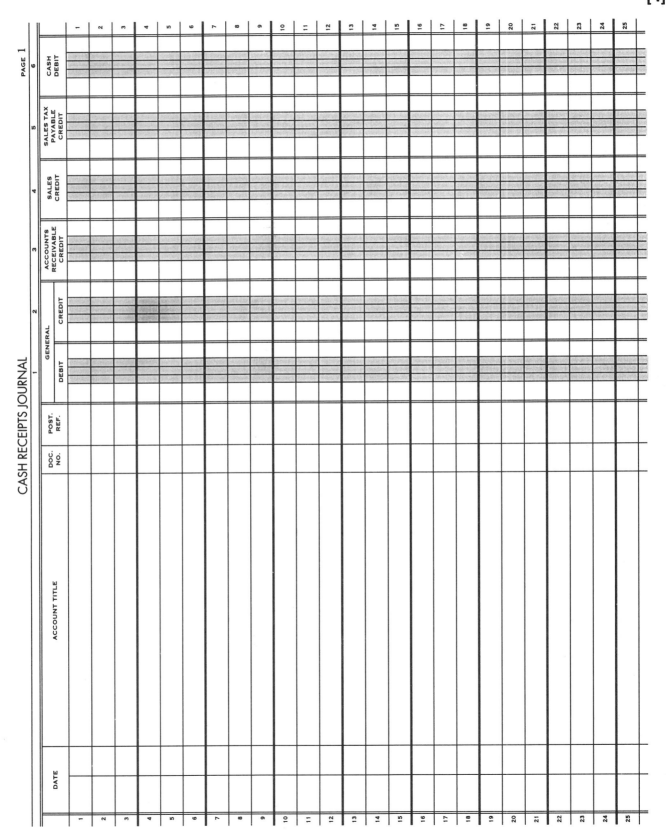

21-1 ON YOUR OWN, p. 586

Forming a partnership

	Rice Patch Balance Sheet June 30, 20--		
ASSETS			
Current Assets:			
Cash		$ 12,379.10	
Accounts Receivable	$ 3,191.40		
Less Allowance for Uncollectible Accounts	63.80	3,127.60	
Merchandise Inventory		18,402.30	
Supplies		571.25	
Total Current Assets			$ 34,480.25
Plant Assets:			
Equipment			8,076.50
Total Assets			$ 42,556.75
LIABILITIES			
Accounts Payable			$ 10,556.75
OWNERS' EQUITY			
David Rice, Capital			32,000.00
Total Liabilities and Owner's Equity			$ 42,556.75

21-1 ON YOUR OWN (concluded)

[5]

CASH RECEIPTS JOURNAL   PAGE 1

DATE	ACCOUNT TITLE	DOC. NO.	POST. REF.	GENERAL DEBIT	GENERAL CREDIT	ACCOUNTS RECEIVABLE CREDIT	SALES CREDIT	SALES TAX PAYABLE CREDIT	CASH DEBIT

21-2 WORK TOGETHER, p. 592

Admitting partners to an existing partnership [4–7]

GENERAL JOURNAL
PAGE 6

DATE	ACCOUNT TITLE	DOC. NO.	POST. REF.	DEBIT	CREDIT

21-2 WORK TOGETHER (concluded)

[4–7]

CASH RECEIPTS JOURNAL PAGE 12

DATE	ACCOUNT TITLE	DOC. NO.	POST. REF.	GENERAL DEBIT	GENERAL CREDIT	ACCOUNTS RECEIVABLE CREDIT	SALES CREDIT	SALES TAX PAYABLE CREDIT	CASH DEBIT

21-2 ON YOUR OWN, p. 593

Admitting partners to an existing partnership [8-11]

GENERAL JOURNAL PAGE 9

DATE	ACCOUNT TITLE	DOC. NO.	POST. REF.	DEBIT	CREDIT

21-2 ON YOUR OWN (concluded)

[8–11]

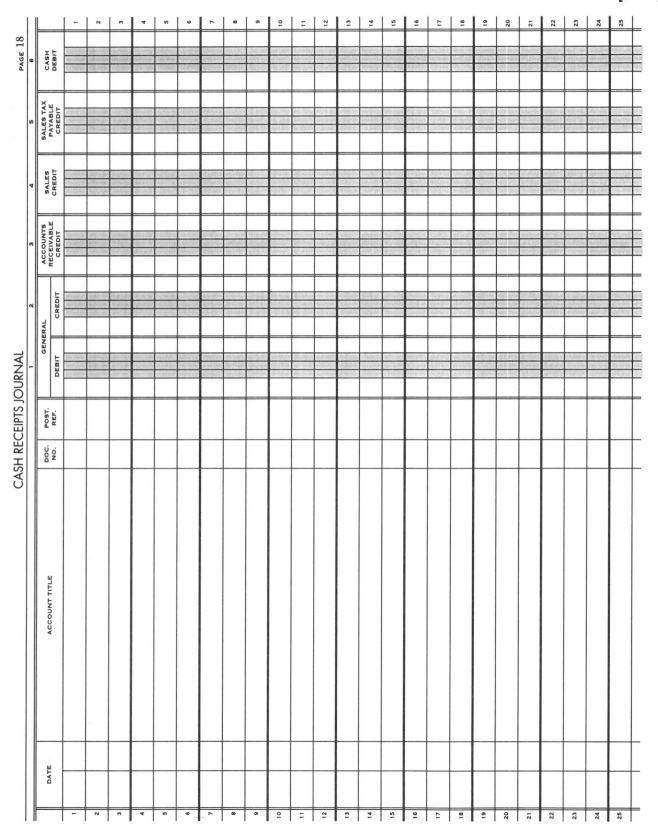

21-1/21-2 APPLICATION PROBLEMS, p. 595

Forming a partnership; admitting a partner with no change in total equity

Application Problem 21-1

CASH RECEIPTS JOURNAL — PAGE 1

DATE	ACCOUNT TITLE	DOC. NO.	POST. REF.	GENERAL DEBIT	GENERAL CREDIT	ACCOUNTS RECEIVABLE CREDIT	SALES CREDIT	SALES TAX PAYABLE CREDIT	CASH DEBIT

Application Problem 21-2

GENERAL JOURNAL — PAGE 12

DATE	ACCOUNT TITLE	DOC. NO.	POST. REF.	DEBIT	CREDIT

Name _____ Date _____ Class _____

21-1/21-2 APPLICATION PROBLEMS

Extra form

Blank Cash Receipts Journal form with columns for Date, Account Title, Doc. No., Post. Ref., General Debit, General Credit, Accounts Receivable Credit, Sales Credit, Sales Tax Payable Credit, and Cash Debit.

21-3 – 21-5 APPLICATION PROBLEMS, p. 596

Admitting a partner with equity equal to new partner's investment; admitting a partner with equity greater than new partner's investment; admitting a partner when goodwill is recognized

Application Problem 21-3

CASH RECEIPTS JOURNAL — PAGE 13

DATE	ACCOUNT TITLE	DOC. NO.	POST. REF.	GENERAL DEBIT	GENERAL CREDIT	ACCOUNTS RECEIVABLE CREDIT	SALES CREDIT	SALES TAX PAYABLE CREDIT	CASH DEBIT

Application Problem 21-4

The general journal for this problem appears on page 362.

CASH RECEIPTS JOURNAL — PAGE 14

DATE	ACCOUNT TITLE	DOC. NO.	POST. REF.	GENERAL DEBIT	GENERAL CREDIT	ACCOUNTS RECEIVABLE CREDIT	SALES CREDIT	SALES TAX PAYABLE CREDIT	CASH DEBIT

Application Problem 21-5

The general journal for this problem appears on page 362.

CASH RECEIPTS JOURNAL — PAGE 5

DATE	ACCOUNT TITLE	DOC. NO.	POST. REF.	GENERAL DEBIT	GENERAL CREDIT	ACCOUNTS RECEIVABLE CREDIT	SALES CREDIT	SALES TAX PAYABLE CREDIT	CASH DEBIT

Chapter 21 Organizational Structure of a Partnership • 361

21-3 – 21-5 APPLICATION PROBLEMS (concluded)

Application Problem 21-4

GENERAL JOURNAL — PAGE 7

DATE	ACCOUNT TITLE	DOC. NO.	POST. REF.	DEBIT	CREDIT

Application Problem 21-5

GENERAL JOURNAL — PAGE 3

DATE	ACCOUNT TITLE	DOC. NO.	POST. REF.	DEBIT	CREDIT

21-6 MASTERY PROBLEM, p. 597

Forming and expanding a partnership

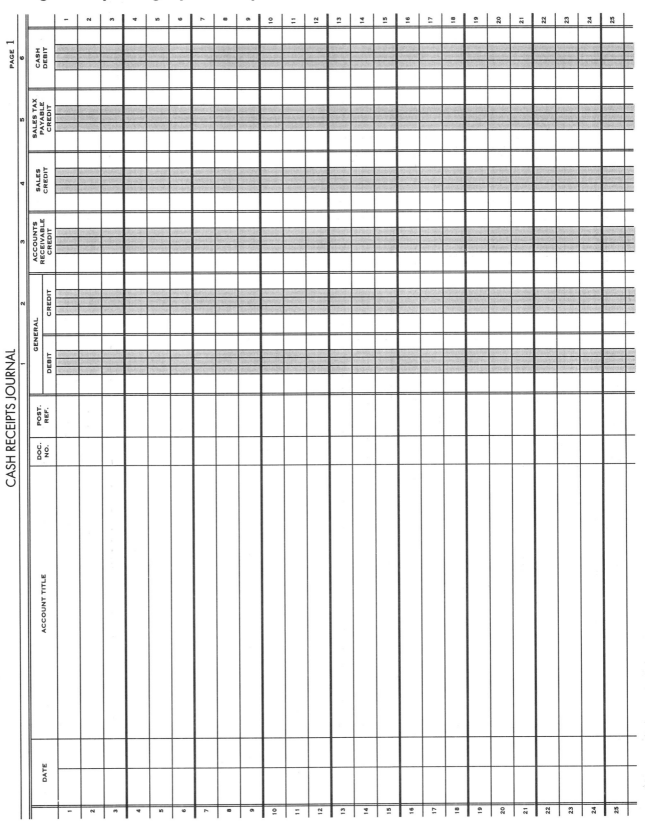

21-6 MASTERY PROBLEM (concluded)

GENERAL JOURNAL

PAGE 1

DATE	ACCOUNT TITLE	DOC. NO.	POST. REF.	DEBIT	CREDIT

21-7 CHALLENGE PROBLEM, p. 598

Forming and expanding a partnership

CASH RECEIPTS JOURNAL — PAGE 8

21-7 CHALLENGE PROBLEM (concluded)

GENERAL JOURNAL

PAGE 4

DATE	ACCOUNT TITLE	DOC. NO.	POST. REF.	DEBIT	CREDIT

22-1 WORK TOGETHER, p. 608

Calculating partnership earnings and journalizing partnership withdrawals [5a]

Fixed percentage:

[5b]

Percentage of total equity:

[5c]

Interest on equity plus fixed percentage:

22-1 WORK TOGETHER (continued)

[5d]

Interest on equity, salary, and fixed percentage:

[6]

GENERAL JOURNAL PAGE 7

	DATE	ACCOUNT TITLE	DOC. NO.	POST. REF.	DEBIT	CREDIT	
1							1
2							2
3							3
4							4
5							5
6							6
7							7
8							8
9							9
10							10
11							11
12							12
13							13
14							14

22-1 WORK TOGETHER (concluded)

[6]

CASH PAYMENTS JOURNAL PAGE 12

DATE	ACCOUNT TITLE	CK. NO.	POST. REF.	GENERAL DEBIT	GENERAL CREDIT	ACCOUNTS PAYABLE DEBIT	CASH CREDIT

22-1 WORK TOGETHER

Extra form

GENERAL JOURNAL

PAGE _____

DATE	ACCOUNT TITLE	DOC. NO.	POST. REF.	DEBIT	CREDIT

22-1 ON YOUR OWN, p. 609

Calculating partnership earnings and journalizing partnership withdrawals [7a]

Fixed percentage:

[7b]

Percentage of total equity:

[7c]

Interest on equity plus fixed percentage:

22-1 ON YOUR OWN (continued)

[7d]

Interest on equity, salary, and fixed percentage:

[8]

GENERAL JOURNAL PAGE 4

	DATE	ACCOUNT TITLE	DOC. NO.	POST. REF.	DEBIT	CREDIT	
1							1
2							2
3							3
4							4
5							5
6							6
7							7
8							8
9							9
10							10
11							11
12							12
13							13
14							14

22-1 ON YOUR OWN (concluded)

[8]

CASH PAYMENTS JOURNAL PAGE 8

DATE	ACCOUNT TITLE	CK. NO.	POST. REF.	GENERAL DEBIT	GENERAL CREDIT	ACCOUNTS PAYABLE DEBIT	CASH CREDIT

22-1 ON YOUR OWN

Extra form

GENERAL JOURNAL

DATE	ACCOUNT TITLE	DOC. NO.	POST. REF.	DEBIT	CREDIT

22-2 WORK TOGETHER, p. 618

End-of-fiscal-period-work for a partnership

Maria and Kelso Shop
Work Sheet
For Year Ended December 31, 20--

	ACCOUNT TITLE	INCOME STATEMENT DEBIT	INCOME STATEMENT CREDIT	BALANCE SHEET DEBIT	BALANCE SHEET CREDIT	
13	Maria Delgado, Capital				93 600 00	13
14	Maria Delgado, Drawing			17 600 00		14
15	Oren Kelso, Capital				50 400 00	15
16	Oren Kelso, Drawing			10 400 00		16
17	Income Summary					17
18	Sales		133 510 00			18
19	Advertising Expense	2 400 00				19
20	Depr. Expense—Equipment	3 063 00				20
21	Depr. Expense—Truck	2 250 00				21
22	Insurance Expense	1 225 00				22
23	Miscellaneous Expense	4 347 00				23
24	Rent Expense	18 000 00				24
25	Supplies Expense—Service	18 807 00				25
26	Supplies Expense—Office	3 475 00				26
27	Truck Expense	13 250 00				27
28	Uncollectible Accounts Expense	293 00				28
29	Utilities Expense	4 900 00				29
30		72 010 00	133 510 00	291 860 00	230 360 00	30
31	Net Income	61 500 00			61 500 00	31
32		133 510 00	133 510 00	291 860 00	291 860 00	32

22-2 WORK TOGETHER (continued)

[4]

Maria and Kelso Shop
Income Statement
For Year Ended December 31, 20--

			% OF NET SALES
Operating Revenue:			
Sales			
Operating Expenses:			
Advertising Expense			
Depreciation Expense—Equipment			
Depreciation Expense—Truck			
Insurance Expense			
Miscellaneous Expense			
Rent Expense			
Supplies Expense—Service			
Supplies Expense—Office			
Truck Expense			
Uncollectible Accounts Expense			
Utilities Expense			
Total Operating Expenses			
Net Income			

[5]

Maria and Kelso Shop
Distribution of Net Income Statement
For Year Ended December 31, 20--

Maria Delgado:		
8% Interest on Equity		
Salary		
Share of Remaining Net Income		
Total Share of Net Income		
Oren Kelso:		
8% Interest on Equity		
Salary		
Share of Remaining Net Income		
Total Share of Net Income		
Total Net Income		

22-2 WORK TOGETHER (continued)

[6]

Maria and Kelso Shop
Owners' Equity Statement
For Year Ended December 31, 20--

Maria Delgado:					
Capital, January 1, 20--					
Share of Net Income					
Less Withdrawals					
Net Increase in Capital					
Capital, December 31, 20--					
Oren Kelso:					
Capital, January 1, 20--					
Share of Net Income					
Less Withdrawals					
Net Increase in Capital					
Capital, December 31, 20--					
Total Owners' Equity, December 31, 20--					

22-2 WORK TOGETHER (concluded)

[7]

GENERAL JOURNAL PAGE 15

DATE	ACCOUNT TITLE	DOC. NO.	POST. REF.	DEBIT	CREDIT

22-2 ON YOUR OWN, p. 618

End-of-fiscal-period-work for a partnership

Lowe and Ray Gallery
Work Sheet
For Year Ended December 31, 20--

	ACCOUNT TITLE	INCOME STATEMENT DEBIT	INCOME STATEMENT CREDIT	BALANCE SHEET DEBIT	BALANCE SHEET CREDIT	
13	Jeffery Lowe, Capital				66 000 00	13
14	Jeffery Lowe, Drawing			21 000 00		14
15	Mona Ray, Capital				60 000 00	15
16	Mona Ray, Drawing			21 000 00		16
17	Income Summary					17
18	Sales		115 450 00			18
19	Advertising Expense	1 320 00				19
20	Depr. Expense—Equipment	4 737 00				20
21	Depr. Expense—Truck	3 740 00				21
22	Insurance Expense	845 00				22
23	Miscellaneous Expense	1 980 00				23
24	Rent Expense	18 480 00				24
25	Supplies Expense—Service	12 962 00				25
26	Supplies Expense—Office	2 396 00				26
27	Truck Expense	11 277 00				27
28	Uncollectible Accounts Expense	198 00				28
29	Utilities Expense	2 915 00				29
30		60 850 00	115 450 00	250 476 00	195 876 00	30
31	Net Income	54 600 00			54 600 00	31
32		115 450 00	115 450 00	250 476 00	250 476 00	32

22-2 ON YOUR OWN (continued)

[8]

Lowe and Ray Gallery
Income Statement
For Year Ended December 31, 20--

			% OF NET SALES
Operating Revenue:			
Sales			
Operating Expenses:			
Advertising Expense			
Depreciation Expense—Equipment			
Depreciation Expense—Truck			
Insurance Expense			
Miscellaneous Expense			
Rent Expense			
Supplies Expense—Service			
Supplies Expense—Office			
Truck Expense			
Uncollectible Accounts Expense			
Utilities Expense			
Total Operating Expenses			
Net Income			

[9]

Lowe and Ray Gallery
Distribution of Net Income Statement
For Year Ended December 31, 20--

Jeffery Lowe:		
8% Interest on Equity		
Salary		
Share of Remaining Net Income		
Total Share of Net Income		
Mona Ray:		
8% Interest on Equity		
Salary		
Share of Remaining Net Income		
Total Share of Net Income		
Total Net Income		

22-2 ON YOUR OWN (continued)

[10]

Lowe and Ray Gallery
Owners' Equity Statement
For Year Ended December 31, 20--

Jeffery Lowe:			
Capital, January 1, 20--			
Share of Net Income			
Less Withdrawals			
Net Increase in Capital			
Capital, December 31, 20--			
Mona Ray:			
Capital, January 1, 20--			
Share of Net Income			
Less Withdrawals			
Net Increase in Capital			
Capital, December 31, 20--			
Total Owners' Equity, December 31, 20--			

22-2 ON YOUR OWN (concluded)

[11]

GENERAL JOURNAL
PAGE 12

DATE	ACCOUNT TITLE	DOC. NO.	POST. REF.	DEBIT	CREDIT

22-3 WORK TOGETHER, p. 623

Liquidation of a partnership

Cash	$12,500.00
Supplies	1,250.00
Office Equipment	15,000.00
Accumulated Depreciation—Office Equipment	8,250.00
Truck	25,500.00
Accumulated Depreciation—Truck	18,300.00
Accounts Payable	1,250.00
Jason Edson, Capital	13,450.00
Peggy Karam, Capital	13,000.00

[3]

GENERAL JOURNAL PAGE 4

	DATE	ACCOUNT TITLE	DOC. NO.	POST. REF.	DEBIT	CREDIT	
1							1
2							2
3							3
4							4
5							5
6							6
7							7
8							8
9							9
10							10
11							11
12							12
13							13
14							14
15							15
16							16
17							17
18							18
19							19
20							20

22-3 WORK TOGETHER (concluded)

[3]

CASH RECEIPTS JOURNAL PAGE 6

DATE	ACCOUNT TITLE	DOC. NO.	POST. REF.	GENERAL DEBIT	GENERAL CREDIT	ACCOUNTS RECEIVABLE CREDIT	SALES CREDIT	SALES TAX PAYABLE CREDIT	CASH DEBIT

CASH PAYMENTS JOURNAL PAGE 8

DATE	ACCOUNT TITLE	CK. NO.	POST. REF.	GENERAL DEBIT	GENERAL CREDIT	ACCOUNTS PAYABLE DEBIT	CASH CREDIT

22-3 ON YOUR OWN, p. 623

Liquidation of a partnership

Cash	$ 8,750.00
Supplies	850.00
Office Equipment	17,500.00
Accumulated Depreciation—Office Equipment	9,625.00
Truck	29,750.00
Accumulated Depreciation—Truck	21,350.00
Accounts Payable	875.00
Denise Oxley, Capital	13,000.00
Charles Tatum, Capital	12,000.00

[4]

GENERAL JOURNAL PAGE 5

DATE	ACCOUNT TITLE	DOC. NO.	POST. REF.	DEBIT	CREDIT

22-3 ON YOUR OWN (concluded)

[4]

CASH RECEIPTS JOURNAL — PAGE 8

DATE	ACCOUNT TITLE	DOC. NO.	POST. REF.	GENERAL DEBIT	GENERAL CREDIT	ACCOUNTS RECEIVABLE CREDIT	SALES CREDIT	SALES TAX PAYABLE CREDIT	CASH DEBIT

CASH PAYMENTS JOURNAL — PAGE 10

DATE	ACCOUNT TITLE	CK. NO.	POST. REF.	GENERAL DEBIT	GENERAL CREDIT	ACCOUNTS PAYABLE DEBIT	CASH CREDIT

22-1 APPLICATION PROBLEM, p. 625

Calculating partnership earnings [1]

Fixed percentage:

[2]

Percentage of total equity:

[3]

Interest on equity plus fixed percentage:

22-1 APPLICATION PROBLEM (concluded)

[4]

Salary plus fixed percentage:

[5]

Interest on equity, salary, and fixed percentage:

[6]

Interest on equity, salary, and fixed percentage (deficit):

22-2 APPLICATION PROBLEM, p. 625

Journalizing partners' withdrawals

GENERAL JOURNAL
PAGE 6

	DATE	ACCOUNT TITLE	DOC. NO.	POST. REF.	DEBIT	CREDIT	
1							1
2							2
3							3
4							4
5							5
6							6
7							7
8							8
9							9
10							10
11							11
12							12
13							13
14							14
15							15
16							16
17							17
18							18
19							19
20							20
21							21
22							22
23							23
24							24
25							25
26							26
27							27
28							28
29							29
30							30
31							31
32							32

22-2 APPLICATION PROBLEM (concluded)

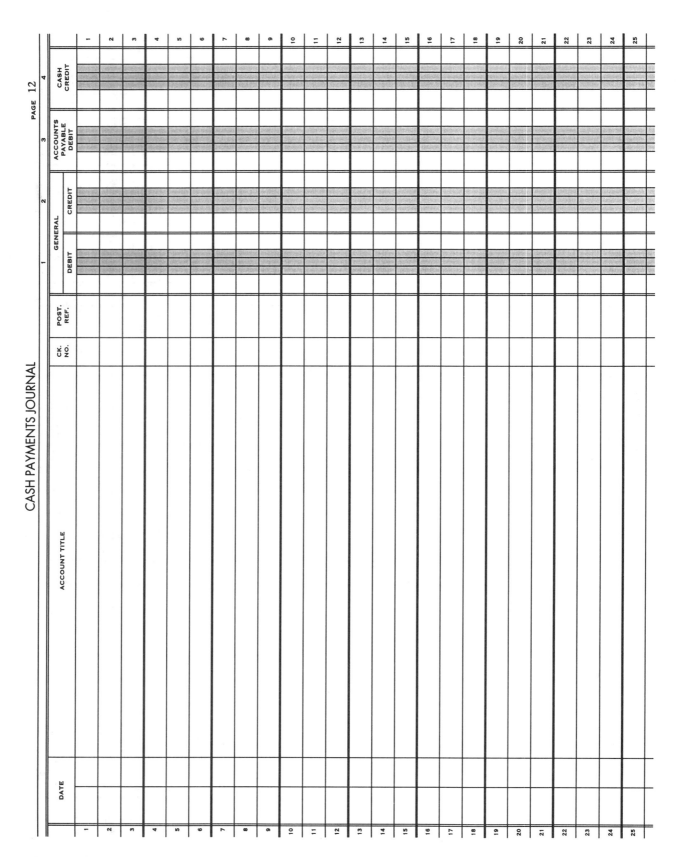

22-3 APPLICATION PROBLEM, p. 625

Completing end-of-fiscal-period work for a partnership

Plantasia
Work Sheet
For Year Ended December 31, 20--

	ACCOUNT TITLE	TRIAL BALANCE DEBIT	TRIAL BALANCE CREDIT	ADJUSTMENTS DEBIT	ADJUSTMENTS CREDIT	INCOME STATEMENT DEBIT	INCOME STATEMENT CREDIT	BALANCE SHEET DEBIT	BALANCE SHEET CREDIT
1	Cash	42711 80						42711 80	
2	Petty Cash	200 00						200 00	
3	Accounts Receivable	1952 66						1952 66	
4	Allowance for Uncollectible Accounts		19 52		(a) 1176				1366 8
5	Supplies—Plants	9118 90			(b) 7522 97			1595 93	
6	Supplies—Office	1808 10			(c) 1390 00			418 10	
7	Prepaid Insurance	1322 71			(d) 490 00			832 71	
8	Equipment	12254 00						12254 00	
9	Accum. Depr.—Equipment		2325 00		(e) 1225 00				3550 00
10	Truck	6000 00						6000 00	
11	Accum. Depr.—Truck		1830 00		(f) 900 00				2730 00
12	Accounts Payable		5948 52						5948 52
13	Susan Poole, Capital		23400 00						23400 00
14	Susan Poole, Drawing	4400 00						4400 00	
15	Ann Dodd, Capital		12600 00						12600 00
16	Ann Dodd, Drawing	2600 00						2600 00	
17	Income Summary								
18	Sales		53404 09				53404 09		
19	Advertising Expense	960 00				960 00			
20	Depr. Expense—Equipment			(e) 1225 00		1225 00			
21	Depr. Expense—Truck			(f) 900 00		900 00			
22	Insurance Expense			(d) 490 00		490 00			
23	Miscellaneous Expense	1738 96				1738 96			
24	Rent Expense	7200 00				7200 00			
25	Supp. Expense—Plants			(b) 7522 97		7522 97			
26	Supplies Expense—Office			(c) 1390 00		1390 00			
27	Truck Expense	5300 00				5300 00			
28	Uncollectible Accounts Expense			(a) 1176		1176			
29	Utilities Expense	1960 00				1960 00			
30		99527 13	99527 13	11645 13	11645 13	28804 09	53404 09	72965 20	48365 20
31	Net Income					24600 00			24600 00
32						53404 09	53404 09	72965 20	72965 20

22-3 APPLICATION PROBLEM (continued)

[1]

Plantasia
Income Statement
For Year Ended December 31, 20--

				% OF NET SALES
Operating Revenue:				
Sales				
Operating Expenses:				
Advertising Expense				
Depreciation Expense—Equipment				
Depreciation Expense—Truck				
Insurance Expense				
Miscellaneous Expense				
Rent Expense				
Supplies Expense—Plants				
Supplies Expense—Office				
Truck Expense				
Uncollectible Accounts Expense				
Utilities Expense				
Total Operating Expenses				
Net Income				

[2]

Plantasia
Distribution of Net Income Statement
For Year Ended December 31, 20--

Susan Poole:		
65.0% of Net Income		
Ann Dodd:		
35.0% of Net Income		
Total Net Income		

22-3 APPLICATION PROBLEM (continued)

[3]

Plantasia
Owners' Equity Statement
For Year Ended December 31, 20--

Susan Poole:			
Capital, January 1, 20--			
Share of Net Income			
Less Withdrawals			
Net Increase in Capital			
Capital, December 31, 20--			
Ann Dodd:			
Capital, January 1, 20--			
Share of Net Income			
Less Withdrawals			
Net Increase in Capital			
Capital, December 31, 20--			
Total Owners' Equity, December 31, 20--			

22-3 APPLICATION PROBLEM (continued)

[4]

Plantasia
Balance Sheet
December 31, 20--

ASSETS			
Current Assets:			
Cash			
Petty Cash			
Accounts Receivable			
Less Allowance for Uncollectible Accounts			
Supplies—Plants			
Supplies—Office			
Prepaid Insurance			
Total Current Assets			
Plant Assets:			
Equipment			
Less Accumulated Depr.—Equipment			
Truck			
Less Accumulated Depr.—Truck			
Total Plant Assets			
Total Assets			
LIABILITIES			
Accounts Payable			
Total Liabilities			
OWNERS' EQUITY			
Susan Poole, Capital			
Ann Dodd, Capital			
Total Owners' Equity			
Total Liabilities and Owners' Equity			

22-3 APPLICATION PROBLEM (continued)

[5, 6]

GENERAL JOURNAL PAGE 12

DATE	ACCOUNT TITLE	DOC. NO.	POST. REF.	DEBIT	CREDIT

22-3 APPLICATION PROBLEM

Extra form

GENERAL JOURNAL

DATE	ACCOUNT TITLE	DOC. NO.	POST. REF.	DEBIT	CREDIT

22-4 APPLICATION PROBLEM, p. 626

Liquidating a partnership

GENERAL JOURNAL PAGE 7

	DATE	ACCOUNT TITLE	DOC. NO.	POST. REF.	DEBIT	CREDIT	
1							1
2							2
3							3
4							4
5							5
6							6
7							7
8							8
9							9
10							10
11							11
12							12
13							13
14							14
15							15
16							16
17							17
18							18
19							19
20							20
21							21
22							22
23							23
24							24
25							25
26							26
27							27
28							28
29							29
30							30
31							31

22-4 APPLICATION PROBLEM (concluded)

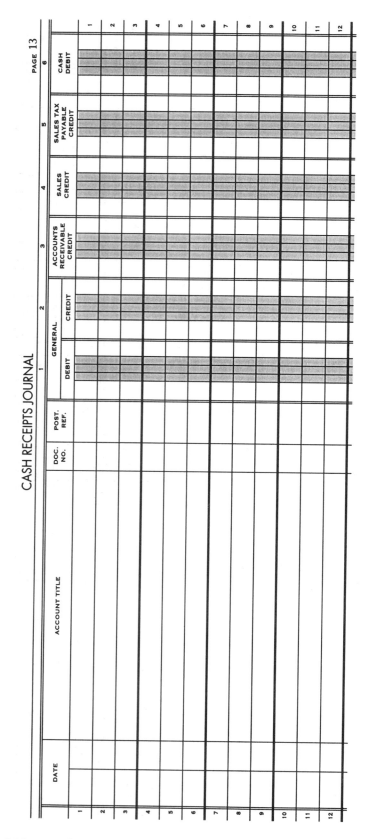

22-5 MASTERY PROBLEM, p. 627

Completing end-of-fiscal-period work for a partnership

J & L Service
Work Sheet
For Year Ended December 31, 20--

#	ACCOUNT TITLE	TRIAL BALANCE DEBIT	TRIAL BALANCE CREDIT	ADJUSTMENTS DEBIT	ADJUSTMENTS CREDIT	INCOME STATEMENT DEBIT	INCOME STATEMENT CREDIT	BALANCE SHEET DEBIT	BALANCE SHEET CREDIT
1	Cash	3016584						3016584	
2	Petty Cash	30000						30000	
3	Accounts Receivable	179938						179938	
4	Allowance for Uncollectible Accounts		2798		(a) 10700				13498
5	Supplies—Service	840307			(b) 693242			147065	
6	Supplies—Office	160000			(c) 128089			31911	
7	Prepaid Insurance	121887			(d) 45155			76732	
8	Equipment	1362100						1362100	
9	Accum. Depr.—Equipment		214100		(e) 136200				350300
10	Truck	1200000						1200000	
11	Accum. Depr.—Truck		271500		(f) 160000				431500
12	Accounts Payable		549032						549032
13	Sarah Saxon, Capital		1500000						1500000
14	Sarah Saxon, Drawing	800000						800000	
15	Jane Rolf, Capital		1200000						1200000
16	Jane Rolf, Drawing	1000000						1000000	
17	Income Summary								
18	Sales		8283826				8283826		
19	Advertising Expense	80000				80000			
20	Depr. Expense—Equipment			(e) 136200		136200			
21	Depr. Expense—Truck			(f) 160000		160000			
22	Insurance Expense			(d) 45155		45155			
23	Miscellaneous Expense	1602440				1602440			
24	Rent Expense	960000				960000			
25	Supplies Expense—Service			(b) 693242		693242			
26	Supplies Expense—Office			(c) 128089		128089			
27	Truck Expense	488000				488000			
28	Uncollectible Accounts Expense			(a) 10700		10700			
29	Utilities Expense	180000				180000			
30		12021256	12021256	1173386	1173386	4483826	8283826	7844330	4044330
31	Net Income					3800000			3800000
32						8283826	8283826	7844330	7844330

22-5 MASTERY PROBLEM (continued)

[1]

J & L Service
Income Statement
For Year Ended December 31, 20--

			% OF NET SALES
Operating Revenue:			
Sales			
Operating Expenses:			
Advertising Expense			
Depreciation Expense—Equipment			
Depreciation Expense—Truck			
Insurance Expense			
Miscellaneous Expense			
Rent Expense			
Supplies Expense—Service			
Supplies Expense—Office			
Truck Expense			
Uncollectible Accounts Expense			
Utilities Expense			
Total Operating Expenses			
Net Income			

[2]

J & L Service
Distribution of Net Income Statement
For Year Ended December 31, 20--

Sarah Saxon:		
10.0% Interest on Equity		
Salary		
Share of Remaining Net income		
Total Share of Net Income		
Jane Rolf:		
10.0% Interest on Equity		
Salary		
Share of Remaining Net income		
Total Share of Net Income		
Total Net Income		

22-5 MASTERY PROBLEM (continued)

[3]

J & L Service
Owners' Equity Statement
For Year Ended December 31, 20--

Sarah Saxon:			
Capital, January 1, 20--			
Share of Net Income			
Less Withdrawals			
Net Increase in Capital			
Capital, December 31, 20--			
Jane Rolf:			
Capital, January 1, 20--			
Share of Net Income			
Less Withdrawals			
Net Increase in Capital			
Capital, December 31, 20--			
Total Owners' Equity, December 31, 20--			

22-5 MASTERY PROBLEM (continued)

[4]

J & L Service
Balance Sheet
December 31, 20--

ASSETS			
Current Assets:			
Cash			
Petty Cash			
Accounts Receivable			
Less Allowance for Uncollectible Accounts			
Supplies—Service			
Supplies—Office			
Prepaid Insurance			
Total Current Assets			
Plant Assets:			
Equipment			
Less Accumulated Depr.—Equipment			
Truck			
Less Accumulated Depr.—Truck			
Total Plant Assets			
Total Assets			
LIABILITIES			
Accounts Payable			
Total Liabilities			
OWNERS' EQUITY			
Sarah Saxon, Capital			
Jane Rolf, Capital			
Total Owners' Equity			
Total Liabilities and Owners' Equity			

22-5 MASTERY PROBLEM (continued)

[5, 6]

GENERAL JOURNAL — PAGE 12

DATE	ACCOUNT TITLE	DOC. NO.	POST. REF.	DEBIT	CREDIT

22-5 MASTERY PROBLEM

Extra form

GENERAL JOURNAL

DATE	ACCOUNT TITLE	DOC. NO.	POST. REF.	DEBIT	CREDIT

22-6 CHALLENGE PROBLEM, p. 627

Completing end-of-fiscal-period work for a partnership

D & E Sales
Work Sheet
For Year Ended December 31, 20--

	ACCOUNT TITLE	TRIAL BALANCE DEBIT	TRIAL BALANCE CREDIT	ADJUSTMENTS DEBIT	ADJUSTMENTS CREDIT	INCOME STATEMENT DEBIT	INCOME STATEMENT CREDIT	BALANCE SHEET DEBIT	BALANCE SHEET CREDIT
1	Cash	6806 99						6806 99	
2	Petty Cash	400 00						400 00	
3	Accounts Receivable	560 36						560 36	
4	Allowance for Uncollectible Accounts		12 33		(a) 34 52				46 85
5	Merchandise Inventory	12646 40		(b) 354 69				12291 71	
6	Supplies—Sales	1285 46			(c) 629 88			655 58	
7	Supplies—Office	914 94			(d) 411 72			503 22	
8	Prepaid Insurance	1260 72			(e) 642 97			617 75	
9	Equipment	11597 00						11597 00	
10	Accum. Depr.—Equipment		2331 00		(f) 1159 70				3490 70
11	Truck	7340 00						7340 00	
12	Accum. Depr.—Truck		1512 04		(g) 734 00				2246 04
13	Accounts Payable		4839 02						4839 02
14	Theresa Doron, Capital		24250 00						24250 00
15	Theresa Doron, Drawing	6000 00						6000 00	
16	Roy Eden, Capital		21500 00						21500 00
17	Roy Eden, Drawing	5000 00						5000 00	
18	Income Summary			(b) 354 69		354 69			
19	Sales		44176 74				44176 74		
20	Purchases	28869 38				28869 38			
21	Purchases Returns and Allowances		317 56				317 56		
22	Advertising Expense	750 00				750 00			
23	Depr. Expense—Equipment			(f) 1159 70		1159 70			
24	Depr. Expense—Truck			(g) 734 00		734 00			
25	Insurance Expense			(e) 642 97		642 97			
26	Miscellaneous Expense	928 00				928 00			
27	Rent Expense	8400 00				8400 00			
28	Supplies Expense—Sales			(c) 629 88		629 88			
29	Supplies Expense—Office			(d) 411 72		411 72			
30	Truck Expense	5227 94				5227 94			
31	Uncollectible Accounts Expense			(a) 34 52		34 52			
32	Utilities Expense	951 50				951 50			
33		98938 69	98938 69	3967 48	3967 48	49094 30	44494 30	51772 61	56372 61
34	Net Loss						4600 00	4600 00	
35						49094 30	49094 30	56372 61	56372 61

22-6 CHALLENGE PROBLEM (continued)

[1]

D & E Sales
Income Statement
For Year Ended December 31, 20--

				% OF NET SALES
Operating Revenue:				
Sales				
Cost of Merchandise Sold:				
Merchandise Inventory, Jan. 1, 20--				
Purchases				
Less Purchases Returns & Allowances				
Total Cost of Mdse. Available for Sale				
Less Mdse. Inventory, Dec. 31, 20--				
Cost of Merchandise Sold				
Gross Profit on Operations				
Operating Expenses:				
Advertising Expense				
Depreciation Expense—Equipment				
Depreciation Expense—Truck				
Insurance Expense				
Miscellaneous Expense				
Rent Expense				
Supplies Expense—Sales				
Supplies Expense—Office				
Truck Expense				
Uncollectible Accounts Expense				
Utilities Expense				
Total Operating Expenses				
Net Loss				

22-6 CHALLENGE PROBLEM (continued)

[2]

D & E Sales
Distribution of Net Income Statement
For Year Ended December 31, 20--

Theresa Doran:		
10% Interest on Equity		
Salary		
Less Share of Net Deficit		
Total Share of Net Loss		
Roy Eden:		
10% Interest on Equity		
Salary		
Less Share of Net Deficit		
Total Share of Net Loss		
Total Net Loss		

Computation of share of net deficit:

[3]

D & E Sales
Owners' Equity Statement
For Year Ended December 31, 20--

Theresa Doran:		
Capital, January 1, 20--		
Share of Net Loss		
Plus Withdrawals		
Net Decrease in Capital		
Capital, December 31, 20--		
Roy Eden:		
Capital, January 1, 20--		
Share of Net Loss		
Plus Withdrawals		
Net Decrease in Capital		
Capital, December 31, 20--		
Total Owners' Equity, December 31, 20--		

22-6 CHALLENGE PROBLEM (concluded)

[4]

D & E Sales

Balance Sheet

December 31, 20--

ASSETS			
Current Assets:			
Cash			
Petty Cash			
Accounts Receivable			
Less Allowance for Uncollectible Accounts			
Merchandise Inventory			
Supplies—Sales			
Supplies—Office			
Prepaid Insurance			
Total Current Assets			
Plant Assets:			
Equipment			
Less Accumulated Depr.—Equipment			
Truck			
Less Accumulated Depr.—Truck			
Total Plant Assets			
Total Assets			
LIABILITIES			
Accounts Payable			
Total Liabilities			
OWNERS' EQUITY			
Theresa Doran, Capital			
Roy Eden, Capital			
Total Owners' Equity			
Total Liabilities and Owners' Equity			

23-1 WORK TOGETHER, p. 640

ON YOUR OWN, p. 640

Journalizing governmental operating budgets [6, 7]

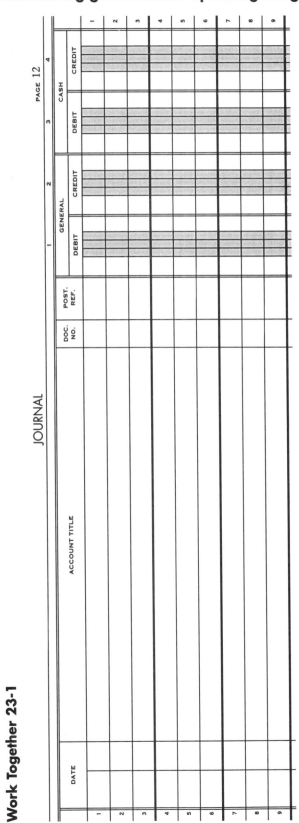

Name ______________________ Date ____________ Class ____________

23-1 WORK TOGETHER ON YOUR OWN

Extra form

JOURNAL

PAGE

					1	2	3	4	
	DATE	ACCOUNT TITLE	DOC. NO.	POST. REF.	GENERAL DEBIT	GENERAL CREDIT	CASH DEBIT	CASH CREDIT	
1									1
2									2
3									3
4									4
5									5
6									6
7									7
8									8
9									9
10									10
11									11
12									12
13									13
14									14
15									15
16									16
17									17
18									18
19									19
20									20
21									21
22									22
23									23
24									24
25									25

23-2 WORK TOGETHER, p. 644

Journalizing governmental revenue transactions [4]

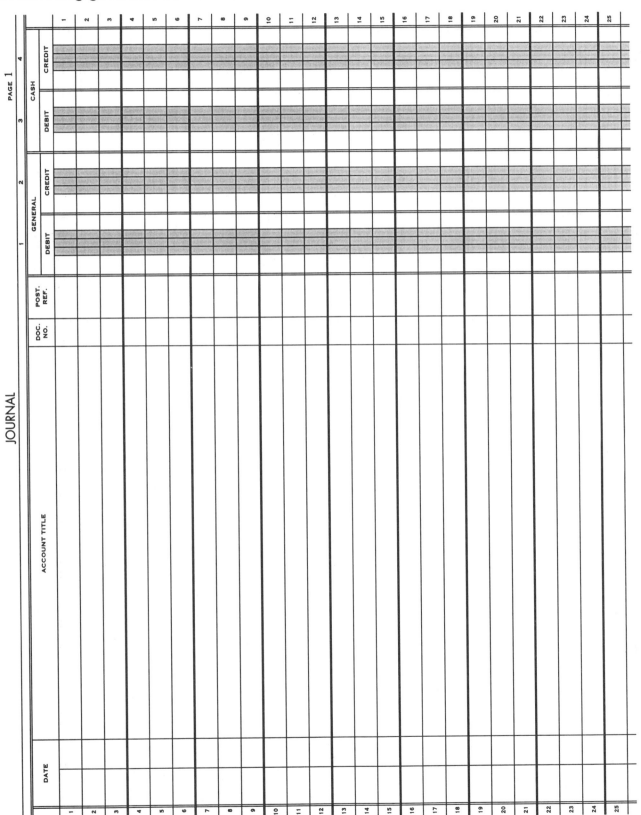

23-2 WORK TOGETHER

Extra form

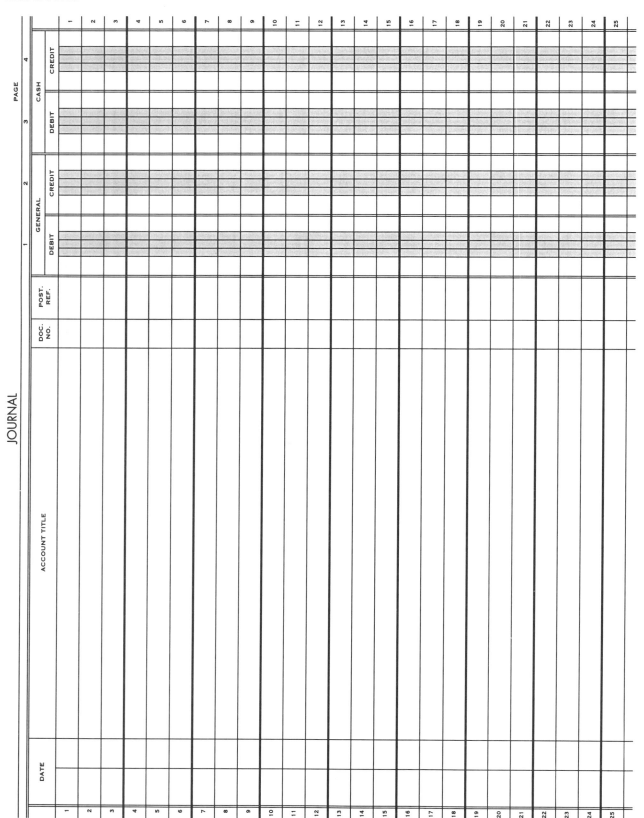

23-2 ON YOUR OWN, p. 644

Journalizing governmental revenue transactions [5]

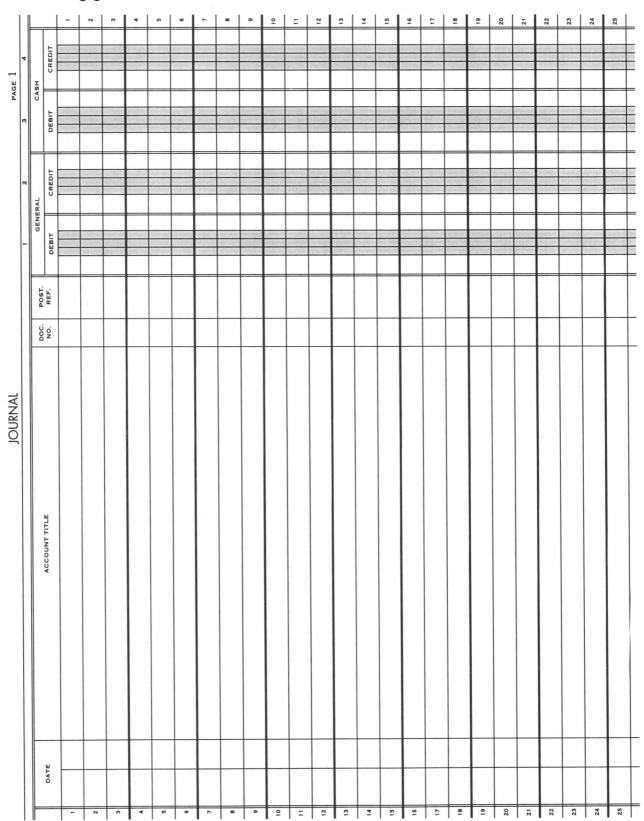

23-2 ON YOUR OWN

Extra form

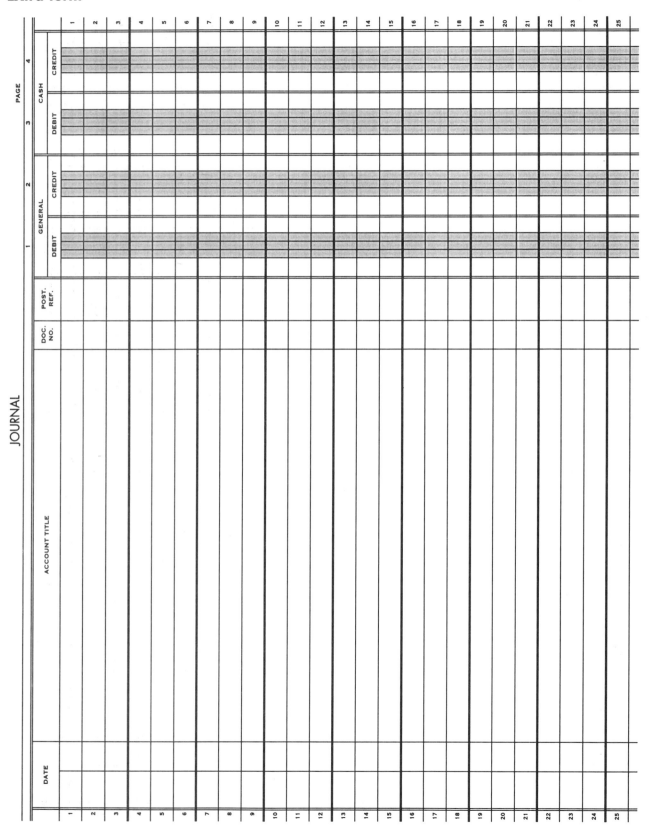

23-3 WORK TOGETHER, p. 651

Journalizing governmental encumbrances, expenditures, and other transactions [5]

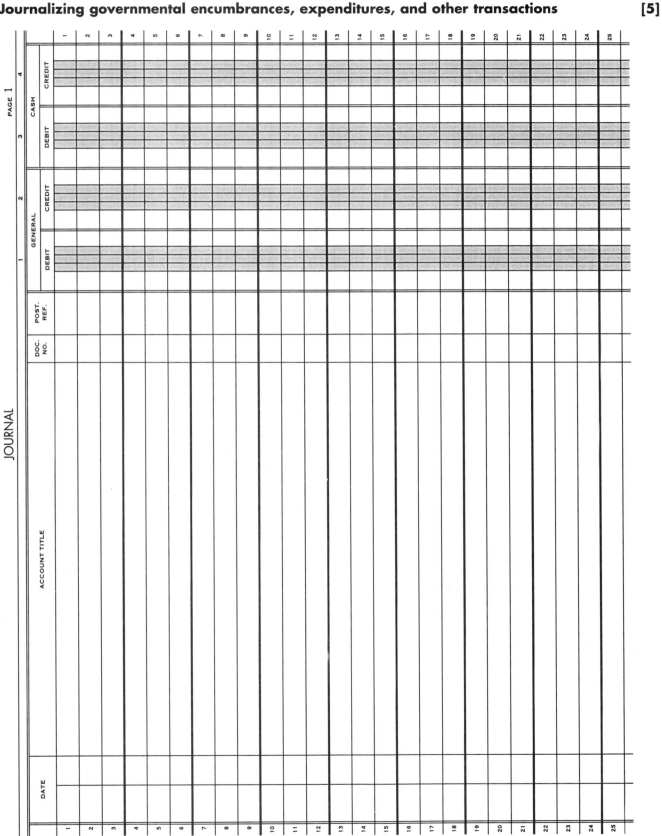

23-3 WORK TOGETHER

Extra form

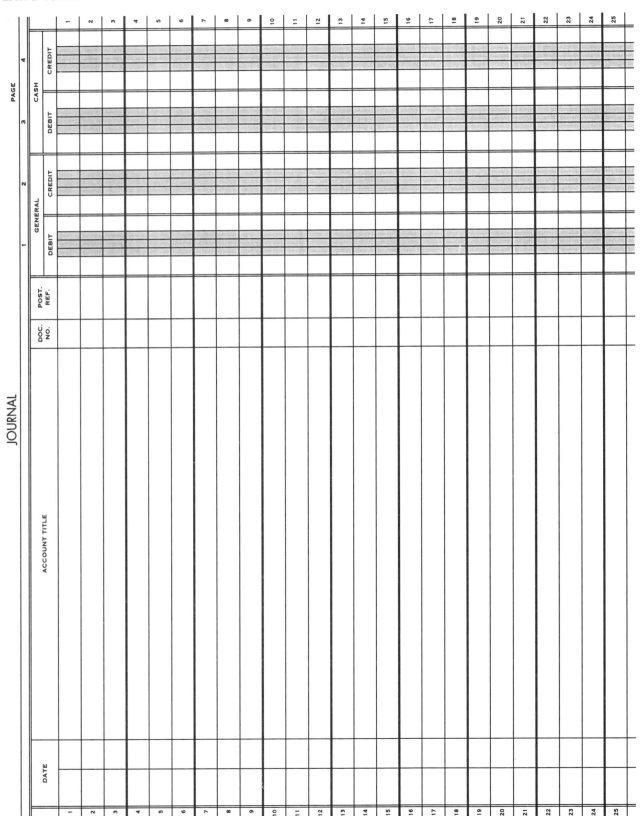

23-3 ON YOUR OWN, p. 652

Journalizing governmental encumbrances, expenditures, and other transactions [6]

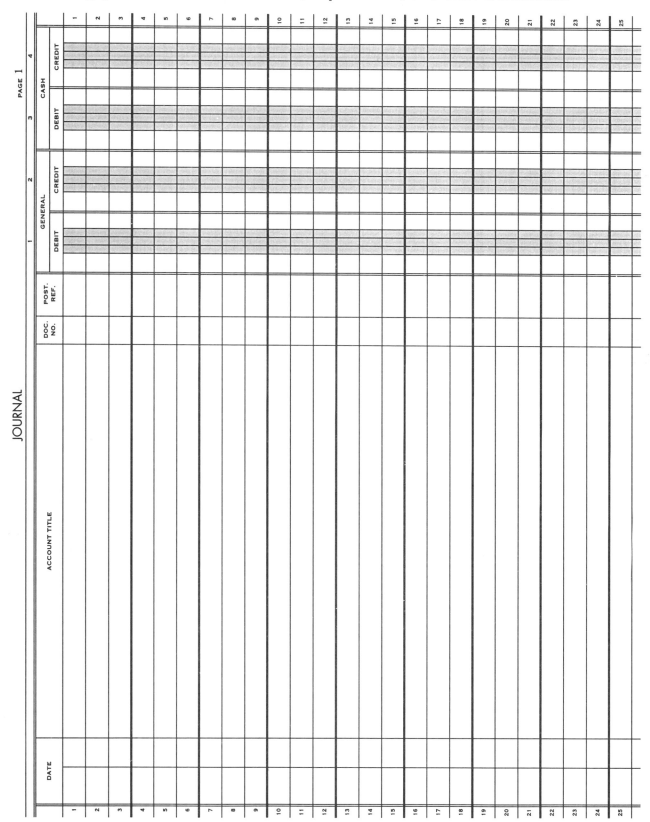

23-3 ON YOUR OWN

Extra form

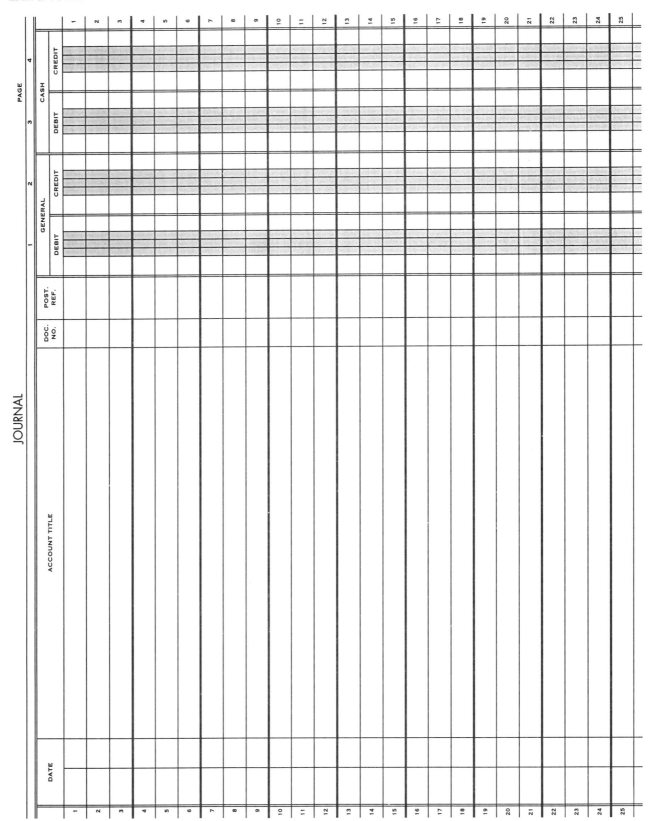

23-1 APPLICATION PROBLEM, p. 654

Journalizing governmental operating budgets

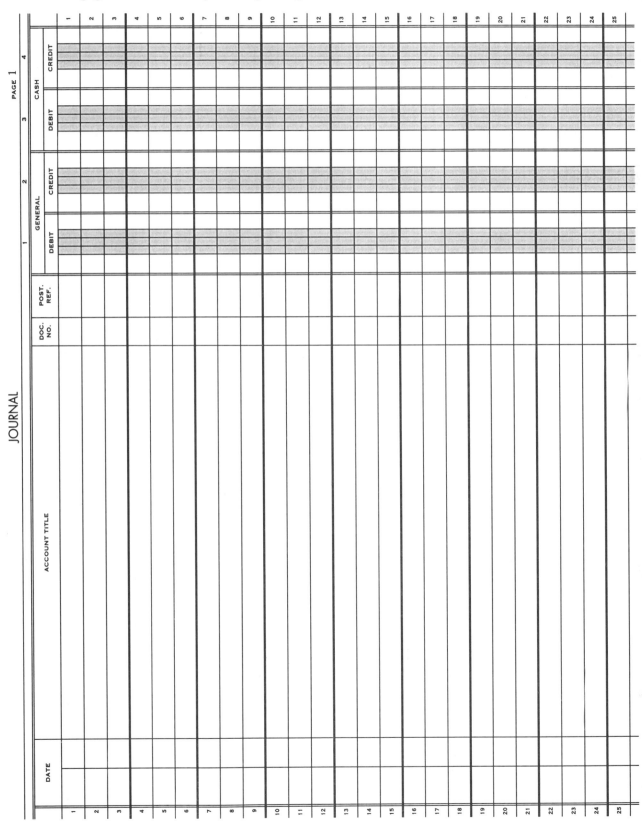

23-1 APPLICATION PROBLEM

Extra form

23-2 APPLICATION PROBLEM, p. 654

Journalizing governmental revenue transactions

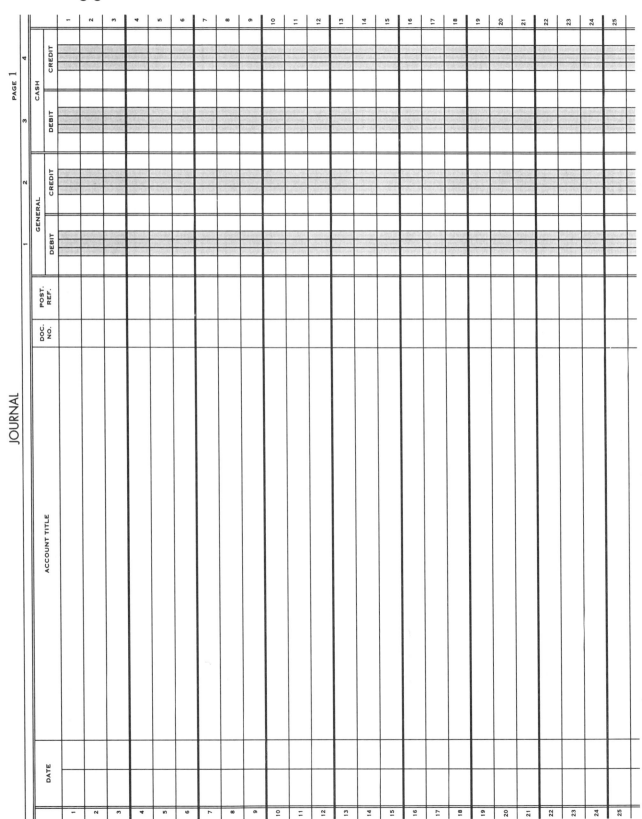

23-2 APPLICATION PROBLEM

Extra form

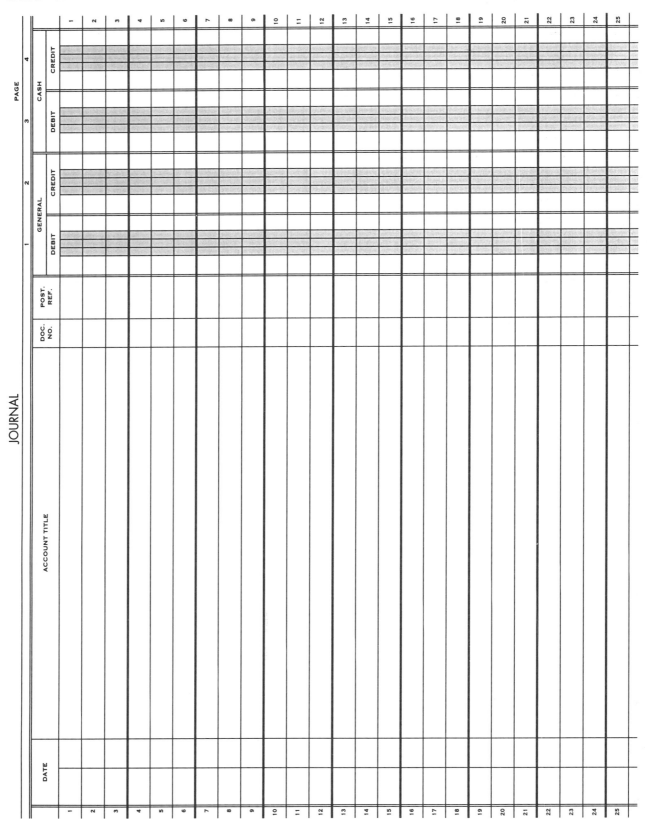

23-3 APPLICATION PROBLEM, p. 654

Journalizing governmental encumbrances, expenditures, and other transactions

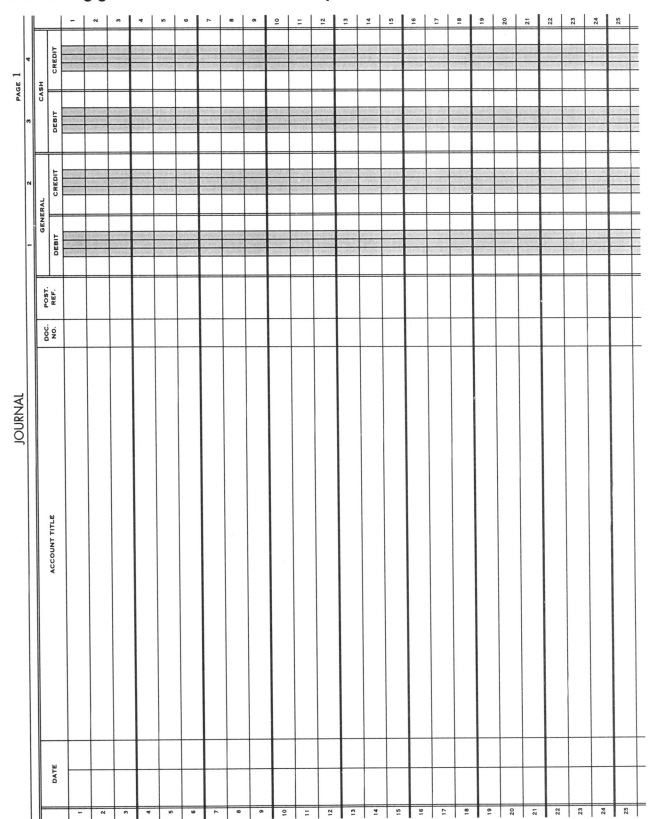

23-3 APPLICATION PROBLEM

Extra form

23-4 MASTERY PROBLEM, p. 655

Journalizing governmental transactions

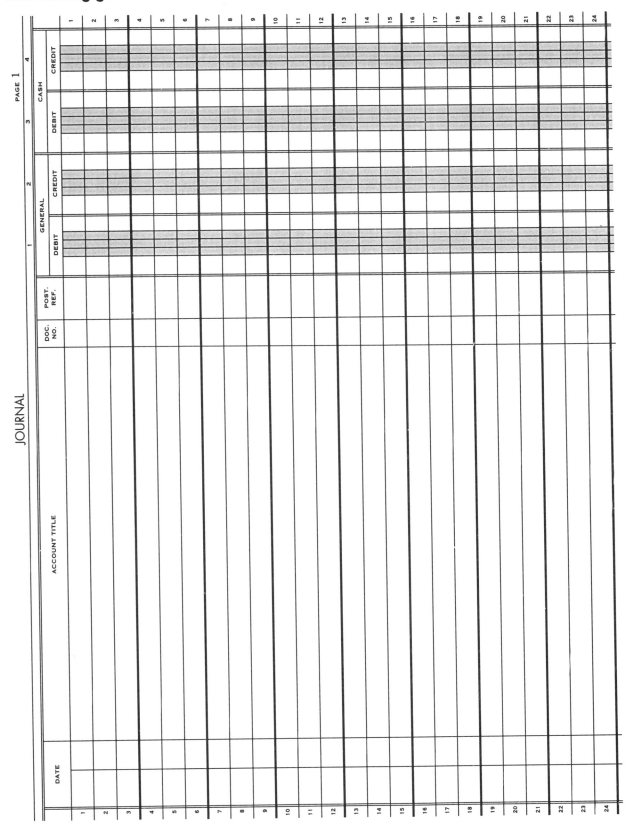

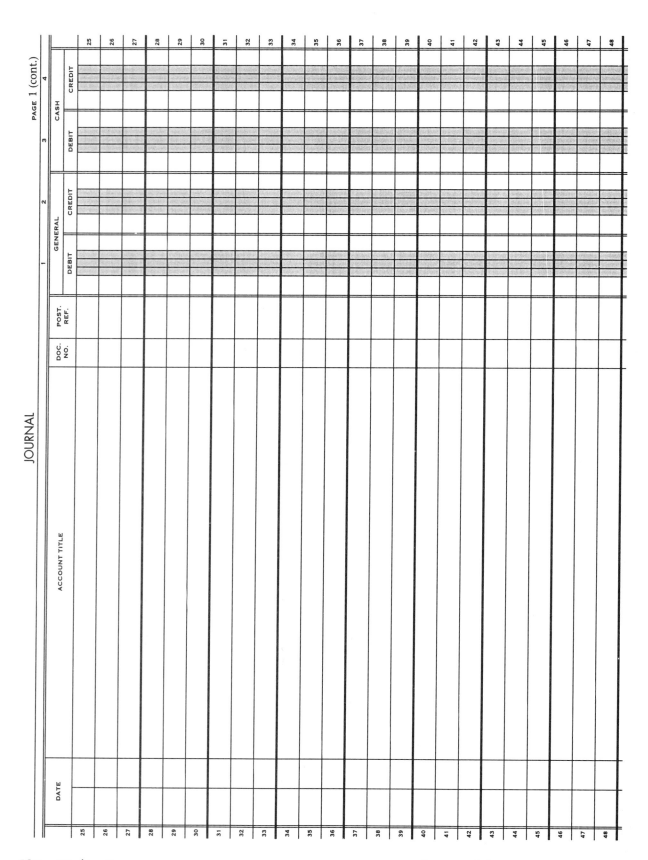

23-5 CHALLENGE PROBLEM, p. 656

Journalizing governmental transactions

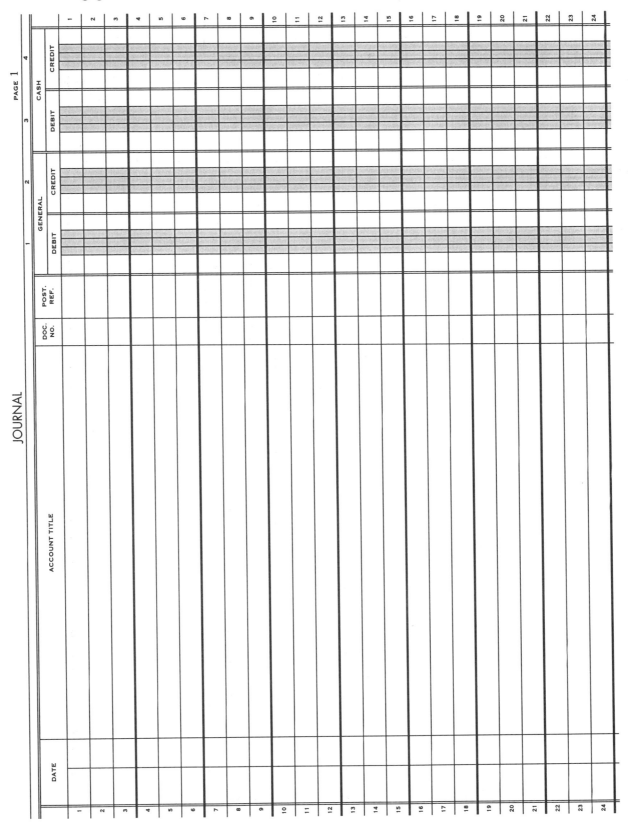

Chapter 23 Budgeting and Accounting for a Not-for-Profit Organization • 427

23-5 CHALLENGE PROBLEM (concluded)

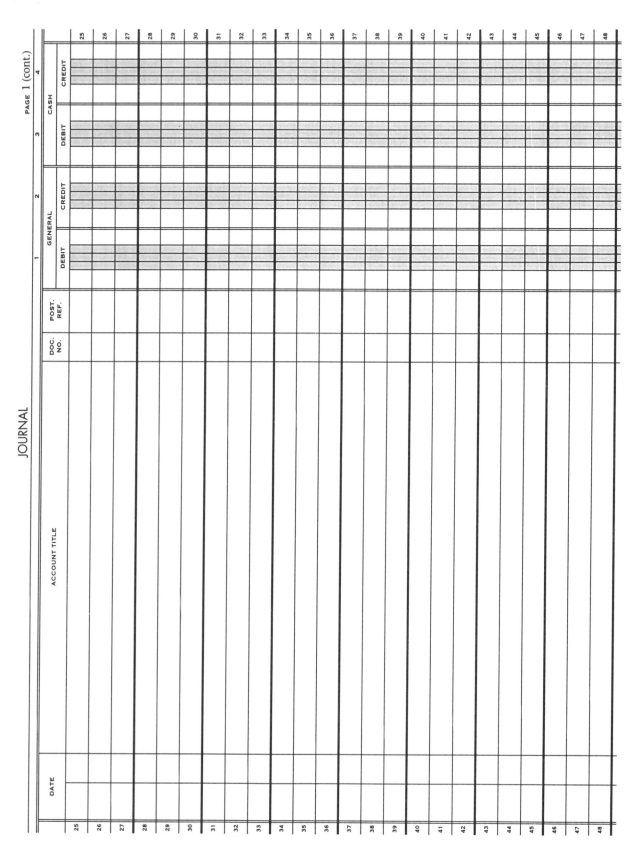

24-1 WORK TOGETHER, p. 667

Preparing a work sheet for a governmental organization [5, 6]

Town of Anoka General Fund
Work Sheet
For Year Ended December 31, 20--

#	ACCOUNT TITLE	TRIAL BALANCE DEBIT	TRIAL BALANCE CREDIT	ADJUSTMENTS DEBIT	ADJUSTMENTS CREDIT	REVENUES/EXPENDITURES DEBIT	REVENUES/EXPENDITURES CREDIT	BALANCE SHEET DEBIT	BALANCE SHEET CREDIT
1	Cash	71 651 00							
2	Taxes Receivable—Current								
3	Allow. for Uncoll. Taxes—Curren.								
4	Taxes Receivable—Delinquen.	12 197 00							
5	Allow. for Uncoll. Taxes—Delinquent		6 824 00						
6	Interest Receivable								
7	Allow. for Uncoll. Interest								
8	Inventory of Supplies								
9	Investments—Short Term		33 108 00						
10	Accounts Payable								
11	Notes Payable		8 550 00						
12	Unreserved Fund Balance		15 50 00						
13	Reserve for Encumb.—Current Year								
14	Reserve for Encumb.—Prior Year								
15	Reserve for Inventory of Supplies								
16	Property Tax Revenue		1600 411 00						
17	Interest Revenue		7 485 00						
18	Other Revenue		2 230 00						
19	Expend.—Personnel, Gen. Gov't	258 472 00							
20	Expend.—Supplies, Gen. Gov't	10 495 00							
21	Expend.—Other Chgs., Gen. Gov't	113 060 00							
22	Expend.—Cap. Outlays, Gen. Gov't	16 978 00							
23	Expend.—Personnel, Pub. Saf.	549 712 00							
24	Expend.—Supplies, Pub. Saf.	18 663 00							
25	Expend.—Other Chgs., Pub. Saf.	153 818 00							
26	Expend.—Cap. Outlays, Pub. Saf.	87 493 00							
27	Expend.—Personnel, Pub. Wks.	112 186 00							

Chapter 24 Financial Reporting for a Not-for-Profit Organization • 429

24-1 WORK TOGETHER (concluded)

[5, 6]

#	ACCOUNT TITLE	TRIAL BALANCE DEBIT	TRIAL BALANCE CREDIT	ADJUSTMENTS DEBIT	ADJUSTMENTS CREDIT	REVENUES/EXPENDITURES DEBIT	REVENUES/EXPENDITURES CREDIT	BALANCE SHEET DEBIT	BALANCE SHEET CREDIT
28	Expend.—Supplies, Pub. Wks.	5 895 00							
29	Expend.—Other Chgs., Pub. Wks.	96 224 00							
30	Expend.—Cap. Outlays, Pub. Wks.	50 781 00							
31	Expend.—Personnel, Rec.	56 400 00							
32	Expend.—Supplies, Rec.	4 708 00							
33	Expend.—Other Chgs., Rec.	25 545 00							
34	Expend.—Cap. Outlays, Rec.	14 330 00							
35	Estimated Revenues	1 611 450 00							
36	Appropriations		1 579 051 00						
37	Budgetary Fund Balance		32 399 00						
38	Encumb.—Supplies, Pub. Wks.	1 550 00							
39		3 271 608 00	3 271 608 00						
40									
41									
42									
43									
44									
45									
46									
47									
48									
49									
50									
51									
52									
53									
54									

24-1 ON YOUR OWN, p. 667

Preparing a work sheet for a governmental organization [7, 8]

Town of Annandale General Fund
Work Sheet
For Year Ended December 31, 20--

#	ACCOUNT TITLE	TRIAL BALANCE DEBIT	TRIAL BALANCE CREDIT	ADJUSTMENTS DEBIT	ADJUSTMENTS CREDIT	REVENUES/EXPENDITURES DEBIT	REVENUES/EXPENDITURES CREDIT	BALANCE SHEET DEBIT	BALANCE SHEET CREDIT
1	Cash	77 187 00							
2	Taxes Receivable—Current								
3	Allow. for Uncoll. Taxes—Current								
4	Taxes Receivable—Delinquent	10 586 00							
5	Allow. for Uncoll. Taxes—Delinquent		5 918 00						
6	Interest Receivable								
7	Allow. for Uncoll. Interest								
8	Inventory of Supplies								
9	Investments—Short Term								
10	Accounts Payable		35 714 00						
11	Notes Payable								
12	Unreserved Fund Balance		27 319 00						
13	Reserve for Encumb.—Current Year		1 900 00						
14	Reserve for Encumb.—Prior Year								
15	Reserve for Inventory of Supplies								
16	Property Tax Revenue		1 490 195 00						
17	Interest Revenue		6 515 00						
18	Other Revenue		3 790 00						
19	Expend.—Personnel, Gen. Gov't	231 404 00							
20	Expend.—Supplies, Gen. Gov't	11 277 00							
21	Expend.—Other Chgs., Gen. Gov't	110 888 00							
22	Expend.—Cap. Outlays, Gen. Gov't	15 663 00							
23	Expend.—Personnel, Pub. Saf.	538 790 00							
24	Expend.—Supplies, Pub. Saf.	16 921 00							
25	Expend.—Other Chgs., Pub. Saf.	150 093 00							
26	Expend.—Cap. Outlays, Pub. Saf.	87 500 00							
27	Expend.—Personnel, Pub. Wks.	111 962 00							

24-1 ON YOUR OWN (concluded)

[7, 8]

	ACCOUNT TITLE	TRIAL BALANCE DEBIT	TRIAL BALANCE CREDIT		
28	Expend.—Supplies, Pub. Wks.	4924 00			
29	Expend.—Other Chgs., Pub. Wks.	95675 00			
30	Expend.—Cap. Outlays, Pub. Wks.	5000 00			
31	Expend.—Personnel, Rec.	14000 00			
32	Expend.—Supplies, Rec.	3943 00			
33	Expend.—Other Chgs., Rec.	24856 00			
34	Expend.—Cap. Outlays, Rec.	13782 00			
35	Estimated Revenues	150150 00			
36	Appropriations		148500 00		
37	Budgetary Fund Balance		1650 00		
38	Encumb.—Supplies, Recreation	1900 00			
39		307285 100	307285 100		

Columns: 1 Trial Balance Debit, 2 Trial Balance Credit, 3 Adjustments Debit, 4 Adjustments Credit, 5 Revenues/Expenditures Debit, 6 Revenues/Expenditures Credit, 7 Balance Sheet Debit, 8 Balance Sheet Credit

Name _____ Date _____ Class _____

24-2 WORK TOGETHER, p. 671

Preparing financial statements for a governmental organization

The work sheet from Work Together 24-1 is needed to complete this problem.

Town of Anoka Annual Operating Budget—General Fund For Year Ended December 31, 20--		
ESTIMATED REVENUES		
Property Tax	$1,600,411.00	
Interest	9,000.00	
Other	2,039.00	
Total Estimated Revenues		$1,611,450.00
ESTIMATED EXPENDITURES AND BUDGETARY FUND BALANCE		
General Government:		
Personnel	$ 268,550.00	
Supplies	63,800.00	
Other Charges	27,925.00	
Capital Outlays	39,725.00	
Total General Government		$ 400,000.00
Public Safety:		
Personnel	$ 398,500.00	
Supplies	125,750.00	
Other Charges	126,250.00	
Capital Outlays	160,500.00	
Total Public Safety		811,000.00
Public Works:		
Personnel	$ 135,800.00	
Supplies	49,250.00	
Other Charges	56,775.00	
Capital Outlays	24,726.00	
Total Public Works		266,551.00
Recreation:		
Personnel	$ 38,600.00	
Supplies	23,800.00	
Other Charges	16,550.00	
Capital Outlays	22,550.00	
Total Recreation		101,500.00
Total Estimated Expenditures		$1,579,051.00
Budgetary Fund Balance		32,399.00
Total Estimated Expenditures and Budgetary Fund Balance		$1,611.450.00

24-2 WORK TOGETHER (continued)

[5]

Town of Anoka General Fund

Statement of Revenues, Expenditures, and Changes in Fund Balance—Budget and Actual

For Year Ended December 31, 20--

	BUDGET	ACTUAL	VARIANCE—FAVORABLE (UNFAVORABLE)
Revenues:			
Property Tax Revenue			
Interest Revenue			
Other Revenue			
Total Revenues			
Expenditures:			
General Government			
Public Safety			
Public Works			
Recreation			
Total Expenditures			
Excess of Revenues Over Expenditures			
Less Outstanding Encumbrances, Dec. 31, 20--			
Increase in Unreserved Fund Balance for Year			
Unreserved Fund Balance, Jan. 1, 20--			
Unreserved Fund Balance, Dec. 31, 20--			

24-2 WORK TOGETHER (concluded)

[6]

Town of Anoka General Fund
Balance Sheet
December 31, 20--

ASSETS			
Cash			
Taxes Receivable—Delinquent			
Less Allowance for Uncoll. Taxes —Delinquent			
Interest Receivable			
Less Allowance for Uncollectible Interest			
Inventory of Supplies			
Total Assets			
LIABILITIES AND FUND EQUITY			
Liabilities:			
Accounts Payable			
Fund Equity:			
Unreserved Fund Balance			
Reserve for Encumbrances—Prior Year			
Reserve for Inventory of Supplies			
Total Fund Equity			
Total Liabilities and Fund Equity			

24-2 WORK TOGETHER

Extra form

24-2 ON YOUR OWN, p. 671

Preparing financial statements for a governmental organization

The work sheet from On Your Own 24-1 is needed to complete this problem.

Town of Annandale
Annual Operating Budget—General Fund
For Year Ended December 31, 20--

ESTIMATED REVENUES		
Property Tax	$1,490,195.00	
Interest	7,638.00	
Other	3,667.00	
Total Estimated Revenues		$1,501,500.00
ESTIMATED EXPENDITURES AND BUDGETARY FUND BALANCE		
General Government:		
Personnel	$259,250.00	
Supplies	54,500.00	
Other Charges	23,775.00	
Capital Outlays	31,873.00	
Total General Government		$369,398.00
Public Safety:		
Personnel	$425,550.00	
Supplies	101,375.00	
Other Charges	118,266.00	
Capital Outlays	150,000.00	
Total Public Safety		795,191.00
Public Works:		
Personnel	$127,900.00	
Supplies	54,921.00	
Other Charges	55,316.00	
Capital Outlays	25,550.00	
Total Public Works		263,687.00
Recreation:		
Personnel	$19,650.00	
Supplies	10,950.00	
Other Charges	7,624.00	
Capital Outlays	18,500.00	
Total Recreation		56,724.00
Total Estimated Expenditures		$1,485,000.00
Budgetary Fund Balance		16,500.00
Total Estimated Expenditures and Budgetary Fund Balance		$1,501,500.00

24-2 ON YOUR OWN (continued)

[7]

Town of Annandale General Fund

Statement of Revenues, Expenditures, and Changes in Fund Balance—Budget and Actual

For Year Ended December 31, 20--

	BUDGET	ACTUAL	VARIANCE—FAVORABLE (UNFAVORABLE)
Revenues:			
Property Tax Revenue			
Interest Revenue			
Other Revenue			
Total Revenues			
Expenditures:			
General Government			
Public Safety			
Public Works			
Recreation			
Total Expenditures			
Excess of Revenues Over Expenditures			
Less Outstanding Encumbrances, Dec. 31, 20--			
Increase in Unreserved Fund Balance for Year			
Unreserved Fund Balance, Jan. 1, 20--			
Unreserved Fund Balance, Dec. 31, 20--			

24-2 ON YOUR OWN (concluded)

[8]

Town of Annandale General Fund
Balance Sheet
December 31, 20--

ASSETS			
Cash			
Taxes Receivable—Delinquent			
Less Allowance for Uncoll. Taxes —Delinquent			
Interest Receivable			
Less Allowance for Uncollectible Interest			
Inventory of Supplies			
Total Assets			
LIABILITIES AND FUND EQUITY			
Liabilities:			
Accounts Payable			
Fund Equity:			
Unreserved Fund Balance			
Reserve for Encumbrances—Prior Year			
Reserve for Inventory of Supplies			
Total Fund Equity			
Total Liabilities and Fund Equity			

24-2 ON YOUR OWN

Extra form

24-3 WORK TOGETHER, p. 674

Journalizing adjusting and closing entries for a governmental organization [5, 6]

The work sheet from Work Together 24-1 is needed to complete this problem.

JOURNAL PAGE 40

24-3 WORK TOGETHER (concluded)

[5, 6]

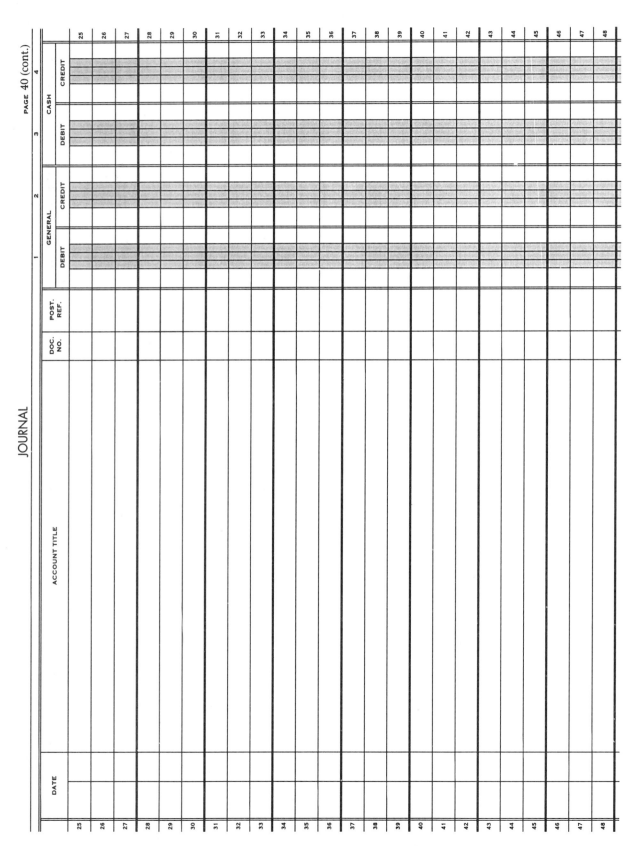

24-3 ON YOUR OWN, p. 674

Journalizing adjusting and closing entries for a governmental organization [7, 8]

The work sheet from On Your Own 24-1 is needed to complete this problem.

JOURNAL PAGE 52

DATE	ACCOUNT TITLE	DOC. NO.	POST. REF.	GENERAL DEBIT	GENERAL CREDIT	CASH DEBIT	CASH CREDIT

24-3 ON YOUR OWN (concluded)

[7, 8]

JOURNAL

PAGE 52 (cont.)

	DATE	ACCOUNT TITLE	DOC. NO.	POST. REF.	1 GENERAL DEBIT	2 GENERAL CREDIT	3 CASH DEBIT	4 CASH CREDIT	
25									25
26									26
27									27
28									28
29									29
30									30
31									31
32									32
33									33
34									34
35									35
36									36
37									37
38									38
39									39
40									40
41									41
42									42
43									43
44									44
45									45
46									46
47									47
48									48

24-1 APPLICATION PROBLEM, p. 676

Preparing a work sheet for a governmental organization [1, 2]

The work sheet prepared in this problem is needed to complete Application Problems 24-2 and 24-3.

Town of Winona General Fund
Work Sheet
For Year Ended December 31, 20--

	ACCOUNT TITLE	TRIAL BALANCE DEBIT	TRIAL BALANCE CREDIT	ADJUSTMENTS DEBIT	ADJUSTMENTS CREDIT	REVENUES/EXPENDITURES DEBIT	REVENUES/EXPENDITURES CREDIT	BALANCE SHEET DEBIT	BALANCE SHEET CREDIT
1	Cash	74 130 00							
2	Taxes Receivable—Current								
3	Allow. for Uncoll. Taxes—Current								
4	Taxes Receivable—Delinquent	17 700 00							
5	Allow. for Uncoll. Taxes—Delinquent		7 960 00						
6	Interest Receivable								
7	Allow. for Uncoll. Interest								
8	Inventory of Supplies								
9	Investments—Short Term								
10	Accounts Payable		3 432 00						
11	Notes Payable								
12	Unreserved Fund Balance		41 244 00						
13	Reserve for Encumb.—Current Year		2 240 00						
14	Reserve for Encumb.—Prior Year								
15	Reserve for Inventory of Supplies								
16	Property Tax Revenue		1459 000 00						
17	Interest Revenue		4 756 00						
18	Other Revenue		9 020 00						
19	Expend.—Personnel, Gen. Gov't	250 050 00							
20	Expend.—Supplies, Gen. Gov't	12 100 00							
21	Expend.—Other Chgs., Gen. Gov't	124 510 00							
22	Expend.—Cap. Outlays, Gen. Gov't	14 500 00							
23	Expend.—Personnel, Pub. Saf.	414 700 00							
24	Expend.—Supplies, Pub. Saf.	21 850 00							
25	Expend.—Other Chgs., Pub. Saf.	168 420 00							
26	Expend.—Cap. Outlays, Pub. Saf.	80 980 00							
27	Expend.—Personnel, Pub. Wks.	157 730 00							

24-1 APPLICATION PROBLEM (concluded)

[1, 2]

ACCOUNT TITLE	TRIAL BALANCE DEBIT	TRIAL BALANCE CREDIT	ADJUSTMENTS DEBIT	ADJUSTMENTS CREDIT	REVENUES/EXPENDITURES DEBIT	REVENUES/EXPENDITURES CREDIT	BALANCE SHEET DEBIT	BALANCE SHEET CREDIT
Expend.—Supplies, Pub. Wks.	6150 00							
Expend.—Other Chgs., Pub. Wks.	52170 00							
Expend.—Cap. Outlays, Pub. Wks.	4630 00							
Expend.—Personnel, Rec.	55250 00							
Expend.—Supplies, Rec.	2157 00							
Expend.—Other Chgs., Rec.	2775 00							
Expend.—Cap. Outlays, Rec.	1044 00							
Estimated Revenues	147695 00							
Appropriations		146754 00						
Budgetary Fund Balance		941 00						
Encumb.—Supplies, Gen Gov't	224 00							
	3035 49 00	3035 49 00						

24-2 APPLICATION PROBLEM p. 676

Preparing financial statements for a governmental organization [1]

The work sheet prepared in Application Problems 24-1 is needed to complete this problem.

Town of Winona General Fund

Statement of Revenues, Expenditures, and Changes in Fund Balance—Budget and Actual

For Year Ended December 31, 20--

	BUDGET	ACTUAL	VARIANCE—FAVORABLE (UNFAVORABLE)
Revenues:			
Property Tax Revenue			
Interest Revenue			
Other Revenue			
Total Revenues			
Expenditures:			
General Government			
Public Safety			
Public Works			
Recreation			
Total Expenditures			
Excess of Revenues Over Expenditures			
Less Outstanding Encumbrances, Dec. 31, 20--			
Increase in Unreserved Fund Balance for Year			
Unreserved Fund Balance, Jan. 1, 20--			
Unreserved Fund Balance, Dec. 31, 20--			

24-2 APPLICATION PROBLEM (concluded)

[2]

Town of Winona General Fund
Balance Sheet
December 31, 20--

ASSETS			
Cash			
Taxes Receivable—Delinquent			
Less Allowance for Uncoll. Taxes —Delinquent			
Interest Receivable			
Less Allowance for Uncollectible Interest			
Inventory of Supplies			
Total Assets			
LIABILITIES AND FUND EQUITY			
Liabilities:			
Accounts Payable			
Fund Equity:			
Unreserved Fund Balance			
Reserve for Encumbrances—Prior Year			
Reserve for Inventory of Supplies			
Total Fund Equity			
Total Liabilities and Fund Equity			

24-3 APPLICATION PROBLEM, p. 676

Journalizing adjusting and closing entries for a governmental organization [1, 2]

The work sheet prepared in Application Problem 24-1 is needed to complete this problem.

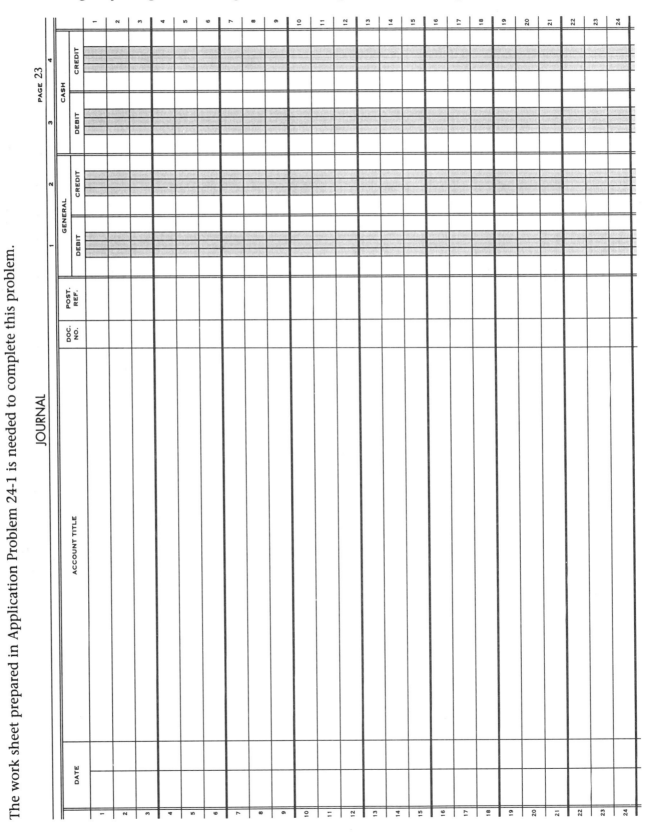

24-3 APPLICATION PROBLEM (concluded)

[1, 2]

JOURNAL — PAGE 23 (cont.)

DATE	ACCOUNT TITLE	DOC. NO.	POST. REF.	GENERAL DEBIT	GENERAL CREDIT	CASH DEBIT	CASH CREDIT

24-4 MASTERY PROBLEM, p. 677

Completing the end-of-fiscal-period work for a governmental organization [1, 2]

Town of Duluth General Fund
Work Sheet
For Year Ended December 31, 20--

	ACCOUNT TITLE	TRIAL BALANCE DEBIT	TRIAL BALANCE CREDIT	ADJUSTMENTS DEBIT	ADJUSTMENTS CREDIT	REVENUES/EXPENDITURES DEBIT	REVENUES/EXPENDITURES CREDIT	BALANCE SHEET DEBIT	BALANCE SHEET CREDIT
1	Cash	103 390 00							
2	Taxes Receivable—Current								
3	Allow. for Uncoll. Taxes—Current		6 940 00						
4	Taxes Receivable—Delinquent	10 430 00							
5	Allow. for Uncoll. Taxes—Delinquent		6 940 00						
6	Interest Receivable								
7	Allow. for Uncoll. Interest								
8	Inventory of Supplies								
9	Investments—Short Term		2 934 00						
10	Accounts Payable								
11	Notes Payable		35 550 00						
12	Unreserved Fund Balance		1 870 00						
13	Reserve for Encumb.—Current Year								
14	Reserve for Encumb.—Prior Year								
15	Reserve for Inventory of Supplies								
16	Property Tax Revenue		1265 000 00						
17	Interest Revenue		6 680 00						
18	Other Revenue		8 120 00						
19	Expend.—Personnel, Gen. Gov't.	211 640 00							
20	Expend.—Supplies, Gen. Gov't.	10 490 00							
21	Expend.—Other Chgs., Gen. Gov't.	106 550 00							
22	Expend.—Cap. Outlays, Gen. Gov't.	12 300 00							
23	Expend.—Personnel, Pub. Saf.	397 540 00							
24	Expend.—Supplies, Pub. Saf.	18 620 00							
25	Expend.—Other Chgs., Pub. Saf.	144 150 00							
26	Expend.—Cap. Outlays, Pub. Saf.	7 230 00							
27	Expend.—Personnel, Pub. Wks.	92 200 00							

24-4 MASTERY PROBLEM (continued)

[1, 2]

	ACCOUNT TITLE	TRIAL BALANCE DEBIT	TRIAL BALANCE CREDIT	ADJUSTMENTS DEBIT	ADJUSTMENTS CREDIT	REVENUES/EXPENDITURES DEBIT	REVENUES/EXPENDITURES CREDIT	BALANCE SHEET DEBIT	BALANCE SHEET CREDIT
28	Expend.—Supplies, Pub. Wks.	5 25 0 00							
29	Expend.—Other Chgs., Pub. Wks.	44 75 0 00							
30	Expend.—Cap. Outlays, Pub. Wks.	39 60 0 00							
31	Expend.—Personnel, Rec.	48 22 0 00							
32	Expend.—Supplies, Rec.	1 85 0 00							
33	Expend.—Other Chgs., Rec.	23 48 0 00							
34	Expend.—Cap. Outlays, Rec.	8 87 0 00							
35	Estimated Revenues	1280 0 00 00							
36	Appropriations		1240 0 00 00						
37	Budgetary Fund Balance		40 0 00 00						
38	Encumb.—Supplies, Gen Gov't	1 87 0 00							
39		2633 5 00 00	2633 5 00 00						
40									
41									
42									
43									
44									
45									
46									
47									
48									
49									
50									
51									
52									
53									
54									

24-4 MASTERY PROBLEM (continued)

[3]

Town of Duluth General Fund
Statement of Revenues, Expenditures, and Changes in Fund Balance—Budget and Actual
For Year Ended December 31, 20--

	BUDGET	ACTUAL	VARIANCE—FAVORABLE (UNFAVORABLE)
Revenues:			
Property Tax Revenue			
Interest Revenue			
Other Revenue			
Total Revenues			
Expenditures:			
General Government			
Public Safety			
Public Works			
Recreation			
Total Expenditures			
Excess of Revenues Over Expenditures			
Less Outstanding Encumbrances, Dec. 31, 20--			
Increase in Unreserved Fund Balance for Year			
Unreserved Fund Balance, Jan. 1, 20--			
Unreserved Fund Balance, Dec. 31, 20--			

24-4 MASTERY PROBLEM (continued)

[4]

Town of Duluth General Fund
Balance Sheet
December 31, 20--

ASSETS			
Cash			
Taxes Receivable—Delinquent			
Less Allowance for Uncoll. Taxes —Delinquent			
Interest Receivable			
Less Allowance for Uncollectible Interest			
Inventory of Supplies			
Total Assets			
LIABILITIES AND FUND EQUITY			
Liabilities:			
Accounts Payable			
Fund Equity:			
Unreserved Fund Balance			
Reserve for Encumbrances—Prior Year			
Reserve for Inventory of Supplies			
Total Fund Equity			
Total Liabilities and Fund Equity			

24-4 MASTERY PROBLEM (continued)

[5, 6]

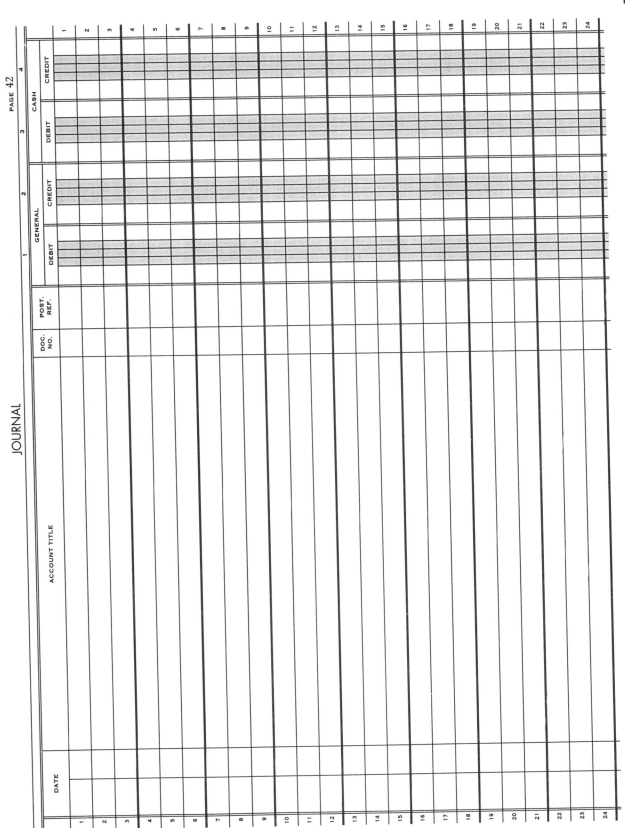

24-4 MASTERY PROBLEM (concluded)

[5, 6]

JOURNAL — PAGE 42 (cont.)

DATE	ACCOUNT TITLE	DOC. NO.	POST. REF.	GENERAL DEBIT	GENERAL CREDIT	CASH DEBIT	CASH CREDIT

24-5 CHALLENGE PROBLEM, p. 679

Completing end-of-fiscal-period work for a governmental organization [1, 2]

Town of Plymouth General Fund
Work Sheet
For Year Ended December 31, 20--

	ACCOUNT TITLE	TRIAL BALANCE DEBIT	TRIAL BALANCE CREDIT	ADJUSTMENTS DEBIT	ADJUSTMENTS CREDIT	REVENUES/EXPENDITURES DEBIT	REVENUES/EXPENDITURES CREDIT	BALANCE SHEET DEBIT	BALANCE SHEET CREDIT
1	Cash	56 148 00							
2	Taxes Receivable—Current								
3	Allow. for Uncoll. Taxes—Current								
4	Taxes Receivable—Delinquent	28 074 00							
5	Allow. for Uncoll. Taxes—Delinquent		11 225 00						
6	Interest Receivable								
7	Allow. for Uncoll. Interest								
8	Inventory of Supplies								
9	Investments—Short Term		35 816 00						
10	Accounts Payable								
11	Notes Payable		63 450 00						
12	Unreserved Fund Balance		1 076 00						
13	Reserve for Encumb.—Current Year								
14	Reserve for Encumb.—Prior Year								
15	Reserve for Inventory of Supplies								
16	Property Tax Revenue		1455 900 00						
17	Interest Revenue		9 885 00						
18	Other Revenue		15 973 00						
19	Expend.—Personnel, Gen. Gov't.	260 520 00							
20	Expend.—Supplies, Gen. Gov't.	14 394 00							
21	Expend.—Other Chgs., Gen. Gov't.	129 975 00							
22	Expend.—Cap. Outlays, Gen. Gov't.	15 168 00							
23	Expend.—Personnel, Pub. Saf.	483 590 00							
24	Expend.—Supplies, Pub. Saf.	21 973 00							
25	Expend.—Other Chgs., Pub. Saf.	175 843 00							
26	Expend.—Cap. Outlays, Pub. Saf.	85 745 00							
27	Expend.—Personnel, Pub. Wks.	113 225 00							

24-5 CHALLENGE PROBLEM (continued)

[1, 2]

ACCOUNT TITLE	TRIAL BALANCE DEBIT	TRIAL BALANCE CREDIT	ADJUSTMENTS DEBIT	ADJUSTMENTS CREDIT	REVENUES/EXPENDITURES DEBIT	REVENUES/EXPENDITURES CREDIT	BALANCE SHEET DEBIT	BALANCE SHEET CREDIT
Expend.—Supplies, Pub. Wks.	6 687 00							
Expend.—Other Chgs., Pub. Wks.	52 684 00							
Expend.—Cap. Outlays, Pub. Wks.	48 820 00							
Expend.—Personnel, Rec.	56 855 00							
Expend.—Supplies, Rec.	2 678 00							
Expend.—Other Chgs., Rec.	28 910 00							
Expend.—Cap. Outlays, Rec.	10 960 00							
Estimated Revenues	1 485 840 00							
Appropriations		1 511 160 00						
Budgetary Fund Balance	25 320 00							
Encumb.—Supplies, Pub. Saf.	1 076 00							
	3 104 485 00	3 104 485 00						

24-5 CHALLENGE PROBLEM (continued)

[3]

Town of Plymouth General Fund

Statement of Revenues, Expenditures, and Changes in Fund Balance—Budget and Actual

For Year Ended December 31, 20--

	BUDGET	ACTUAL	VARIANCE—FAVORABLE (UNFAVORABLE)
Revenues:			
Property Tax Revenue			
Interest Revenue			
Other Revenue			
Total Revenues			
Expenditures:			
General Government			
Public Safety			
Public Works			
Recreation			
Total Expenditures			
Excess of Expenditures Over Revenues			
Plus Outstanding Encumbrances, Dec. 31, 20--			
Decrease in Unreserved Fund Balance for Year			
Unreserved Fund Balance, Jan. 1, 20--			
Unreserved Fund Balance, Dec. 31, 20--			

24-5 CHALLENGE PROBLEM (continued)

[4]

Town of Plymouth General Fund
Balance Sheet
December 31, 20--

ASSETS				
Cash				
Taxes Receivable—Delinquent				
Less Allowance for Uncoll. Taxes —Delinquent				
Interest Receivable				
Less Allowance for Uncollectible Interest				
Inventory of Supplies				
Total Assets				
LIABILITIES AND FUND EQUITY				
Liabilities:				
Accounts Payable				
Fund Equity:				
Unreserved Fund Balance				
Reserve for Encumbrances—Prior Year				
Reserve for Inventory of Supplies				
Total Fund Equity				
Total Liabilities and Fund Equity				

24-5 CHALLENGE PROBLEM (continued)

[5, 6]

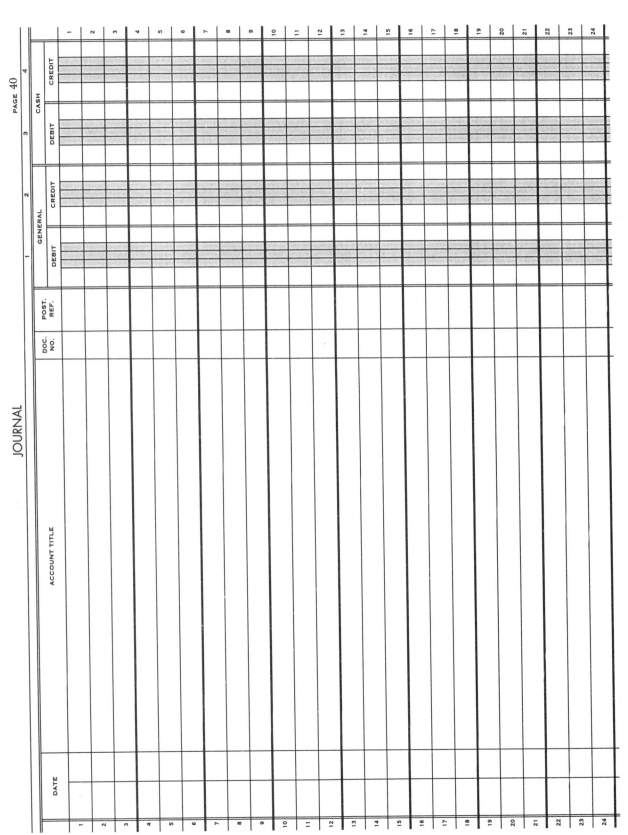

24-5 CHALLENGE PROBLEM (concluded)

[5, 6]

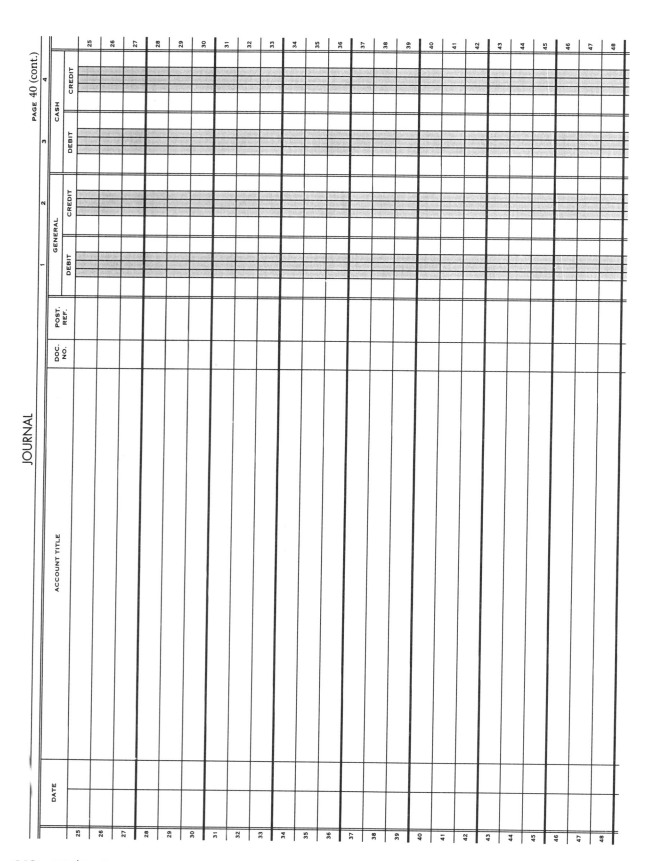

24-5 CHALLENGE PROBLEM

Extra form

Blank journal form with columns for Date, Account Title, Doc. No., Post. Ref., General Debit, General Credit, Cash Debit, and Cash Credit.

24-5 CHALLENGE PROBLEM

Extra form

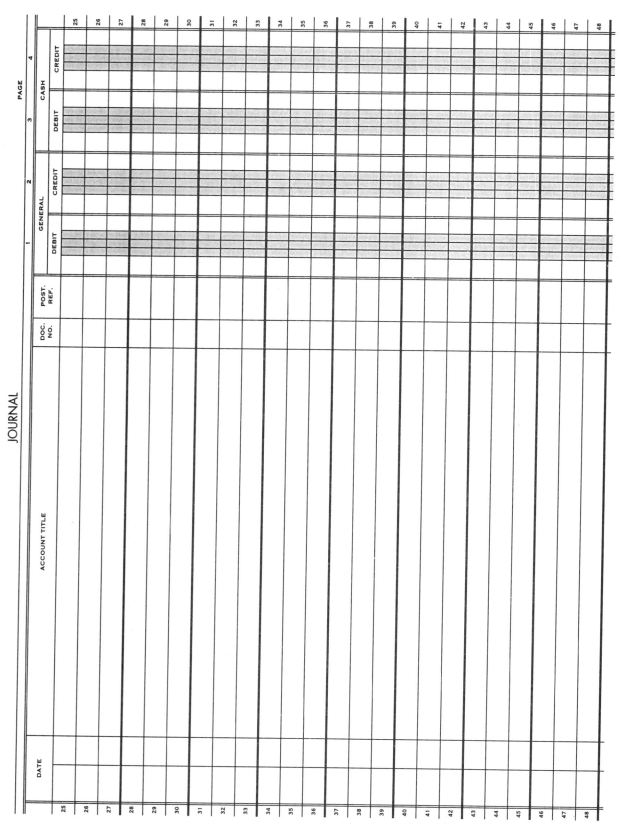